ORGANIZATIONAL BEHAVIOR IN SPORT MANAGEMENT

ORGANIZATIONAL BEHAVIOR IN SPORT MANAGEMENT

Eric W. MacIntosh, PhD
University of Ottawa

Laura J. Burton, PhD
University of Connecticut

Human Kinetics

Library of Congress Cataloging-in-Publication Data

Names: MacIntosh, Eric W., 1977- author. | Burton, Laura J., author.
Title: Organizational behavior in sport management / Eric MacIntosh, Laura J. Burton.
Description: Champaign, IL : Human Kinetics, [2019] | Includes
  bibliographical references and index.
Identifiers: LCCN 2017038346 (print) | LCCN 2017040217 (ebook) | ISBN
  9781492552390 (e-book) | ISBN 9781492552383 (print)
Subjects: | MESH: Sports | Workplace--psychology | Interprofessional
  Relations | Physical Education and Training--organization & administration
  | Organizational Culture | Personnel Management
Classification: LCC GV713 (ebook) | LCC GV713 (print) | NLM QT 260 | DDC
  796.06--dc23
LC record available at https://lccn.loc.gov/2017038346

ISBN: 978-1-4925-5238-3 (print)

The web addresses cited in this text were current as of March 2018, unless otherwise noted.

Acquisitions Editor: Diana Vincer; **Developmental and Managing Editor:** Carly S. O'Connor; **Copyeditor:** Tom Tiller; **Indexer:** Beth Nauman-Montana; **Permissions Manager:** Dalene Reeder; **Graphic Designer:** Whitney Milburn; **Cover Designer:** Keri Evans; **Cover Design Associate:** Susan Rothermel Allen; **Photograph (cover):** Andrey Popov/iStock/Getty Images (left) and ferrantraite/E+/Getty Images (right); **Photo Production Manager:** Jason Allen; **Senior Art Manager:** Kelly Hendren; **Illustrations:** © Human Kinetics, unless otherwise noted; **Printer:** McNaughton & Gunn

Printed in the United States of America   10 9 8 7 6 5 4 3

The paper in this book is certified under a sustainable forestry program.

Human Kinetics
1607 N. Market Street
Champaign, IL 61820
USA

United States and International
Website: **US.HumanKinetics.com**
Email: info@hkusa.com
Phone: 1-800-747-4457

Canada
Website: **Canada.HumanKinetics.com**
Email: info@hkcanada.com

E7082

Tell us what you think!
Human Kinetics would love to hear what we
can do to improve the customer experience.
Use this QR code to take our brief survey.

CONTENTS

Part II Managing the Individual

45

Part III Managing the Group

Part IV Managing the Organization 165

PREFACE

As a field of research, organizational behavior (OB) is concerned with the full range of people who work in an organization, from the leadership and management core to the employees who "make the engine run" and the volunteers who often fill many needed roles. In sport organizations, OB extends to the specialized roles of coaches, athletes, and officials that form the essence of the competitive product on the field of play. Consequently, the study of OB in sport considers many different stakeholders, as well as the various attitudes, beliefs, and values that make up a sport and its culture. Moreover, the topics addressed by OB are vast, complex, dynamic, and of great importance to practicing sport managers.

In this book, we consider both the classical research conducted in OB in general and the evolution of sport management in particular. From a functionalist management perspective, many of the classical studies have focused on understanding the best way to manage people, as if to say that staff members operate under the direct control of those who work in management. Of course, anyone who knows a thing or two about human psychology and behavior knows that people are not controllable; rather, they hold their own values, beliefs, objectives, and principles and possess the power to both act and react as they choose. It would be inaccurate, however, to say that OB models do not have predictive or practicable utility—they clearly do. Indeed, both classical and contemporary OB research and practice touch on ways in which people's attitudes can shape their behavior and offer guidance for management concerned with the welfare of employees.

In this text, we provide information about the individual's intrapersonal aspects and interpersonal relationships as well as the organizational processes that we believe are fundamental to working in a sport organization. We focus equally on what leaders and managers should understand in regard to human behavior and on what each person brings to the work situation in terms of attitudes, thoughts, perceptions, and skills. As a result, instead of treating the employee as someone to be managed in a particular way, we emphasize individual needs, desires, interests, and empowerment at work. In this context, we discuss the roles of administrators, volunteers, players, coaches, general managers, presidents, service employees, and others who work in sport organizations; moreover, we examine both how they behave independently and how they interact with each other.

Most of us spend a huge proportion of our time at work, and it makes sense that the field of OB works to explain the attitudes and behaviors that influence us at work. And yet, in sport management to date, no single text has provided an account of what it is like to work for a sport organization while also chronicling the various OB topics (historical and contemporary) of managerial importance. With that gap in mind, this textbook addresses key questions pertaining to why we do what we do at work, why others behave as they do, and how our interpretations of situations are subject to our biases.

ORGANIZATION OF THE TEXT

This book is organized into four main parts: Organizational Behavior in Sport Organizations, Managing the Individual, Managing the Group, and Managing the Organization. This sequence is purposeful in that we want readers to begin by appreciating the employee, then understand the building blocks of OB research as it relates to the group and the organization. Throughout the text, we examine the variety of stakeholders in sport and treat them as being independent of the organization. That is, they hold their own beliefs and values and act in their own interests while contributing—sometimes positively, sometimes negatively—to the pursuit of group and organizational objectives.

Each chapter begins with a list of learning objectives to help readers organize the information presented. In addition, each chapter includes a special section, titled In the Boardroom, that highlights a particular subject or topic addressed in the chapter. Case studies are also included in each chapter to help illustrate particular topics and facilitate focused discussion in class. Each chapter concludes with discussion questions to help ensure that chapter objectives are met.

Part I, which includes the book's first three chapters, introduces concepts that set the stage for the rest of the text. It also covers the importance of strategy, diversity, and integrity—three topics that are foundational to success for contemporary sport managers. Chapter 1 highlights the similarities and differences between enduring and temporary sport organizations and introduces open systems theory to provide readers with a working knowledge of how an organization's operations are influenced by its context. Chapter 2 follows with an examination of the need to proactively manage diversity and develop inclusive management practices. And chapter 3 explores the importance of understanding ethics and ethical behavior in organizations, especially in light of the pervasive ethical challenges that characterize sport at all levels.

In part II, we focus on understanding the individual and appreciating the various types of attitudes, values, and behaviors that a person may bring to work. This part of the book provides models and frameworks that are critical to building and maintaining a solid knowledge base in organizational behavior, regardless of whether you are a student, a practicing manager, an employee, or simply a person who is interested in human behavior. More specifically, chapter 4 explores how personality, emotions, attitudes, and motivations affect the ways in which individuals work in a sport organization. Chapters 5 and 6 examine motivation, training, and job satisfaction as critical components in supporting individuals' work. And chapters 7 and 8 address ways to reduce stress in the work environment and enhance organizational socialization of the individual. These part II chapters provide readers with a toolkit to use that highlights important management situations involving both the intrapersonal aspects and interpersonal relationships they will encounter at work.

In part III, we detail concepts that help people manage a group, as well as their own role in a group. This section also presents some ways in which people can integrate and function well within a group or team. Several of the theories and concepts presented here illustrate the dynamic nature of OB concepts, insofar as the individual is a functioning actor in a group who sometimes holds power and influence and at other times must perform a particular role that is necessary for achieving desired outcomes. In chapter 9, we address the critical role of leadership in the organization, discuss ways of leading others, and cover self-leadership and leadership development. Chapter 10 addresses decision making and explores both the routine (programmed) decisions and the nonroutine (nonprogrammed) decisions made on a daily basis. Chapter 11 examines the concept of a team, the importance of team development in the context of sport organizations, and ways in which team effectiveness is affected by cohesion and social loafing. Chapter 12 covers conflict, negotiation, and power and highlights some of the realities that characterize work in sport organizations.

Part IV addresses three key topics of OB at the organizational level: communication, culture, and change. Of course, these factors affect the individual and group levels, but they also appear in a compelling and dynamic context when viewed from the organizational perspective. In chapter 13, we detail the basic process of interpersonal communication and the various ways in which a person interprets and decodes messages that influence group, organizational, and cross-cultural contexts. Chapter 14 explores both the superficial and the deeper meanings of organizational culture and examines the holistic nature of this concept. In chapter 15, we address the many types of change faced by sport organizations, which range from rules and regulations imposed by regulatory bodies to internal mechanisms that influence how work gets performed in an organization.

INSTRUCTOR GUIDE

The print book is accompanied by an instructor guide, which includes chapter objectives; answers to the chapter-ending discussion questions from the text; answers to the discussion questions for each chapter's case study; suggestions for integrating the case studies into your own lectures; links to relevant websites; suggested readings; and ideas for assignments, lab activities, essay topics, and class projects. Ancillary products supporting this text are free to adopting instructors. Contact your Sales Manager for details about how to access HK *Propel*, our ancillary delivery and learning platform.

The theories presented in this book, as well as the positions taken and even the references cited, reflect our own preferences and experiences, both as teachers and as researchers of sport management. We hope that our collective orientation provides an opportunity for other teachers to bring up their own views, practices, and theories, regardless of whether they align with what is presented here. As members of a growing field that helps sport organizations and their people feel valued, we know that dialogue enables learning and understanding, and we hope that purpose is served well by this textbook.

ACKNOWLEDGMENTS

Thanks to my former and current students, who openly discussed how the topics of organizational behavior influenced them and their work-related endeavors and continue to motivate and inspire my teaching and research; to Keith and Marie M., Jim W., Simon G., and Jason B. for their friendly reviews of some chapters; to the external reviewers for their commentary; and finally, to the Human Kinetics staff for their tireless and professional work.

—Eric MacIntosh

Thanks to my current and former students, who provided the inspiration for this project and shared their insights and their experiences of organizational behavior in the sport industry. I would also like to thank the staff at Human Kinetics. We could not have done this without your incredible attention to detail and exceptional professionalism through every step of the process.

—Laura Burton

PART I

ORGANIZATIONAL BEHAVIOR IN SPORT ORGANIZATIONS

Research on organizational behavior (OB) has a long history of combining information from psychology and sociology, as well as administrative concepts, in order to explain how people go about their work. In the sport management setting, borrowing from these other disciplines is helpful but not sufficient, given that sport is characterized by many unique aspects and nuances. Here in part I, therefore, we not only introduce key concepts from these other disciplines but also indicate areas where sport management differs from the general organizational behavior literature.

The three chapters included in this section introduce topics that are fundamental for today's sport manager. Chapter 1 begins by discussing the importance of OB in sport, then addresses what we view as a critical resource for sport organizations—that is, human capital. This chapter discusses the importance of a people-centered approach for management and includes the concept of open systems theory, revealing how various outcomes are produced

through the people who perform the work, and the importance of appreciating both the internal and external working environment in sport organizations.

Chapter 2 discusses the strategic importance of diversity as an asset in sport organizations. More specifically, the chapter highlights the importance of proactively managing diversity in order to reap its full benefits. The discussion defines stereotypes, prejudice, and discrimination, all of which affect the experiences and influence the behaviors of individuals who work in diverse organizations. The chapter closes with a discussion of how diversity training affects organizational outcomes.

Given the pervasive ethical challenges faced by individuals at all levels of sport—from youth through the international and professional ranks—it is critical to examine ethical behavior in sport organizations. To meet this need, chapter 3 examines ethics, morals, and values and the ways in which they influence individuals who work in sport organizations. The chapter also examines the application of ethics to the decision-making process, as well as ways in which an organization can foster a climate that supports ethical behavior.

OB strategy, proactive management of diversity, and ethical decision making lie at the heart of good management and undergird the designing of a workforce that is inclusive, just, and fair. Thus, in examining these key topics, the first three chapters of the book set the scene for what is to come in addressing the three levels of OB—that is, the individual, interpersonal, and organizational processes.

Chapter 1

Importance of Organizational Behavior in Sport

Chapter Objectives

After studying this chapter, you will be able to

- define organizational behavior,
- discuss the three basic levels of management understanding related to organizational behavior,
- appreciate the need to create a people-centered focus in an organization,
- discuss open systems theory,
- explain the need for human knowledge as capital, and
- articulate the importance of organizational behavior for contemporary sport management.

Business is conducted by people, for people, and through people. Even today, when technology plays an increased and critical role in our lives, a sport organization cannot exist without the people who conceive it in the first place and those who work toward accomplishing its mission, vision, and objectives as set forth by its leaders. In every sector of the sport industry—from grassroots club sport to the high-performance sector—the people who run and contribute to sport organizations are crucial to each organization's daily challenges, trials and tribulations, and, ultimately, success or failure.

The field of organizational behavior (OB) involves the scientific study of individual behavior, group dynamics, and structural choices in organizations (Nelson, Quick,

Armstrong, & Condie, 2015). Put simply, OB researchers study people, what they think of and do in their jobs and in their groups, and, more generally, how an organization operates and performs. Such researchers find a wide array of opportunities to examine organizational behavior in the sport industry. For instance, employed work may be performed on either a part-time or a full-time basis in either the amateur or the professional sport industry.

Furthermore, both part-time and full-time work can be done in either an enduring or a temporary organization. Enduring organizations (e.g., the National Hockey League's Montreal Canadiens) have a long and storied history, whereas temporary organizations (e.g., an organizing committee for a sport event—for instance, the 2018

Commonwealth Games) exist for a defined and relatively short period of time. Temporary sport organizations typically rely more heavily on volunteers, particularly at higher levels of performance (e.g., the Olympics) and in the amateur sector both nationally and locally (e.g., Canada Games, club-based sport competitions). Of course, volunteers are also invaluable to enduring organizations, where they support various initiatives, such as community fundraising campaigns. At the amateur level, however, many organizations lack the budget to hire paid staff and therefore rely largely on unpaid volunteers for their success and even for their survival.

The work performed in the sport industry engages many stakeholders, who are also part of what makes sport operations both attractive and specialized. Full-time employees, sport volunteers, athletes, coaches, trainers, administrative support staffers—all of these people have various levels of attachment to their work and to their sport organizations. For instance, the factors that motivate full-time employees to excel at their jobs and advance in their companies are likely to differ from the factors that motivate individuals to volunteer their time without any particular expected return on investment. Differences also exist in their attitudes toward work and their behavior in group and organizational settings. Sport organizations are also distinguished by the variety of actors who may hold relevant technical expertise—sometimes with very different skill sets—such as coaches, players, and administrators.

As sport management began to emerge as a field of study in classrooms across the United States and Canada in the 1980s, scholars borrowed from parent disciplines—such as sport psychology, sociology, and business administration—in order to learn more about the factors that make working in and for sport organizations unique (e.g., transformational leadership in sport administration or coaching, marketing segmentation for sport orga-

nizations, the marketing of and through sport). Sport management scholars also began organizing conferences, both in North America (e.g., North American Society for Sport Management, n.d.) and abroad in order to discuss the field and its future. In these formative years of sport management scholarship, the study of people's organizational behavior often concentrated on coaches and administrators. As the field matured, research also addressed other stakeholder issues (e.g., volunteers, gender, ethics, race), marketing literature was further developed, and the study of human resource management in sport organizations emerged.

Thus the study of people in sport organizations was garnering more interest. This growth resulted in part from the increased understanding of the importance of knowledge acquisition relative to the field of sport management and the realization that human capital is one of the most important resources in an organization, regardless of sector. This resource-based view, or RBV (see Barney, 1991), posited that firms are more likely to enjoy sustained advantages if they control resources that are not substitutable and are valuable, rare, and imperfectly imitable. The RBV approach has helped sport management researchers determine the ways in which sport is unique and the ways in which it is similar to other industries.

Acquiring and developing both tangible and intangible resources is crucial to the successful management of an organization. This process requires us to appreciate both the external environment and the internal context of the organization. External forces acting on the organization include economic, political, sociocultural, legal, ecological, demographic, and technological factors. In this competitive global ecosystem, "knowledge and human capital have become essential strategic resources . . . , [and] the process of fostering their creation and deployment has emerged as one of the most important areas of strategic management" (Szymanksi & Wolfe, 2017,

p. 26). In these days of fierce competition and rapid change, it is critical that management scholars recognize and understand that attracting, developing, and retaining human talent is a prerequisite for success.

IMPORTANCE OF UNDERSTANDING OB

In any type of sport organization—large or small, for-profit or not-for-profit—people want to find meaning and fulfillment in their work while contributing to the success of the organization. From the viewpoint of the organization, it competes not only with other entities in the sport industry but also with those in other industries for consumer interest and disposable dollars. Meeting this challenge requires leadership grounded in a strong understanding of an array of topics addressed by the field of organizational behavior. We characterize these topics as falling into three basic levels of management understanding related to OB:

1. *Individual factors:* personality, perceptions, attitudes, motivation, satisfaction, personal values, personal ethics, misbehavior, stress, well-being, emotional disposition, self-handicapping tendencies, citizenship in the company, leadership, followership, emotional intelligence, self-awareness

2. *Interpersonal and group factors:* development of group and team building, group and team dynamics, interpersonal relationships within groups, group decision making, leadership, followership, commitment to group goals, commitment to the group, communication within and outside of the group, creativity in team projects, group norms, virtual teams

3. *Organizational factors:* change, culture, socialization, leadership, diversity, outcomes, power and politics in the organization, governance, structure, social networks

Appreciating these levels of understanding, and the ways in which they influence each other, enables us to develop a fundamental understanding of what makes people tick in work life. For example, some individuals have a personality that is predictive of experiencing high levels of stress. When such a person experiences high stress that goes uncontrolled—or lacks the needed support from the group or organization to overcome or deal with the stress—then the person's health and work may suffer. The consequences of poorly managed stress can also spill over into the person's performance in a group or team. The obvious implication here is that if the group or team underperforms, then the result for the organization itself could be affected. Thus we see the how the three levels of understanding can overlap and interact. As a result, sport managers must be well versed in the full range of OB topics in order to provide a positive and healthy work environment.

Most people spend the majority of their working lives away from their families and with their colleagues in various organizational settings, from the cubicle to the boardroom to the video room to the field. Given this huge commitment, it makes sense to try to develop a purposeful understanding of our work in sport. The ways in which we experience work, and the settings in which we pursue our careers, can bring challenge, despair, and (hopefully) happiness. Thus quality of life itself provides strong motivation for both aspiring and practicing sport managers to study and understand OB.

The resource-based view of the firm considers the fact that what is (or is not) readily available can assist (or hinder) management in producing desirable outcomes for the organization. In almost all scenarios, the critical resource for performing work derives from people, and sport managers may work with a wide range of people, such as athletes, coaches, athletic support personnel (e.g., athletic trainers, strength and conditioning specialists), and volunteers. If a needed skill set or piece of knowledge is not readily available, then the manager faces the difficult and important task of either finding new talent in new or different places (e.g., finding new ways to recruit) or developing current personnel to meet the organization's needs (e.g., through further education, mentoring, or experience). Thus it is helpful for any manager to have a sense of what people want from work, of the skills and attributes they bring to the job, and of how their needs and desires may or may not align with the organization's objectives and goals.

Self-awareness and OB knowledge can go a long way toward helping you experience optimal individual fulfillment in your work. Knowledge of OB subject matter can also help you understand why others behave as they do, both individually and in groups. Understanding people's attitudes and behaviors is helpful regardless of whether you are an aspiring sport leader, a manager by title or trade, a new member of an organization, or a person seeking work.

CREATING A PEOPLE-CENTERED STRATEGY

To fully understand contemporary viewpoints on OB, we must appreciate key historical factors that have affected both management and employees. Until recently (in historical terms), the employee had been merely an afterthought. However, in the last 100 years or so, many improvements have been made in working conditions that allow workers to feel appreciated. For instance, the value of the individual person, as well as individual rights and well-being, have been asserted and affirmed by the Emancipation Proclamation, the rise of unionization efforts, and the establishment of legal regulations on labor.

These and other contextual factors have influenced academic literature on work. For example, Maslow's hierarchy of needs (posited in 1943) and Herzberg's motivation-hygiene theory (see chapter 6) highlighted for management the importance of understanding workers and their attitudes and needs as related to their jobs and their work environments. This research was conducted after the appearance of unions, when employees were starting to gain more rights and privileges, but before the establishment of many of the rights and regulations that govern work practices in modern organizations. Although both sets of research were challenged, they were also widely adopted and proved to be instrumental in forming further research ideas about the creation of person-centered work. Indeed,

IN THE BOARDROOM
Using Important Organizational Documents to Make Sense of Work

Key organizational documents such as mission, vision, and values statements can help you learn what top leadership is looking for when it comes to daily work life. Such documents should be included in an organization's strategic and emergent planning activities, in which leadership lays out what is most important to the organization. Understanding these documents can help you make sense of your work because they articulate broad objectives and goals that provide a road map for determining acceptable (and unacceptable) forms of behavior at work.

they continue to be discussed in literary and practical management situations, and their seminal contributions are invaluable to the study of organizational behavior. Other researchers have highlighted the fact that the core of organizational work is performed by skilled people who bring a range of aptitudes, abilities, and interests to the job. For example, Mintzberg (1994) argued that organizational leaders should enhance their people's performance by engaging in strategic planning activities aimed at becoming and remaining competitive.

Consequently, at the core, the study and practice of OB must be about understanding the individual first. Moreover, given the need to get things done in teams and groups in sport organizations, managers must begin with a fundamentally sound understanding of the human resource component of work life and of the various behaviors that either help or hinder a person in pursuing group (or team) and organizational goals.

Managing any organization requires a deep appreciation and understanding of people as the critical resource. Whether as an entry-level employee, a volunteer, or a seasoned professional, each person in the organization carries a level of responsibility for helping the organization achieve a variety of objectives. In other words, each individual is an actor in the midst of the various group and organizational activities that contribute to the strategic management process. This process has been described as consisting of four parts (Chappelet & Bayle, 2005):

1. Analysis
2. Vision
3. Action
4. Control

In this model, the process is led and managed by the human side of the enterprise. More specifically, employees' and volunteers' decisions, actions, and behaviors have consequences that are influenced by the people with whom they work. Sometimes this requires a manager to initiate various recruiting and hiring practices; at other times, it requires interpersonal communication with a colleague or subordinate. It may also mean that a person assumes a particular role in order to help lead a change initiative. Ultimately, any strategic management activity involves discussions of the need for human resources and various types of knowledge that can benefit the organization through the key components of analysis, vision, action, and control (O'Boyle, 2017).

Strategic thinking in sport management must also account for the fact that each organization is different and that the context—whether internal or external (e.g., specific to the club or part of a larger environment, such as that of high-performance amateur sport)—can influence the decisions made by the organization's leadership (O'Boyle, 2017). These decisions, of course, carry implications for people both inside and outside of the organization, and research has highlighted the need to consider both internal and external stakeholders. For instance, some sport management literature has acknowledged the need for sport and event managers to recognize the stakeholders in policy development—including primary stakeholders such as coaches and athletes—as part of a deliberative and democratic process (MacIntosh & Parent, 2017; Thibault, Kihl, & Babiak, 2010). Part of the rationale for this idea holds that the stakeholder has a vested interest in the organization and a desire to succeed. For example, given that sport organizations rely on athletes to use their aptitudes and skills to produce a high-quality product for sale to sponsors and fans, it makes strategic sense to include this stakeholder group in decision making. When sport managers include athletes in the process of policy development, they can produce a better environment for work and operations.

It is vital that managers possess the ability to accurately analyze the environment, build on the organization's vision, and take the action required to achieve desired outcomes. For instance, when a deficit or apparent weakness appears in a particular area of the organization, management must find ways to address it. Sometimes the answer involves recruiting and hiring someone who brings a needed skill set. That new person will bring a unique set of skills, aptitudes, and personality characteristics that will influence how he or she behaves. That behavior may be productive, innocuous, or potentially harmful to the organization. For more on how human psychology produces attitudes toward work that are reflected in behavior, see chapter 4. More generally, as we discuss throughout this book, individual personality, needs, wants, and motivations carry several implications for individual job performance and for working in groups.

ORGANIZATIONS AS OPEN SYSTEMS

Open systems theory holds that an organization receives inputs from the external environment, transforms them into specific services or goods (throughputs), and delivers those goods or services to the environment as outputs (Chelladurai, 2014). Sport organizations are complex open systems characterized by various interacting components that influence the organization's people, technologies, structures, and purposes (Nelson et al., 2015). In this model, management can use an external focus to secure needed resources and support for the various internal initiatives it desires to undertake.

Consider the example of a local sport-event company tasked with running a 5K fundraiser (see figure 1.1). The company will gather various inputs, such as raw materials for the event (e.g., registration forms, time-keeping devices, T-shirts, water cups), recruit volunteers to help on race day, and acquire technology to facilitate online registration. The company will then create a variety of throughputs, such as customizing the registration forms and uploading them to a social media site to enable online registration, training volunteers to provide the best experience for participants, and designing a logo for the event. The output will consist of the event itself—the 5K fundraiser. Based on lessons learned during this process, the company will consider how to improve its staging of the next event, perhaps by being more selective in volunteer recruitment or by using a different company to provide the T-shirts (i.e., a different input).

As you can see even in this simplified example, the sheer variety and number of stakeholders who contribute to the success of a team, club, or sport event require sport managers to appreciate a

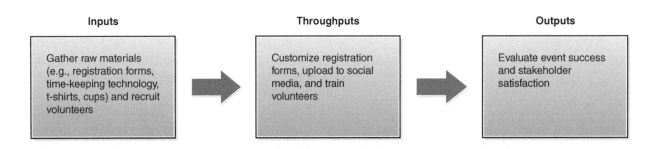

Inputs	Throughputs	Outputs
Gather raw materials (e.g., registration forms, time-keeping technology, t-shirts, cups) and recruit volunteers	Customize registration forms, upload to social media, and train volunteers	Evaluate event success and stakeholder satisfaction

Figure 1.1 Simplified open systems concept.

wide range of interests (e.g., participant, volunteer), needs (e.g., amount of funds raised), and wants (e.g., participant enjoyment of the event). In addition, an event of this nature often involves both autonomous work and group work, and each person who helps make the event happen brings personal attitudes, skills, and aptitudes. Thus, in order to evaluate how the event worked—that is, whether it was successful or unsuccessful—we need to have a working understanding of OB topics.

To reiterate the upshot of open systems theory, "the organization works by taking inputs, converting them into throughputs, and delivering outputs to its task environment" (Nelson et al., 2015, p. 6). As illustrated by figure 1.1, this simple explanation is intuitive, understandable, and relatable. For sport organizations, however, the process is not necessarily so neat and tidy, because the outcome of sport competition is unpredictable; on any given day, players, coaches, officials, managers, and fans do not know the outcome of a game. Hence, the notion of linearity between input, throughput, and output—though intuitive and appealing—does little to explain competitive performance.

The sport world is also distinguished, particularly at the professional and team levels, by the substitutability of the players and coaching staff, who in themselves constitute various inputs into the system. For instance, imagine the challenges for marketing and promotions staff when the most popular player (a fan favorite) is transferred or traded to another team at midseason. All the work they have done to market that player is now out of date, and they must therefore create new throughputs almost immediately in order to produce new outcomes. For many sport organizations at the professional level, this is a fairly common phenomenon that influences a variety of jobs in the organization.

In addition, sport organizations do not operate in a bubble; rather, their boundaries are permeable. For example, the National Football League was long able to ignore (or, some might say, cover up) the problems caused by concussions and repeated subconcussive blows to the head, including long-term brain damage suffered by many of its former players. However, as the media, the families of players, and NFL fans have begun to speak out, the league has been forced to acknowledge the inherent dangers of playing football. In response, it has adopted new rules in an effort to make the game safer, such as preventing players from returning to action immediately after sustaining a concussion. New rules require new learning and behavioral adaptations in order to arrive at the desired outcomes for the league and its players.

As this example illustrates, the open systems perspective must consider how the external environment affects an organization and its ways of functioning. To consider another example, social media platforms enable consumers to voice opinions (favorable or unfavorable) about organizations, teams, athletes, coaches, officials, and game- and sport-related experiences. The development of this technology has also allowed consumer-generated content to be shared quickly and widely. As a result, sport organizations and their managers must be attuned to the external environment and respond appropriately (e.g., in the form of throughputs) when the need arises.

Thus the permeable boundaries of sport organizations make the job of sport managers complex, because at any given time external factors may force them to make internal adaptations in the workforce. In other words, external realities require managers to be flexible, adaptable, and ready to respond. This requirement means that sport managers must develop a strong sense of the organization's internal strengths, weaknesses, and human resources.

Although open systems theory provides a tidy way to conceptualize how work is done, it does not necessarily allow for the intricacies of some factors, such as a person's personality or disposition at work. Nor does it account for the dynamic internal and external environments of the organization.

ACQUIRING KNOWLEDGE AND EXPERIENCE IN SPORT MANAGEMENT

Students of sport management must gain knowledge of the unique features of sport; for example, it is intangible, perishable, subjective, unpredictable, and emotion laden (Mullin, Hardy, & Sutton, 2014). In addition, given that sport is most often consumed socially (with friends and family) and that it occurs in public spaces, a sport organization's operations are influenced by a variety of stakeholders. This reality requires students to appreciate both the organization's internal work and the ways in which it is affected by the external environment. As a result, when seeking employees, an increasing number of sport organizations are looking not just for people who are educated in how a given sport works but also for people who have relevant experience as a volunteer, athlete, coach, or intern. Through education and experience in sport, people can integrate theory and practice—an important asset to sport organizations that desire this kind of human capital.

In addition, in many of today's sport organizations, hiring managers seek people who possess both general knowledge of the relevant sport and—even more important—strong knowledge of management principles, understanding of how the sport system operates (e.g., at the club, national, or international level), and strong people skills (e.g., communication, leadership). Increasingly, potential employees are also expected to possess relevant education and a knowledge base in sport

management, as well as direct experience in a sport organization through either volunteering or an internship. Knowledge of sport management and of sport system operations is an essential resource that comes from the classroom, the field of play, work experience, and volunteer work. For hiring managers, then, one crucial activity is to find people who are equipped with both sport and sport-organization knowledge and experience. It is equally important for the sport organization to develop the incoming talent and increase the person's knowledge base for the benefit of the organization.

Heisig (2009) noted two types of knowledge that are important for management: explicit and tacit. Knowledge is explicit if it is easily written, articulated, and codified, as is the case with many of the organizational documents used by sport organizations. For example, the NCAA produces a number of resources (e.g., handbooks, manuals, online materials) that explain various rules and protocols for athlete well-being, safety, and compliance. Tacit knowledge is harder to articulate and is often unstated; it is developed through experience and deepened through the various problem-solving trials experienced by a person, group, or organization. Nonaka and Takeuchi (1995) noted that the mastery of various tasks often takes the tacit form because it is developed through years of experience. This type of knowledge is context specific and is developed through the individual's interaction with his or her internal and external environments. In some cases, it becomes codified, thus becoming explicit knowledge in formal organizational documents. From an organizational standpoint, both forms of knowledge are important in informing the expected procedures at work, the structures in which work takes place, the communication channels that can lead to getting work done accurately and on time, and, ultimately, both individual and organizational performance.

A growing body of research in sport management examines how knowledge is formed and used in sport organizations to teach members and develop their talent. Much of this research addresses how organizations like the International Olympic Committee (IOC) use and store various forms of knowledge, which can help future organizing committees (e.g., Halbwirth & Toohey, 2001). In another example, O'Reilly and Knight (2007) addressed best practices for knowledge management that can help sport organizations remain competitive. More recently, Parent, MacDonald, and Goulet (2013) emphasized the key roles played by individuals with tacit knowledge of sport events and examined how sport organizations can use people with direct experience and knowledge of the sport and the sport system to help manage sport events. Essentially, this type of research highlights the fact that for many sport organizations it is critical to build on people's knowledge bases and skill sets developed through experience in the sport system.

Ultimately, it is good practice to hire people who are educated in the world of sport (thus the rise of sport management programs around the world) and who have some experience working within a sport organization. Students who are equipped with knowledge and experience relevant to both sport management and the understanding of human behavior will be prepared to make the transition to full-time employment in the sport industry.

SUMMARY

Although understanding human behavior is a lifelong pursuit (and perhaps one that is impossible to achieve fully), it is nonetheless a worthy and necessary endeavor for good management. Even those who are most educated in organizational behavior face the reality that each person is different and possesses his or her own values, beliefs, and assumptions about work and life—and that these individual factors affect the person's attitudes and behaviors. Therefore, as we try to show in this book, even the best frameworks and theories cannot fully explain or predict a person's reactions, motives for work, or perceptions of what is important for the organization.

At this juncture in sport management research, we have learned much from the classical theories developed in the parent disciplines, and we have set forth a body of literature that accounts for some of the unique features of the sport industry. Even so, the field of sport management

IN THE BOARDROOM
Human Knowledge as Capital in Staging Sport Events

In both enduring and temporary sport organizations, one main function of managers is to find smart, reliable, and hard-working people who can serve as a source of knowledge. When it comes to staging major sporting events, the acquisition and creation of knowledge help the organization store, apply, and transfer expertise for the next iteration of the event. In order to do so, organizations manage knowledge in explicit forms (e.g., mission statements, corporate objectives found in strategic planning documents) and in tacit forms developed through experience. As a student, you can acquire knowledge both through formal in-class study and through practical experience in sport organizations. Both of these types of learning can help you understand the nuances of sport, develop the skills necessary for working effectively with other people, and appreciate the intricacy of the sport organization's stakeholder environment through the organization's operations.

Planning to Launch a New Sport Team

In 2017, the National Hockey League (NHL) welcomed a new franchise in the form of the Las Vegas Golden Knights. For the organization's management team, preparing for the first puck drop was no doubt a monumental task. One major aspect of this preparation involved recruiting and hiring the support personnel (coaches, trainers, administrators) and drafting and signing the players for the team's inaugural season. Because the team is located in a city with a certain reputation (thus the nickname Sin City), the management group probably made personnel decisions with an eye toward off-ice factors such as personality. Teams located in less provocative environments (e.g., Minneapolis, Winnipeg) may have had very different conversations regarding an individual's personality or predisposition toward risky or harmful behavior. Would a team in Las Vegas want a high-risk personality among its core personnel?

Gambling and partying are major factors in Las Vegas society and culture. They contribute to the city's reputation ("What happens in Vegas stays in Vegas") and carry serious implications for the team and its ownership. Thus they necessitate sophisticated organizational policies in response (e.g., game-day curfews, rules regarding gambling). Given these realities, it was critical for the organization to carefully select each person hired, including coaches, players, and administrative staff. Of course, it is important for any professional sport team to create clearly articulated rules, policies, and regulations regarding employee behavior. But for the Golden Knights, located in Sin City, it was especially important to focus on establishing such policies in the early years of the organization. Equally important is the organization's follow-through on any disciplinary matters related to issues such as missed curfews or gambling troubles. More generally, it is crucial for any organization to reinforce key messages and important values in order to effectively manage its people and their behavior.

Case Study Questions

1. As general manager (GM) for the Golden Knights, it is critical for you to acquire human capital in order to build a successful franchise. Would you place more emphasis on recruiting veterans or rookies players? Why?

2. In light of open systems theory, how might management guard against risky behavior among the team's players? In other words, what sorts of things could management do to help players integrate safely and productively into the city?

3. If you were the GM for a visiting team (e.g., Detroit Red Wings), how would you police your players? Is it fair to impose specific player rules depending on the city in which the team is playing?

has much more to address. For instance, the frameworks borrowed from other disciplines to explain behavior in sport management were created in different time periods and referred largely to working-class white males; as a result, we now need a more contemporary and direct focus on sport organizations and their people. Thus when we consider the teachings of the parent disciplines and the early research in sport, we must challenge some widely held assumptions about work life and about the meaning of work that were rooted in the periods in which the research was conducted.

To put it another way, sport management practice and research can benefit from examining the realities of today's sport organizations that are vastly different from those of even 10 years ago. The research conducted to date has helped us explain and even predict aspects of work life, but organizations, groups, and individuals in the workforce are different now than they were 50 years ago. Consider, for instance, the current prevalence of dual-income families, geographically dispersed work, and workforces connected via technology. Moreover, such factors are constantly changing in response to the various external forces that act on the organization and on the individual's life.

When viewed as resources, human beings—and their ability to acquire and develop knowledge—can be seen as organizational assets that should be managed. Consequently, managers and researchers must consider the levels of management understanding related to OB and how they intersect to produce various outcomes for the individual, the group, and the organization as a whole.

DISCUSSION QUESTIONS

1. What are the three basic levels of management understanding related to OB?
2. What is an open systems view of an organization?
3. Why is human capital considered a resource for organizations?
4. Describe why it is important to engage in strategic planning and why managers should remain flexible and adaptable to the external environment.
5. What is the difference between tacit and explicit forms of knowledge?

Chapter 2

Understanding Diversity

Chapter Objectives

After studying this chapter, you will be able to

- describe diversity and differentiate surface- and deep-level diversity;
- explain the importance of diversity as an asset for sport organizations;
- describe management approaches that maximize the benefits of diversity for sport organizations;
- differentiate the concepts of stereotyping, prejudice, and discrimination; and
- explain how implicit bias affects individuals' selection and work experiences in sport organizations.

If properly managed, diversity can be a key asset to any sport organization. Fostering an inclusive environment for all employees and stakeholders can provide benefits such as reduced employee turnover, more time spent engaged in work-related tasks, and other positive behaviors by employees. It can also provide a strategic advantage because it allows an organization to respond effectively to the needs of diverse consumers, fans, participants, players, and other important stakeholders. Sport fans and participants are incredibly diverse, and organizations that constructively engage the diversity of their constituents are more likely to succeed and grow. Thus diversity is important not only to an organization's "bottom line" but also to its ability to support and celebrate the differences that its employees and stakeholders bring to their work and play.

Throughout this book, we use Cunningham's (2015) definition of diversity as "the presence of socially meaningful differences among members of a dyad or group" (p. 6). These differences can include both surface-level and deep-level factors. Surface-level differences involve readily observable characteristics, such as age, sex, physical ability, and race. Because these differences are easily observed, we tend to use them to make quick judgements about how we fit into an organization. In contrast, deep-level differences take less apparent forms—such as information diversity and value diversity—which require interaction between people in order to become known. Information diversity, for instance, involves differences based on knowledge, functional training, and tenure in an organization; it often results from differing levels of education or work-related experience, such as holding (or not) a law degree or graduate degree in business administration or serving (or not) as a representative of a local political or business organization. Value diversity, on the other hand, involves differences in values, attitudes, and beliefs—for example, valuing work experience more than a college degree or valuing time spent with family and friends more than working on weekends (Cunningham, 2015). Although these categories are distinct constructs, they are also connected; for instance, one study (Cunningham, 2006) found that when surface-level diversity increased among coaches, their perceptions of deep-level diversity also increased.

One of the most amazing things about working in sport is that it is universal— you can travel to any area of the world and interact with people who play, watch, and love to talk about sport. Depending on where you go, of course, the sport of choice may be hockey, basketball, cross-country skiing, or the world's most popular sport of soccer—but the general appeal of sport is experienced everywhere. Because

sport is universal, participant and fan communities are bound to include diversity; therefore, organizations that want to support their participants and fans must reflect and engage those differences. One example can be found in ESPN, which recognizes the importance of diversity in fulfilling its mission: "To serve sports fans wherever sports are watched, listened to, discussed, debated, read about or played" (ESPN, "About," n.d., n.p.). To help it fulfill this mission, ESPN seeks to recruit, hire, develop, and retain talented people who represent the organization's globally diverse group of fans. To find out more about the importance of diversity in ESPN's employment practices, check out the organization's career website at https://jobs.espncareers.com.

As sport organizations continue to become more diverse, the ways in which they work also change. These changes relate to the shift to a more service-based

IN THE BOARDROOM
Diversity, Inclusion, and Wellness at ESPN

The ESPN Diversity, Inclusion & Wellness team "strives to hire, develop, and retain talented people who represent . . . [the organization's] diverse global fans" (ESPN, "Diversity," n.d., n.p.). ESPN maintains several employee resource groups (ERGs) that are each led by employees and assigned a member of the executive team who serves as a champion for the group. Including more than 2,000 members overall, the ERGs provide a way for employees to connect based on shared interests or backgrounds. Examples include Young Professionals, Women, Asians, People With Disabilities, Latinos, Families, African Americans, and ESPN EQUAL (for gay, lesbian, bisexual, and transgender employees). The collective mission of the ERGs is to do the following (ESPN, "Diversity"):

- Educate and promote cultural diversity
- Network and learn from others
- Develop professional skill sets
- Add value to the business
- Expand the recruitment base
- Support ESPN's community and diversity outreach partnerships

economy in sport (Cunningham, 2015), which of course involves more direct interaction between employees and customers. Indeed, a service-based business succeeds only if it creates high-quality relationships between customers and employees. Researchers have noted that customers who believe they are interacting with people different from themselves experience less satisfaction in the interaction; therefore, building a workforce that reflects the different types of customers engaged by the organization may result in more positive customer service experiences (Cunningham, 2015).

In another ongoing change, both in the sport world and beyond, organizations increasingly use team-based approaches to tackle tasks and projects. In organizations that foster and support a diverse workforce, individuals who work in teams can interact with others who bring a wide variety of experiences, perspectives, and ideas. In this way, their differences can produce better work outcomes for the team and for the organization as a whole. Of course, as we discuss later in this chapter, working in a diverse group also comes with challenges. Therefore, the organization must provide support to help people overcome these challenges in order to make the most of diversity in a work team.

An additional consideration involves the increase in mergers and acquisitions in the sport industry, which sometimes involve global companies and can result in employees working with and for individuals from diverse backgrounds. In 2005, for instance, two of the largest sports apparel organizations merged when Adidas bought Reebok. Though both were international companies, Reebok was headquartered in the United States, whereas Adidas was based in Germany. Thus one of the initial challenges presented by the merger involved how to align the German organizational culture of engineering and design with the more marketing-focused organizational culture of a U.S. company. As this example suggests, the organiza-

tions that best support and foster an inclusive work environment enjoy an advantage in responding effectively to mergers and acquisitions. Furthermore, at the local level (e.g., towns, cities, regions), merging sport organizations may provide new and different perspectives on managing those organizations and better serve the needs of diverse customers (Cunningham, 2015).

Diversity in sport organizations can also be affected by legal mandates. In the United States, for instance, civil rights legislation mandates protection against discrimination based on race, gender, age, sex, physical ability, or religion; in addition, some state laws go further by protecting individuals from discrimination based on sexual orientation or gender identity. The first major U.S. legislation of this type to address the workplace was Title VII of the Civil Rights Act of 1964, which prohibited employment discrimination based on race, color, sex, religion, or national origin. Later, the Civil Rights Act of 1991 and the Lily Ledbetter Fair Pay Act of 2009 added provisions allowing individuals to recover compensatory and punitive damages for intentional violations of Title VII by an employer (U.S. Equal Employment Opportunity Commission, 2009). In another example, Title IX of the Education Amendments of 1972 affords protection for underrepresented groups (e.g., women in sport organizations) and has been used to protect individuals in cases of discrimination, notably sexual harassment. In Canada, the Canadian Human Rights act extends legal protection for individuals regardless of "race, national or ethnic origin, colour, religion, age, sex, sexual orientation, marital status, family status, disability, or conviction for an offence for which a pardon has been granted or in respect of which a record suspension has been ordered" (Canadian Human Rights Act, 2017, n.p.).

Legal mandates notwithstanding, sport organizations that lack a diverse workforce often face ethical challenges, most notably at the senior level (i.e., in the leadership team). One high-profile example can be found in the NFL's struggle to formulate even a barely adequate response to the issue of domestic violence committed by players. In response, calls continue to be made for the league to increase the diversity of its senior leadership—specifically, by including more women—to help it respond more effectively to this issue (Brinson, 2014).

More generally, social pressures have contributed to increased awareness of the need for a diverse workforce in sport organizations (Cunningham, 2015). In this vein, scholar and advocate Richard Lapchick (2016) and his colleagues collect extensive data regarding the racial and gender demographics of employees working in U.S.-based intercollegiate sport organizations and in major professional sport organizations in the United States and beyond. Lapchick and other sport management scholars—including Fink (2016), LaVoi (2016), Burton (2015), Cunningham (2015), and Walker and Melton (2015)—continue to call for an increase in diverse representation in senior leadership positions across sport organizations. The importance of diversity has also been voiced by external stakeholders, such as customers and prospective employees. For example, prospective employees have expressed more positive attitudes toward sport organizations that they believed were more diverse and maintained a more inclusive organizational culture (W. Lee & Cunningham, 2015).

UNDERSTANDING SOCIAL IDENTITY

In order to effectively manage diversity, we must understand the complexities of social identity, which is based on an individual's knowledge of belonging to certain social groups and on the emotional meaning of that belonging (Cox, 1994). For example, if you were asked who you are, you might answer by saying something like the fol-

lowing: "I am an undergraduate majoring in sport management," or "I am African American," or "I am a varsity athlete." Each of these statements might refer to a portion of your social identity. When an individual's social identity differs from the majority of an organization's members, this difference may become more noticeable; in such cases, a person may feel that he or she must act in a way that is not personally natural. For example, in terms of gender diversity, the majority of leadership positions in sport are filled by men (Lapchick, 2016), and women who are members of a male-dominated group or organization may feel pressured to act more like the men in the organization.

In addition, people often view others more favorably and feel more comfortable with them if they have similar social identities. That is, we tend to favor others from our own in-group and to hold more positive feelings toward them than toward people from outside the group. We also tend to exaggerate both the positives of our in-group and the negatives of any out-group (i.e., group other than our own); in fact, we tend to hold stereotypes of the out-group and ignore differences among its members (Hitt, Miller, & Colella, 2015). For example, members of a college sorority or fraternity tend to hold more favorable views not only of fellow members of their own group but also of members of other sororities and fraternities (i.e., their extended in-group) but more negative views of people who are not members of sororities or fraternities (their out-group).

DIVERSITY MANAGEMENT AND INCLUSIVE ORGANIZATIONS

As described earlier in the chapter, there are many reasons for a sport organization to value diversity. A bit later, we will examine individual, group, and organizational outcomes associated with diverse and inclusive organizations. First, however, we describe research examining the *practice* of diversity management, which must be carried out effectively in order for an organization to realize the potential benefits of diversity.

Fink and Pastore (1999) propose a model (figure 2.1) that includes four categories of diversity management, which fall on a continuum ranging from noncompliant with diversity management practices to the most strategically engaged practice of proactive management. Organizations found at the lowest level are considered noncompliant because they do not recognize the benefits associated with diversity or use inclusive practices. In fact, they tend to view inclusive practices as detrimental to effective organizational functioning. As a result, they run the risk of violating laws related to diversity (in places that have such guidelines, such as the United States and Canada) while also failing to consider any potential benefits associated with supporting diversity.

Further along the compliance continuum (Fink & Pastore, 1999), we find organizations that are compliant with legal requirements related to diversity but still fail to recognize the benefits of inclusive management. These organizations comply with laws in order to avoid legal complications but do not fully realize the benefits of having a diverse workforce. To the contrary, individuals who are different from the majority are expected to "fit in" by being like the other employees in the organization. In these organizations, individuals who do not fit with the majority are not supported, and organizational power is held by a few individuals in the majority group.

Still further along the continuum (Fink & Pastore, 1999), we find organizations classified as reactive to diversity management. These organizations recognize that effective management of diversity can lead to positive organizational outcomes—such as reaching different customer groups, generating creative sponsorship campaigns that attract new companies, and implementing diverse programming to attract new members—and therefore work to create

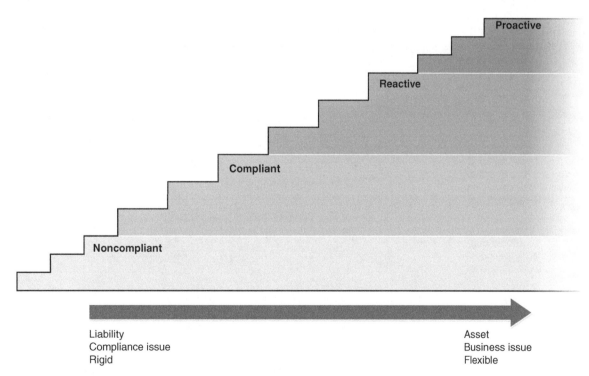

Figure 2.1 Framework for understanding diversity management in sport organizations.

Based on Fink and Pastore (1999, p. 321).

a diverse workforce. However, as reactive organizations, they make only sporadic efforts to implement or build on inclusive practices (e.g., once-a-year diversity training). This intermittent approach fails to fully activate the benefits that a diverse workforce can bring to an organization.

The most inclusive organizational diversity practices are used by proactive organizations (Fink & Pastore, 1999), which realize the full benefits of diversity. In these organizations, all areas are focused on developing and effectively managing a diverse workforce. More specifically, the organization's policies and procedures feature inclusive work practices, and power is shared by many individuals in order to maximize the benefits of diversity in the workforce.

We also highlight the multi-level model of organizational inclusiveness described by Cunningham (2015). This model (figure 2.2) focuses specifically on inclusion, which is described as "the degree to which employees are free to express their individual self and have a sense of workplace connectedness and belonging" (p. 275). The model identifies factors that support an inclusive work environment at the individual, leader, organizational, and macro

levels. At the individual level, inclusiveness and community can be facilitated by intergroup contact—that is, contact with people who are different from each other. This interaction may include difficult dialogues, such as discussing the effects of racism on co-workers, that can help create an inclusive organization. Such conversations can help individuals understand each other, understand differences, challenge counterproductive thinking, and stimulate new ideas about working together to meet the goals of the organization.

Efforts to foster organizational inclusiveness require effective leadership. Leaders who advocate for diversity can influence their employees' attitudes toward diversity; they can also set an expectation for their employees to engage in and promote inclusion in the organization. As Cunningham (2015) noted, when employees "are expected to hold inclusive attitudes and demonstrate inclusive behaviors, they are likely to do so" (p. 277).

Inclusiveness is also affected by factors at the organizational level, including education, programming, and inclusive practices. Organizations that succeed at creating an inclusive environment incorporate

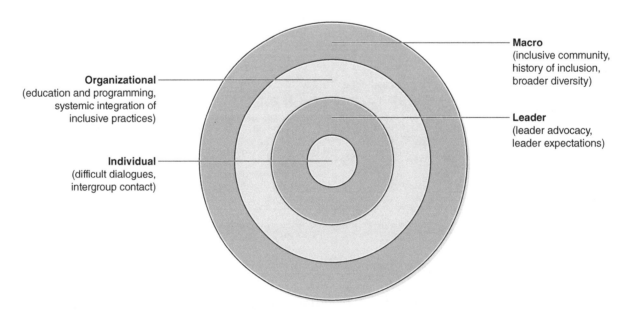

Figure 2.2 Multi-level factors affecting organizational inclusiveness.
Based on Cunningham (2015, pg. 276).

elements of diversity and inclusion into all areas of practice—for example, strategic planning, hiring procedures, and formal policies (Cunningham, 2015).

Finally, inclusive practices are affected at the macro level by the environment in which an organization operates. For instance, inclusive communities tend to be characterized by a larger percentage of people who hold a liberal political ideology, and they often adopt laws to mandate inclusion in the workplace. In turn, organizations located in diverse and politically progressive communities are more likely to implement inclusive work practices (Cunningham, 2015). Similarly, organizations embedded in larger organizations with a history of inclusive practices also tend to foster inclusion. For example, in the United States and Canada, collegiate athletic departments are situated within universities systems and therefore use the same inclusive practices adopted by those institutions.

Another example of inclusive practices can be found in US Lacrosse (n.d.), whose official inclusion statement is as follows:

US Lacrosse seeks to foster a national lacrosse community that encourages understanding, appreciation, and acceptance of all within its membership, volunteer base, and staff. Further, US Lacrosse believes that broad representation and participation add significant value to the lacrosse experience of each of us, and that these valued experiences are enhanced by embracing underrepresented and underserved communities.

The organization also provides a template for member organizations to use in assessing their diversity and inclusion efforts.

OUTCOMES ASSOCIATED WITH DIVERSITY MANAGEMENT

In order to fully realize the benefits of diversity in the workforce, a sport organization must either take the proactive approach proposed by Fink and Pastore (1999) or implement the strategies described in Cunningham's (2015) model of inclusive sport organizations. If diversity is managed effectively, the benefits can be realized by individuals, by the sport organization, and by the society in which the organization operates.

Individual Outcomes

In organizations that value and support employees as individuals, employees exhibit more commitment, deeper satisfaction, and greater involvement (Pellegrino, D'Amato, & Weisberg, 2011). Furthermore, organizations that have a gender-diverse workforce tend to experience less relationship conflict and task conflict (i.e., conflict specific to completing work-related projects) if they also foster a more inclusive and gender-equitable climate (Nishii, 2013). When organizations adopt inclusive management practices, individuals in the organization are more likely to feel that they are valued and treated fairly. In contrast, if individuals believe that they are devalued or treated unfairly, they may exhibit a decline in work performance, develop a desire to leave the organization, or consider filing a lawsuit against it (Colquitt, Conlon, Porter, & Ng, 2001).

When adopting inclusive and proactive strategies to manage diversity, sport managers should help all members feel that their needs are being heard and met—including those in the majority (which, in sport organizations, usually means white heterosexual men). As noted by Hitt and colleagues (2015),

To ensure commitment, satisfaction, and strong performance among those in a majority group, organizational leaders must (1) carefully build and communicate the case for diversity by citing the forces of change discussed earlier and (2) ensure fair decision processes and fair outcomes for all. (p. 46)

Organizational Outcomes

When an organization adopts inclusive practices and takes a proactive approach to diversity management, the resulting benefits on the organization level include increased creativity, greater ability to perform complex tasks, and more effective decision making (Hitt et al., 2015). In one study of sport organizations with a racially diverse staff, those that adopted a proactive approach to managing diversity enjoyed stronger organizational performance—as measured by NACDA Directors' Cup points—than those that did not adopt such a strategy (Cunningham, 2009). Using the same criteria for organizational performance, similar results were found for sport organizations with higher diversity in terms of sexual orientation (Cunningham, 2011).

In a study examining diversity of sport participants (rather than staff), an increase in cultural diversity among players (i.e., in players born in Europe) on an NHL team resulted in better team performance (Kahane, Longley, & Simmons, 2013). However, if the cultural diversity included players from a wide range of European countries, some performance declines were noted. These declines were attributed to challenges associated with language and communication barriers.

Societal Outcomes

Sport organizations have always faced ethical challenges and will continue to do so. One way to minimize these challenges is to recognize the benefits of diversity and adopt an inclusive or proactive strategy for managing it. The alternative can be quite costly. For instance, after winning the 2015 World Cup, five members of the U.S. women's national soccer team filed a wage discrimination lawsuit against U.S. Soccer, the national governing body for the sport. The complaint, filed with the U.S. Equal Employment Opportunity Commission, charged that U.S. Soccer committed wage discrimination by paying the women's team nearly four times less than the men's team even though the women's team was better known and more successful and was exceeding projected revenues by $16 million (Powell, 2016). In April of 2017, the U.S. women's team reached an agreement with the U.S. Soccer Federation. Terms of the new agreement included "generous

IN THE BOARDROOM

Nike Expands Support for Diversity

Mark Parker, who serves as chairman, president, and CEO of Nike, has stated Nike's desire to use "the power of sport to advance equality—on the field and in life" (SGB Media, 2017). One of the many ways in which Nike has put this desire into action is by partnering with organizations that serve diverse communities. In 2017, for instance, Nike announced partnerships with two groups: MENTOR and PeacePlayers International (SGB Media, 2017). MENTOR is a U.S. organization that facilitates high-quality mentoring for youth and connects volunteers to opportunities in their local communities. PeacePlayers is a global organization that uses basketball to help young people unite from divided communities, including individuals living in the Middle East, Northern Ireland, and South Africa. The group trains coaches to support participation in basketball and create opportunities for participants to engage in difficult conversations about race and other issues in their communities.

increases in base pay and match bonuses, better per diem allowances, enhanced travel benefits and increased financial support for players who are pregnant" but this "does not necessarily guarantee equal pay with their male counterparts" (The Guardian, 2017, para. 4).

In another example, after the University of Iowa dismissed longtime field hockey coach Tracey Griesbaum in September 2014, four players filed a civil rights complaint against the university (Ackers, Silfer, Cafone, and Hemeon et al. v. University of Iowa, 2015). The players charged athletic director Gary Barta with a pattern of removing highly qualified female coaches and alleged that the university had discriminated against them on the basis of sex by engaging in practices that were discriminatory or had discriminatory effects as a result of violations of Title VII of the Civil Rights Act of 1964. (See table 2.1 for an overview of U.S. federal laws preventing discrimination in employment.) The players alleged differential treatment of female student-athletes as compared with male student-athletes, including overreaction to complaints by a small group of female student-athletes while failing to reprimand a male coach who physically harmed a group of male student-athletes. As stated in the complaint,

The University's stereotype-motivated reaction to a minority group of females on the team emotionally upset by the methods of the female coach also harms the females who complained. It enables stereotypes about them as well as the coach and completely undermines the experience of the entire team. (p. 5).

Both of these cases could be viewed as hinging in part on a lack of gender diversity—specifically, on the male-dominated leadership of both U.S. Soccer and the University of Iowa's athletic department. In a similar vein, calls have been made by Lapchick (2016) and other scholars—including Hawkins, Carter-Francique, and Cooper (2016)—to increase racial diversity in coaching, especially among football programs in the NCAA Division I Football Bowl Subdivision (FBS). FBS football is typically the largest revenue-generating sport for a Division I athletic program (U.S. Department of Education, 2017), and the majority of the student-athletes participating in it are African American; yet less than 10 percent of those student-athletes are led by a black head coach (Lapchick, 2016). To date, no legal complaints have been brought against universities regarding race discrimination in the hiring of coaches. Nonetheless,

Table 2.1 U.S. Federal Laws Prohibiting Job Discrimination

Title VII of the Civil Rights Act of 1964 (Title VII)	Prohibits employment discrimination based on race, color, religion, sex, or national origin.
Equal Pay Act of 1963 (EPA)	Protects men and women who perform substantially equal work in the same establishment from sex-based wage discrimination.
The Age Discrimination in Employment Act of 1967 (ADEA)	Protects individuals who are 40 years of age or older from employment discrimination.
Titles I and V of the Americans with Disabilities Act of 1990, as amended (ADA)	Prohibit employment discrimination against qualified individuals with disabilities in the private sector and in state and local governments.
Sections 501 and 505 of the Rehabilitation Act of 1973	Prohibit discrimination against qualified individuals with disabilities who work in the federal government.
Title II of the Genetic Information Nondiscrimination Act of 2008 (GINA)	Prohibits employment discrimination based on genetic information about an applicant, employee, or former employee.

it appears that systemic challenges tied to racial discrimination may contribute to the scarcity of black coaches in college football (B. Joseph, 2016).

CHALLENGES TO DIVERSITY IN SPORT ORGANIZATIONS

Having reviewed the myriad benefits associated with diversity when sport organizations manage it inclusively and proactively, we turn now to the challenges that organizations may face when working to establish a diverse and inclusive work environment. These challenges include the ways in which stereotypes influence our thinking and contribute to the development of prejudice; in turn, these two factors influence the behavioral construct of discrimination. When you understand these concepts, you can take steps to overcome any challenges that you may face when working in a diverse and inclusive sport organization.

Stereotyping

Stereotyping involves the "the unconscious or conscious application of (accurate or inaccurate) knowledge of a group in judging a member of the group" (Banaji & Greenwald, 1994, p. 58). Essentially, a stereotype consists of a collection of beliefs held about a group of people, including beliefs about their attributes and skills. These beliefs can act as a key cause of bias against and poor treatment of people who differ from oneself (Cunningham, 2015). Stereotypes are damaging because they fail to take into account the uniqueness of all individuals. In other words, though we may encounter a person who fits a stereotype that we hold, we can just as easily find someone who does not fit that stereotype—for example, an intelligent and studious athlete. Even so, stereotyping can be difficult to overcome, because we tend either to discount information that counters the stereotype or to view an individual who does not fit into it as merely an exception to it.

We see the influence of stereotypes throughout sport organizations, including in sport leadership and in our notions of who is suited to hold a leadership position. For example, women may be stereotyped as lacking the necessary skills and attributes for leadership positions even when evaluators indicate that a woman would be equally likely to succeed when compared with a similarly qualified man (Burton, Grappendorf, & Henderson, 2011). Of course, stereotypes also affect the individual who is subjected to stereotyping. In the phenomenon of stereotype threat, a person is evaluated through the lens of a negative stereotype, which can be detrimental to his or her achievement in a particular role or task (Steele & Aronson, 1995). For instance, stereotype threat has been demonstrated in college sport participation, as female athletes exhibit a decline in performance when exposed to gender and sex stereotypes that view females as less athletically capable than males (Chalabaev, Sarrazin, Fontayne, Boiché, & Clément-Guillotin, 2013). Even though the female participants observed in the study were high-level athletes, they were still affected by stereotyping that ran counter to their own self-identity, thus illustrating how damaging a stereotype can be.

Prejudice

Prejudice typically consists of a negative attitude toward or evaluation of another group or an individual from that group; examples include racism, sexism, homophobia, and ableism. At the same time, Cunningham (2015) cautions us to be aware that prejudice does not always involve a negative attitude. In some cases, we may hold positive attitudes both toward people who are like us (i.e., who are from our in-group) and toward people who are different from us (i.e., from an out-group) yet still be biased because we hold more positive attitudes toward the in-group than toward the out-group.

In order to fully understand how prejudice affects our behavior, we must also understand that prejudice comes in two types: explicit and implicit. We are typically thinking about explicit prejudice when we consider prejudice in general terms. Explicit prejudice involves consciously held attitudes toward a specific group. Explicit or overt forms of prejudice are socially constructed, which means that, based on certain social cues or contexts, we may feel that it is more appropriate to express prejudice toward certain groups. For instance, in the context of sport in the United States, researchers in one study found that it was considered more acceptable to express sexist comments than racist ones when making attributions for a loss (Cunningham, Ferreira, & Fink, 2009).

Not all prejudice, however, is consciously or deliberately expressed (Cunningham, 2015). To the contrary, implicit prejudice operates at an unconscious level and does not require deliberate thought. Thus it can be difficult to recognize because individuals may not believe that they carry it. One readily accessible way to explore whether you hold implicit bias is to take the Implicit Association Tests found on the Project Implicit website. The anonymous tests are completed online, and participants are provided with a debriefing report to help understand and interpret the results.

Discrimination

Discrimination is a behavioral construct that results in unfair and inappropriate treatment of individuals or groups (Cunningham, 2015). It can take the form of either access discrimination or treatment discrimination. In access discrimination, members of a particular group are denied entrance into a particular job or profession. For instance, research has extensively documented access discrimination against women in coaching in both men's and women's sports. More specifically, women continue to face access discrimination in seeking head coaching opportunities in Division I women's sports (Acosta & Carpenter, 2014; LaVoi, 2016) and in seeking coaching positions in men's sports (Walker & Melton, 2015). Moreover, as we can readily observe, this finding holds true beyond the college level: Despite the number of men who coach women's sports, women are not provided with access to coaching positions in men's sports. We do have at least one high-profile exception, in the NBA, where Becky Hammon serves as an assistant coach with the San Antonio Spurs and in 2016 became the first woman to be part of a coaching staff in the NBA All-Star Game. Of course, access discrimination in coaching is not limited to sex discrimination; for example, work by Cunningham and Sagas (2005), among others, has noted that African Americans also find only limited opportunities in coaching.

Treatment discrimination, in contrast, involves actions taken against certain groups when they are members of a sport organization. This form of discrimination can include behaviors denying individuals access to certain information or resources that are necessary in order to complete work or succeed in the profession. It can also include negative behaviors directed toward certain individuals, such as negative comments and hostile acts. Treatment discrimination can occur in combination with access discrimination. For example, in the profession of athletic training, researchers have uncovered both access and treatment discrimination against young female athletic trainers (Burton, Borland, & Mazerolle, 2012). These trainers were often denied opportunities to work in high-profile men's sports (access discrimination), and when they were able to work in men's sports their decisions (e.g., diagnosis of player injuries, criteria for return to play) as sports medicine professionals were constantly scrutinized by male coaches (treatment discrimination). As one participant who had four years of experience working as a full-time athletic trainer noted, "there have been occasions where I've seen them [male coaches] go directly to a male athletic trainer and then ask (in front of me) questions about the exact same thing I was trying to explain to them" (Burton et al., 2012, p. 312).

DOES DIVERSITY TRAINING WORK?

Diversity training is "the educational process whereby people acquire skills, knowledge, attitudes, and abilities pertaining to diversity-related issues" (Cunningham, 2015, p. 312). Such programs help provide valuable skills, knowledge, and abilities to individuals who work in diverse settings, yet they are often met with resistance and therefore have the potential to be more negative than positive for sport organizations. With this caveat in mind, organizations must tailor their diversity training programs to meet their specific needs (Cunningham, 2015).

The many positive outcomes associated with diversity training include the potential for employees to develop improved attitudes and motivation at work, which can increase both morale and satisfaction. In addition, when employees better understand diversity, they are able to engage in more effective diversity-related behaviors (e.g., using more inclusive language). Finally, diversity training can lead to improved organizational compliance with legal mandates, thus avoiding lawsuits related to discriminatory behavior toward employees (Cunningham, 2015).

Among potential negative outcomes, diversity training requires employees to consider sensitive issues (e.g., racism, homophobia), and some employees may resist discussing such topics in a work setting. Furthermore, employees who are part of a gender or racial majority may perceive the training as blaming them for the challenges associated with a diverse workforce. Employees may also question the connection of diversity training to their daily work and wonder how such training can improve organizational effectiveness.

Thus, when an organization considers implementing a diversity training program, it must consider both the potential positive outcomes and the potential negative ones (Cunningham, 2015).

Before embarking on diversity training, the organization should conduct a needs analysis in order to understand where training is needed, who requires training, and what should be included in the training (Roberson, Kulik, & Pepper, 2003). The resulting objectives should be kept in mind as the program is implemented. These objectives should align with the organization's mission and strategic vision and take account of the needs of employees with particular job responsibilities, such as customer interaction. They should also focus on the needs of individual employees; each person comes to the training with unique diversity-related experiences, attitudes about diversity, and behavioral tendencies (Cunningham, 2015).

Here is a list of guiding questions that can be used to support best practices in implementing diversity training in sport organizations.

1. What are the stated objectives of the training session?
2. How do the training objectives align with the objectives of the organization?
3. What are the specific characteristics of the individual stakeholders who will attend the training—for example, in terms of work experience, tenure in the organization, attitudes toward diversity, and experience in working with diverse groups?
4. What stakeholder needs (e.g., of leaders, managers, interns, volunteers) must be met in the training?

Newly emerging work by Bohnet (2016) encourages organizations to focus their diversity training efforts on becoming bias-free organizations. As discussed earlier in this chapter, all individuals hold stereotypes, including implicit bias (i.e., bias below the surface), yet we can also take actions to minimize the influence of those biases in our work. One popular approach for minimizing bias in the hiring process involves using a "blind" audition. For instance, a music director might ask candidates to perform their auditions behind a screen, which allows the director to hear the audition without considering the performer's appearance. In one study, the use of screens led to a dramatic increase in the number of women selected (Goldin & Rouse, 2000).

Some organizations are also seeking to reduce bias in the hiring process by adopting new technology. For instance, services such as GapJumpers, TalentSonar, and Applied allow employers to remove applicants' demographic information and focus only on their potential as employees (Bohnet & Morse, 2016). This sort of approach is only one step toward becoming a bias-free organization, but it is an important one.

Organizations should also consider reviewing any practices that are perceived to be bias free but might in fact negatively affect certain groups. These practices might include self-evaluation of performance (men tend to rate themselves more competent and effective while women tend to underestimate their competence and effectiveness), the scheduling of meetings in the late afternoon or evening (which poses challenges for primary caregivers, who are most often women), and the use of golf outings for networking events (which tends to favor upper-income white men over members of other groups). Another key practice is the use of symbols, artifacts, and ceremonies that demonstrate what the organization values (for more on these considerations, see chapter 14). For instance, when pictures or portraits of past leaders line the halls, consider what they say about the organization's approach to diversity. As these examples indicate, taking steps to build a bias-free organization does not necessarily have to involve expensive or extensive changes; to the contrary, the relatively inexpensive ideas

mentioned here can make a meaningful difference in developing a more inclusive sport organization (Bohnet, 2016).

SUMMARY

Sport organizations will continue to engage diverse fans, employees, participants, and other critical stakeholders. Diversity can occur at both the surface level, in the form of readily identifiable cues, and at a deeper level that requires more substantive inquiry to uncover. Organizations that proactively manage diversity—on both levels—and develop inclusive management practices will reap the benefits of diversity. For instance, individual employees in such organizations are more committed to the organization, less likely to quit or look for new positions, and less likely to bring a lawsuit alleging discriminatory practices. In addition, such organizations benefit from increased creativity and ability to handle complex tasks. In the world of sport, organizations that manage diversity inclusively and proactively can also achieve better on-field performance.

As we strive to reap the many benefits available to sport organizations that proactively manage diversity, we must always be mindful of the influence of stereotyping, prejudice, and discrimination. Though it can be difficult to recognize, we must be aware that implicit prejudice (implicit bias) can affect how individuals are recruited, hired, and retained. To help minimize bias, organizations can implement thoughtful diversity training and take other concrete steps, such as using new technologies that allow employers to consider applicants without reference to their demographic characteristics. Though no sport organization can claim to be completely bias free, we are hopeful that you—the new generation of sport managers and leaders—will aspire to make your sport organizations free of bias and help them maximize the benefits of diversity for all stakeholders.

CASE STUDY

Improving Gender Diversity in Intercollegiate Sport

As athletic director for a major university competing in the NCAA Division I FBS, you have reviewed the latest Racial and Gender Report Card issued by Richard Lapchick (2016) and the latest Head Coaches of Women's Collegiate Teams: A Report on Select Division I Institutions in 2016-2017 produced by Nicole LaVoi (2017). You are troubled by the lack of women and the lack of racial and ethnic diversity (among both men and women) among head coaches at the collegiate level. When you see that your university has received a D grade for the percentage of women in head coaching positions, you decide that you must address the issue. To begin doing so, you initiate an evaluation of employees' work experiences in the athletic department. Specifically, you ask members of the sport management faculty to conduct an anonymous survey to evaluate the department's diversity climate and to help conduct confidential interviews with women who either currently work in the department or have recently left.

After analyzing results of the climate survey and the confidential interviews, the sport management faculty provides you with a report of findings. One significant finding indicates a perceived favoritism toward the older white men in the department, who tend to lead the teams that receive more departmental support in terms of funding, human resources, and marketing and communications staff. In addition, the women coaches who were interviewed after leaving the program described a departmental climate that did not support their ideas and initiatives to improve the experiences of the female student-athletes they coached. These former coaches also described being marginalized in meetings—for example, talked over or ignored when making important points—and left out of important decisions that affected their teams.

After reviewing these findings, you realize that it is past time to make some changes in order to better support your women coaches and to hire and recruit new women into the department.

Case Study Questions

1. How would you describe the climate of the athletic department in question? Evaluate the climate based on the model of an inclusive athletic organization described by Cunningham (2015).

2. Is diversity training needed in this athletic department? Why, or why not? If so, what steps should the department take before embarking on the training?

3. How would you address potential challenges to diversity training from department employees?

DISCUSSION QUESTIONS

1. Consider the other students in your sport management courses, then describe the diversity of this group in terms of both surface and deep-level diversity. As part of your answer, describe how you were able to determine deep-level diversity.

2. Using the model of diversity management put forward by Fink and Pastore (1999), describe how diversity is managed by your favorite sport organization.

3. Define the terms *stereotype, prejudice*, and *discrimination*. To help explain each term, provide examples from sport organizations.

4. Provide definitions for access discrimination and treatment discrimination and use an example from a sport to support your understanding of each type of discrimination.

5. Describe three or four actionable steps that sport organizations can take to become more bias free.

Chapter 3

Ethics in Sport Organizations

Chapter Objectives

After studying this chapter, you will be able to

- define ethics and explain the importance of ethical codes of conduct in organizational behavior,

- articulate why it is important to study ethics in organizational behavior for sport organizations,

- explain ethical decision making in sport organizations, and

- describe current ethical challenges in organizational behavior faced by sport organizations.

Ethics is a critical component of effective organizational behavior, and this is particularly true in the sporting world in light of the pervasive ethical challenges found in sport. Although professional sport has been the scene of numerous high-profile scandals, it is hardly the only sector of sport that requires close consideration of ethics. To the contrary, ethical challenges are faced by employees, managers, and leaders at all levels, from youth sport to secondary schools through intercollegiate and international sport. When faced with these challenges, individuals must make decisions about how to handle unethical behavior by organization members and other key stakeholders, such as fans and boosters.

Unfortunately, some of the most egregious examples of unethical behavior in sport have occurred in just the past decade. Of course, one of the most prominent cases involved the late Joe Paterno, the legend-

ary football coach at Penn State. By all accounts, Paterno generally exhibited the hallmarks of an ethical college football coach and was known as an upstanding member of the university community, but his failure to report allegations of child sexual abuse by his former colleague Jerry Sandusky resulted in immeasurable harm to victims who might otherwise have been spared. Additional allegations charge that other members of the university, including the president and athletic director at the time, also failed to report concerns about Sandusky (Hobson & Boren, 2016). Ethical challenges have also been faced by the most popular professional sport league in the United States—the National Football League. For instance, many observers have argued that the NFL's response to research linking football to concussions and debilitating brain injury has followed a path similar to the denialism exhibited by Big Tobacco in response to research linking cigarettes to lung cancer (Schwarz, Bogdanich, & Williams, 2016).

These scandals, and many others in the world of sport, affect a wide range of people, including employees, customers, fans, and other stakeholders. Moreover, they illustrate the fact that when unethical behavior occurs, it is often known to more than just a select few individuals (or leaders) in the organization. Therefore, in order to minimize ethical scandals, sport organizations must take steps to develop an ethical environment. Critical elements in such an environment include personal integrity, an inclusive mind-set, social responsibility, and global sustainability (i.e., respecting the needs of future generations) (Nahavandi, Denhardt, Denhardt, & Aristigueta, 2013).

ETHICS

Before we discuss ways to support employees in an ethical environment, we must first define the term *ethics*. For the purposes of this chapter, we draw on the work of DeSensi and Rosenberg (2010), who define ethics as consisting of the "principles and concepts of right and wrong conduct and decisions" (p. 4). Thus ethics differs from morality, which involves "expressions of values, attitudes, and lifestyles by specific social groups and individuals" (DeSensi & Rosenberg, 2010, p. 4). We focus here on ethics because it helps determine how individuals should act, whereas morality critiques the "quality and standards of a particular group" (DeSensi & Rosenberg, 2010, p. 4). Because ethical issues plague all levels of sport, it is critical for us to understand ethics when managing and leading individuals in sport organizations.

In the sport world, ethical considerations tend to be guided and explained by three major ethical foundations: deontology, teleology, and existentialism. Deontology describes right behaviors and decisions as being guided by the rules, duties, and norms of conduct agreed on by a community or society (DeSensi & Rosenberg,

2010). The deontological perspective does *not* consider the implications of the behavior or decision. For example, suppose that an athletic director learns that her most successful and respected coach has provided a meal to her team that goes beyond what is allowed by NCAA rules. Using a deontological approach, the athletic director would report the meal to the NCAA as a violation regardless of any sanctions that might be imposed as a result.

In teleology, on the other hand, behavior is judged as right or wrong on the basis of whether it produces good or bad consequences. As noted by DeSensi and Rosenberg (2010), "whenever one weighs the benefits and the costs of some action (or inaction) when confronted with a moral problem, one focuses on the consequences of one's behavior" (p. 56). Returning to the preceding example, if the athletic director considers the fact that sanctioning the coach would diminish the experiences of the team members, then she may gear her decision to minimize the negative effect on the student-athletes.

The third foundation, existentialism, guides behavior not on the basis of what is right or wrong but on the basis of authenticity. As described in existentialism, authenticity is determined by two guiding principles: "that individuals create their own essence and [that] individuals must take responsibility for their own actions" (Pfleegor & Seifried, 2016, p. 393). In other words, each person determines ethical behavior based on what is authentic to him or her. Returning again to the preceding example, if the athletic director takes an existentialist approach, her decision regarding how to handle the NCAA violation will be guided not by what is right or wrong or by the potential outcomes but by what she holds as authentic to herself and her leadership.

Regardless of the ethical foundation used, each individual in a sport organization is responsible for his or her "intentional personal and professional actions and behaviors as a manager within the context of sport" (DeSensi & Rosenberg, 2010, p. 114). This responsibility to act ethically extends to all projects and tasks to which the individual is assigned as a member of the organization—whether as a leader, manager, employee, volunteer, or intern. The following section details some ways in which sport organizations can help guide ethical behavior by all members.

DEVELOPING AN ETHICAL ENVIRONMENT IN SPORT ORGANIZATIONS

Having established a working definition of ethics, we can now examine the four critical elements of an ethical environment: personal integrity, an inclusive mind-set, social responsibility, and global sustainability. We begin with a focus on you. As a current or potential member of a diverse sport organization—for instance, ESPN, Adidas, the National Women's Soccer League, a local YMCA, or your college or university—you are responsible for your own ethical behavior. Accordingly, the first step in developing an ethical environment is to act with personal integrity—meaning that you think and act in a manner congruent with your morals and beliefs.

If this seems like an easy step to take in a sport organization, consider the following example: You are beginning your first day as an event operations intern for an athletic department that competes at the highest level of college football—the NCAA Division I Football Bowl Subdivision. It's game day, and your only responsibility is to ensure that no one but the referees enters the referee locker room before the game. This restriction is designed to ensure that no one unduly influences the referees. Much to your surprise, after the referee crew leaves the locker room, the head umpire and the legendary football coach from your university ask you to unlock the room so that they can speak privately about a personal matter. What do you do? How might your response be influenced by the

three major ethical foundations described earlier in the chapter—deontology, teleology, and existentialism?

The development of an ethical environment also requires the organization to foster and support an inclusive mind-set (a process that is discussed in detail in chapter 2). As described by Cunningham (2015), this type of mind-set can be facilitated by encouraging individuals to engage in (sometimes difficult) conversations with people who differ from us, expecting leaders to advocate for equity and promote inclusion in the organization, and providing education and programming to support inclusion and demonstrate inclusive practices.

The third critical component of an ethical environment is social responsibility. You may be familiar with the term *corporate social responsibility* (CSR), which refers to organizational-level actions that go beyond the goal of generating profit (i.e., benefiting the bottom line) to focus on improving the social well-being of community members and sustaining the environment in which the organization operates. One good example can be found in the Red Sox Foundation, whose mission is to harness "the passion of Red Sox Nation [in order] to make a difference in the lives of children, veterans, families, and communities throughout New England by improving their health, educational, and recreational opportunities" (Red Sox Foundation, n.d.). Among its efforts, the foundation provides support to local health services organizations, scholarships to students engaged in community service, and programming to increase the number of children who play baseball in inner cities. A more in-depth discussion of CSR is provided later in this chapter.

The final component of an ethical environment is global sustainability, which involves "meeting the needs of the present generation in a way that does not compromise the capacity of future generations to meet their needs" (Nahavandi et al., 2013, p. 25). One example of global sustainability is provided by innovative environmental initiatives undertaken by Nike. In an effort to minimize the use of carbon (a significant contributor to greenhouse gas emissions), Nike strives to be part of a low-carbon growth economy. The company uses carbon as a leading indicator to assess sustainability but also recognizes that "sustainability goes way beyond carbon. It means addressing all our impacts on the environment and the communities where we operate, supporting labor rights in supply chains, while continuing to serve the athlete and our business" (Nike, n.d., n.p.). However, even with those stated efforts to address global sustainability, Nike continues to face scrutiny for unsafe labor practices in factories across the developing world. Recent allegations against Nike and other apparel companies include dangerous working conditions for employees at factories in Cambodia and Vietnam (Segran, 2017). All sport organizations must recognize that global sustainability requires a commitment to both the environment and the communities living in that environment, as one cannot be prioritized over the other.

IMPORTANCE OF LEADERSHIP IN DEVELOPING AN ETHICAL ENVIRONMENT

Leadership is critical to fostering and supporting an ethical environment in a sport organization. An organization's level of ethical environment reflects employees' perceptions of the organization's ethical policies, practices, and procedures (K.D. Martin & Cullen, 2006). Leaders shape the ethical environment by setting clear standards for employees and holding them accountable to those standards (Mulki, Jaramillo, & Locander, 2008). They also do so through their own behavior; in other words, ethical leaders help support an ethical environment both directly and indirectly.

Ethical leaders are recognized as "honest, caring, and principled individuals who make fair and balanced decisions" (Brown & Treviño, 2006, p. 597). They can be described in terms of two dimensions: moral person and moral manager (Treviño, Brown, & Pincus-Hartman, 2003). The moral-person component of ethical leadership involves demonstrating concern for others and being approachable, whereas the moral-manager component involves demonstrating behavior and supporting organizational processes that meet moral standards (Brown & Mitchell, 2010, p. 584). For example, the leader of a highly successful sport organization might facilitate an ethical climate for employees by supporting volunteer service projects in the community—not only by providing funds to pay for supplies and feed volunteers (moral manager) but also by joining volunteers on a Saturday to help perform the service work (moral person).

Acting as an ethical leader requires thoughtful action and personal development. Ethical leaders must be able to "identify ethical dilemmas and engage in ethical decision-making processes that require an awareness of personal and professional values" (Hancock & Hums, 2015, p. 120). They must act with the utmost fairness and honesty and be trustworthy. They must also assure all employees and relevant stakeholders that the organization supports reporting unethical behavior. An ethical environment cannot exist if the leader allows unethical behavior to occur or, worse, justifies such behavior (Hancock & Hums, 2015). Here are some best practices that leaders can use to support an ethical climate:

- Set clear expectations regarding ethical behavior. Use and share codes of ethics and codes of conduct with all stakeholders in the sport organization.
- Ensure that leaders of sport organizations model the expected behaviors as provided in the code of ethics and code of conduct.

- Support and reinforce ethical behaviors. Recognize and reward those stakeholders who demonstrate the desired behaviors. For those who do not demonstrate ethical behavior, consider appropriate punishments (including possible removal from the organization if necessary).
- Provide necessary training and support to help develop ethical behavior. This can include hosting seminars and workshops that provide clear expectations of ethical behavior and communicating resources available to stakeholders to help support ethical behavior (e.g., steps regarding how to report unethical behavior by co-workers).

CODES OF ETHICS

Codes of ethics (or ethical policies) are adopted by organizations to serve as guidelines for ethical behavior by all stakeholders. Those who are bound by an organization's code of ethics typically include employees, volunteers, coaches, and athletes. In order to be meaningful, a code of ethics must clearly state basic principles and expectations and address ethical dilemmas that members of the organization may face (DeSensi & Rosenberg, 2010). Furthermore, to ensure that the code is accepted, it should be developed with input from as many members of the organization as possible (DeSensi & Rosenberg, 2010). In addition, to facilitate successful adoption of the code, the organization should address it in orientation sessions for new employees (see chapter 8), make it readily available to all members, and frequently revisit it to ensure that it remains relevant to the needs of the organization's members and continues to meet current professional standards.

Establishing a code of ethics can benefit a sport organization in several ways. On the macro level, for instance, the code helps specify the organization's social responsibilities, and the explicit guidelines laid out in the code help the organization act with fairness and honesty. On the individual level, the code provides stable and permanent guidelines for right and wrong actions by employees and other organizational stakeholders; it can also motivate individuals to act ethically as a result of positive peer pressure.

Codes of ethics are necessary at all levels of sport, and, again, they apply both to members of the organization and to other stakeholders, such as guests, fans, and customers. For instance, as youth sport has grown increasingly specialized, including increased commitment of financial resources for travel to tournaments and the use of specialized coaches (e.g., strength and conditioning coaches), the pressures on those working and volunteering in youth sports has increased as well. To help support ethical behavior many youth sport organizations have recognized the importance of establishing codes of ethics for staff, coaches, and parents. One such organization, USA Hockey, provides a clearly stated code of ethics intended "to provide standards of ethical conduct for coaches involved with USA Hockey and its member organizations" (USA Hockey, n.d., n.p.).

Ethical policies or codes of ethics provide guiding principles that the organization expects employees, volunteers, customers, fans, and other important stakeholders to follow as representatives of that organization. These expectations may address discrimination, harassment, bullying, improper relationships, communication, and the use of drugs (including alcohol and tobacco). The U.S. based National Federation of State High School Associations (NFHS) is an interscholastic athletic association that provides a code of ethics for high school coaches. Following are some of the codes as provided by the NFHS (Coaches Code of Ethics, 2017).

- The coach shall be aware that he or she has a tremendous influence, for either good or ill, on the education of the student and, thus, shall never place the value of winning above the value of instilling the highest ideals of character.

- The coach shall uphold the honor and dignity of the profession. In all personal contact with students, officials, athletic directors, school administrators, the state high school athletic association, the media, and the public, the coach shall strive to set an example of the highest ethical and moral conduct.

- The coach shall take an active role in the prevention of drug, alcohol and tobacco abuse.

Another way to support ethical behavior in a sport organization is to establish a code of conduct, which is similar to a code of ethics but different in that it provides a specific set of guidelines to support ethical behavior. A code of conduct provides a set of rules, responsibilities, or guiding behaviors that are viewed as proper practices for individuals, groups, or the organization as a whole. Most professional leagues and teams have established a code of conduct to guide behavior by employees, coaches, players, fans, and other important stakeholders.

Here are some typical statements in a code of conduct for a team or sport facility:

- Players respect and appreciate all fans.

- Fans are treated in a consistent, professional, and courteous manner by facility and team personnel.

- Fans enjoy the game free from disruptive or unruly behavior, including foul or abusive language or obscene gestures.

- Fans sit only in their ticketed seats and show their tickets when asked to do so.

- Fans who engage in fighting, throw objects, or try to enter the court or field of play are immediately ejected from the game.

- Fans do not display obscene or indecent messages on signs or clothing.

- Fans comply with requests from facility staff regarding operations and emergency response procedures.

ETHICAL DECISION MAKING

In addition to providing guidelines that encourage ethical actions by employees, volunteers, interns, fans, customers, and other stakeholders, sport organizations must also consider ways to support the process of making ethical decisions. Fortunately, several models are available to help us understand how to support ethical decision making. Here, we detail a model recently put forward by Pfleegor and Seifried (2016)—the etho-conventional decision-making model for sport managers (see figure 3.1)—which we believe provides a comprehensive approach to understanding how to best support ethical decision making.

In order to better understand this model, we must briefly describe the foundations of formalism, conventionalism, and interpretivism in sport philosophy. Formalism is the most rigid of the philosophical foundations and requires strict adherence to the rules of a sport (e.g., formal rulebook) or the rules established by a sport organization. In other words, all decisions made on the basis of a formalistic philosophy would strictly follow the rules as written. Conventionalism, in contrast, is the least restrictive foundation. It views strict adherence to rules as limiting the essence or ethos of sport, which conventionalists argue should include adopting novel strategies and ways of enhancing the game. This approach has been criticized for the difficulty that can be encountered in determining whether a given behavior follows the ethos of the sport in question or constitutes cheating. A middle way between formalism and conventionalism is offered by interpretivism, which integrates "adherence to the constitutive rules with conventions, social

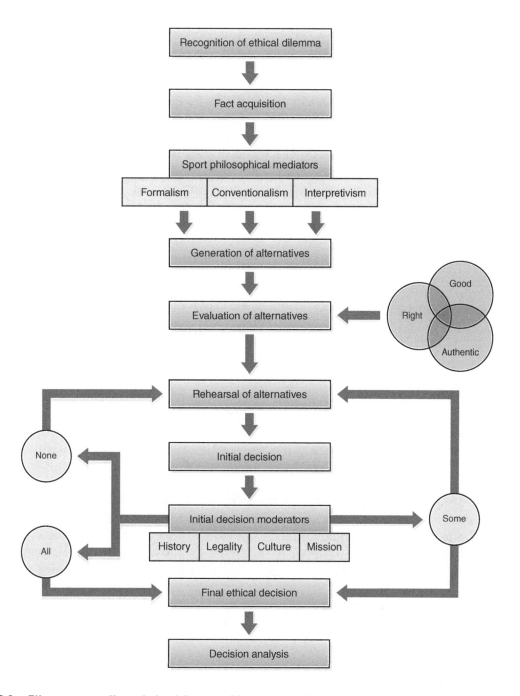

Figure 3.1 Etho-conventional decision-making model for sport managers.

Reprinted by permission from A. Pfleegor and C. Seifried, "Ethical Decisions in Sport: Etho-Conventional Decision Making Model for Sport Managers," *International Journal of Sport Management* 17, (2016): 383-407.

issues, and outside resources to determine right and wrong" (Pfleegor & Seifried, 2016, p. 396).

The first step in the etho-conventional model is to recognize the very existence of an ethical dilemma. Although this step may seem obvious, we must understand that *many* decisions required in sport organizations include an ethical component. Examples include the hiring and firing of personnel, the distribution of academic records and other sensitive personal information, and employee performance evaluations.

The second step is to acquire all information relevant to the dilemma; this process should address both primary (i.e., individuals directly involved in the dilemma) and secondary (i.e., individuals not directly involved with but aware of the dilemma) sources. Next, the information gathered should be interpreted using the three sport philosophy foundations—that is, formalism, conventionalism, or interpretivism—in order to generate alternatives for the decision maker to consider in determining how to address the dilemma. These alternatives are then evaluated through the ethical foundations of deontology, teleology, and existentialism to help the decision maker consider possible actions in terms of what is right, good, and authentic.

After evaluating the available options, the decision maker can develop an initial ethical decision. This decision should then be evaluated further through a filtering process that takes into account any issues of legality, as well as the organization's history, culture, and mission. Once the decision has been filtered through those four factors, the sport manager can make a final ethical decision. After the decision is implemented, the manager should evaluate its positive and negative effects in order to learn and grow from the process.

ETHICAL GUIDELINES IN HUMAN RESOURCE MANAGEMENT

Some ethical considerations are particularly relevant to the area of organizational behavior known as human resource (HR) management. Specifically, ethical behavior is crucial to the HR management processes of hiring and firing employees, socializing new employees into the organization, and meeting ethical obligations to current employees (DeSensi & Rosenberg, 2010).

Ethical responsibilities in the hiring of employees include honestly representing the necessary qualifications for a given position, as well as the responsibilities it entails. For instance, many positions in sport organizations require employees to work on some nights and weekends. In such cases, both the organization as a whole and the specific individuals who carry out the hiring process have an ethical responsibility to be very clear about that expectation when writing the job description and interviewing prospective employees. Further along in the process, when making decisions about hiring, sport managers must do so in a manner that is free of discriminatory elements and complies with applicable federal and state laws. Some sport organizations impose additional requirements, such as anti-nepotism provisions that bar individuals from being hired for positions under a family member's supervision. Of course, managers should hire only those individuals who possess the needed qualifications and capabilities to carry out the duties outlined in the job description.

Ethical considerations also arise in the key processes used to socialize employees into the organization, such as orientation, training, and evaluation. The organization should take care to help new employees understand all expectations associated with employment, including the organization's ethical code or code of conduct. Employees must also be provided with appropriate training in order to carry out their job responsibilities. For example, a new employee in the ticket office of a professional sport team may need to be trained in using the organization's proprietary ticketing software.

Effective employee evaluation is critical to the success of any sport organization and must be conducted in an ethical manner. In order for the process to be ethical, the evaluation must be tailored to criteria that are necessary for performing the stated job responsibilities. Any evaluation instrument used must be reliable and of similar quality to other evaluation instruments. Furthermore, the evaluation system (including any instruments used) must be shared with and supported by the members of the organization. Feedback from the evaluation must be shared with the employee and be used as a tool to help the employee improve and potentially advance in the organization.

Another important ethical consideration with regard to employees involves the nature of the relationship between the employee and the employer. Employees have certain rights (provided in the United States by federal, state, and sometimes local law) that protect them in the hiring and firing process, in receiving a fair wage, and in having their privacy respected. In turn, the employer is obligated, both legally and ethically, to ensure that these rights are maintained. The employer must also be aware that ethical challenges can arise in the power differential between employer and employee; with that in mind, the employer must work to maintain an appropriate balance of power. For example, a new intern working in the athletic marketing office may be eager to gain experience and thus be willing to work every available event. The intern's supervisor must not take advantage of this eagerness; instead, the supervisor should ensure that

the intern works a manageable number of hours while being provided with a meaningful learning experience.

CORPORATE SOCIAL RESPONSIBILITY

At this point in the chapter, we have discussed the importance of ethics in sport organizations and provided resources to help you understand ethics in the context of organizational behavior. In this section, we address the concept of corporate social responsibility as one way in which ethical behavior can be demonstrated in the operations of a sport organization. Corporate social responsibility consists of voluntary actions taken by an organization in order to respond to social and environmental concerns in its operations and its interactions with stakeholders (Van Marrewijk, 2003).

A number of researchers in sport management have examined how organizations undertake CSR actions. In our view, the optimal framework (Babiak & Wolfe, 2009) is one that takes a stakeholder-centric approach to CSR (see figure 3.2). When

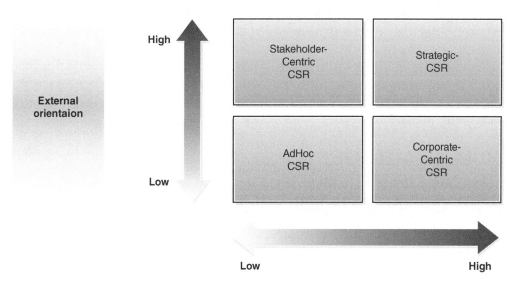

Figure 3.2 Determinants of the adoption of corporate social responsibility in professional sport: a proposed framework.

Reprinted by permission from K. Babiak and R. Wolfe, "Determinants of Corporate Social Responsibility in Professional Sport: Internal and External Factors," *Journal of Sport Management* 23, no 6(2009): 717-742.

IN THE BOARDROOM
NBA FIT: Stakeholder-Centric CSR

The NBA FIT program is a "comprehensive health and wellness platform" (National Basketball Association, n.d., n.p.) that encourages children and adults to engage in physical activity, follow guidelines for proper nutrition, and maintain a healthy lifestyle. The program features a dedicated website that offers resources and information related to working out, tips for maintaining a healthy lifestyle, and a pledge that participants can sign in order to commit to staying fit. The program partners with coaches (including strength and conditioning coaches) and health care experts to share their knowledge in support of physical activity and healthy lifestyle choices. NBA FIT also operates programs in the communities of NBA and WNBA teams—for example, NBA FIT Live Healthy Week (National Basketball Association, n.d.).

sport organizations take this approach, they "align their core competencies using . . . [their] unique abilities to benefit society, thus enabling . . . [them] to fully realize the potential of CSR both for . . . [their] beneficiaries and for the team [i.e., the organization]" (p. 735). From the perspective of organizational behavior, using a stakeholder-centric approach to CSR allows the organization to align its ethical approach to sport and the actions it takes to actualize or implement its ethics. In essence, stakeholder-centric CSR allows the sport organization to "talk the ethical talk and walk the ethical walk." One example of stakeholder-centric CSR is highlighted in the sidebar titled NBA FIT: Stakeholder-Centric CSR.

FUTURE CHALLENGES IN ETHICAL OPERATIONS OF SPORT ORGANIZATIONS

Sport organizations will undoubtedly continue to face ethical challenges in the realm of organizational behavior. We discuss a few of those challenges here—in intercollegiate sport, professional sport, and technology in sport—but this discussion certainly does not provides an exhaustive consideration of what lies ahead. Therefore, we encourage you to contemplate other ongoing ethical challenges, as well as those that may yet arise.

Intercollegiate sport will continue to face ethical challenges in both decision making and leadership due to ongoing pressure to win and increase revenue. Specifically, universities continue to rely on athletics as a marketing tool to increase student applications, increase enrollment of out-of-state students, enhance reputation, and, for a small percentage of universities, bring in considerable revenue. As a result, the pressure to win will continue to be felt by athletic directors, administrators, and coaches. At the same time, these individuals also face other pressures, such as fielding the most talented team possible within the academic requirements of the university and ensuring that student-athletes maintain their academic eligibility according to NCAA requirements. These competing pressures can lead to unethical decisions that carry negative implications for all of a university's stakeholders. To see how the desire to win can take precedence over all else, we need only to review the scandal related to alleged sexual assaults, other crimes, and cover-ups by members of the Baylor University football program

IN THE BOARDROOM
The Knight Commission on Intercollegiate Athletics

Intercollegiate athletic programs—particularly Division I Football Bowl Subdivision (FBS) programs—face significant challenges, including the rising cost of maintaining competitive teams, pressure from stakeholders to win and keep winning, and the need to generate revenue to support their programs. These challenges can lead to ethical issues, including cheating (e.g., fake classes, improper tutoring assistance) geared to keeping athletes academically eligible. In this environment, the Knight Commission on Intercollegiate Athletics seeks to influence policies to better support the academic experiences of student-athletes. The commission has produced reports and built an interactive database that stakeholders in college athletics can use to understand the current state of college sport and the spending it entails (Knight Commission on Intercollegiate Athletics, 2017). As a future employee in a sport organization, you can use resources provided by the Knight Commission on Intercollegiate Athletics and other groups (such as the College Sport Research Institute in Columbia, South Carolina) to stay informed about issues facing collegiate athletic administrators.

under the leadership of then-coach Art Briles (Goodwyn, 2017).

On the professional level, both sport leaders and other stakeholders will continue to face the ethical challenge of how to address the growing crisis of traumatic brain injury in contact sports. The NFL and the NHL need to provide honest and ethical leadership that can serve as an example for those in youth sport and interscholastic and intercollegiate sport. Unfortunately, as of yet, league leaders have chosen to resist honest, significant reforms that would help support retired players who suffer from debilitating injuries as a result of head trauma sustained during their playing days (Lupica, 2016; Branch, 2016).

In addition, ethical challenges will continue to be created by technological developments that enable fast and easy sharing of information. Social media platforms (e.g., Snapchat, Twitter, Instagram, Facebook) can closely link fans with players and employees of sport organizations in exciting ways. Yet for all the positive connections they enable, we have also witnessed the ugliness that can occur when individuals hide behind a screen name. This ugliness was brought to the fore in the summer of 2016 by two prominent sports reporters, Sarah Spain and Julie DiCaro. In a video that quickly went viral, men read tweets posted about Spain and DiCaro that highlighted the harassment and abuse they have experienced on Twitter. (To view the video, search YouTube for "#MoreThanMean." Warning: The content is disturbing.) Another troubling trend involves the use of social media to attack athletes (usually football players) when they are perceived to be responsible for a team's loss. Athletic departments, and coaches in particular, have been quick to respond to such attacks, but more work needs to be done on the issue—perhaps, for example, establishing a social media code of ethics for fans to follow.

SUMMARY

Ethics and integrity are critical to effective organizational behavior in the sport industry, and developing an ethical environment is crucial to minimizing ethical problems.

CASE STUDY
Ethical Challenges in Youth Sport Administration

As fall arrives, you are excited to begin your first season as director of the Smithton Youth Soccer League. Though you look forward to watching the 30 teams play, you also recognize that some coaches and parents have exhibited conduct that does not support the principles of youth sport development, such as fun, fair play, and good sportspersonship. Unfortunately, it is not long into the season before you are approached by a group of disgruntled parents. They allege that the top team in the sixth-grade league (the Smithton Firecrackers) is violating the age requirement established by the league by allowing five players to play on their team who appear to be older and more mature than others in the league. The parents also complain that the coach of the Firecrackers (Coach Sarah) tends to use those five players for the majority of each game and that the scores are therefore lopsided. For example, one parent refers to a game in which her daughter's team lost 11-0 to the "more mature" Firecrackers. The parents also complain that Coach Sarah yells harshly at her players, even though you have received no complaints from parents of players on her team.

Case Study Questions

1. Identify the ethical dilemmas presented in this fictional case study.
2. Evaluate one of these dilemmas by using the etho-conventional decision-making model for sport managers.
3. As director of the Smithton Youth Soccer League, what actions could you take to address the ethical dilemmas identified in question 1?

The development of an ethical environment hinges on personal integrity, an inclusive mind-set, social responsibility, and global sustainability.

Ethics differs from morality. Whereas morality involves expressions of values and attitudes that are specific to certain social groups and individuals, ethics involves concepts and principles that undergird right and wrong decisions. Thus ethics guides behavior, and all members of a sport organization are responsible for their personal and professional actions. This responsibility extends to all projects and tasks assigned to an individual as a member of the organization, whether as a leader, manager, employee, volunteer, or intern. Leaders of sport organizations play an integral role in establishing ethical guidelines and creating an environment that supports ethical decision making. A code of ethics can be used to set expectations for ethical behavior in the organization.

DISCUSSION QUESTIONS

1. Research the code of ethics or code of conduct for a professional sport organization and for a youth sport organization. Compare the two documents, then discuss the reasons for their similarities and differences.

2. Identify an ethical issue faced by a specific sport organization, then apply the etho-conventional model to reach your own decision about how to address the issue.

3. Review CSR activities conducted by a professional sport organization and determine whether they align with Babiak and Wolfe's notion of stakeholder-centric CSR.

4. What future ethical challenges (beyond those mentioned in the chapter) do you think will need to be addressed by leaders of sport organizations?

PART II
MANAGING THE INDIVIDUAL

The first three chapters of the book covered what we consider to be critical aspects of OB for today's sport manager. In part II, we delve into aspects of OB that view the individual as a person, as an actor in organizational life who is responsible for his or her own work pleasure, and as a critical part of the organization. As we contend, a people-centered manager understands the person and his or her interests, needs, and wants; in other words, a people-centered manager views the person as more than a body to fill a spot in the organization.

In addressing personality and attitudes, chapter 4 helps explain why individuals seek out and excel in particular types of work and how employers and managers can use this information to identify, select, and train people for specific positions in sport organizations. The chapter also addresses how attitudes influence behaviors and vice versa. In addition, it discusses the interaction of personality with motivation and satisfaction, thus setting the scene for later chapters in the book.

Chapter 5 examines how individuals learn, which is a critical component of both individual and organizational success because it allows us to construct and implement appropriate training and development programs. These programs must use effective learning processes and goal setting in order to best support employee performance. Learning can occur through classical conditioning, operant conditioning (positive and negative reinforcement), and social learning. This chapter also explores motivation, which is another important component of individual development and successful performance.

Chapter 6 examines job satisfaction, which is of course one of the key outcomes sought by individuals in their work. In addition, the chapter discusses critical psychological states that employees may experience, as well as ways in which managers can help enrich jobs. It also addresses the importance of respecting the employee's voice and considers various ways in which an employee might handle dissatisfying aspects of work.

Job stress affects just about every person who works, but people perceive stress in different ways. With this diversity in mind, chapter 7 discusses various stakeholders in sport and how they experience and deal with stress. The chapter also addresses the differences between eustress and distress and examines what happens in prolonged stressful situations that can lead to burnout. In addition, the chapter covers ways in which managers can recognize stress and help prevent the workplace from becoming an unwell or overly stressed environment for people.

In chapter 8, we examine the process through which a person is recruited, hired, and brought into an organization to perform a job. Specific topics include the formation of the psychological contract, the information that people need in order to integrate into the organization, and the key human resource activities of training and development. The chapter also covers the nature of enduring versus temporary roles in sport and discusses ways in which practicing managers can respond to various scenarios.

Chapter 4

Understanding Personality and Attitudes

Chapter Objectives

After studying this chapter, you will be able to

- describe the traits associated with the Big Five personality model,

- explain how motivation influences a person's behaviors in a work setting,

- describe the interactional approach to understanding personality and behavior,

- discuss the concepts of intelligence and emotional intelligence and how emotional intelligence influences a person's behaviors in a work setting,

- describe how attitudes influence behavior and how behaviors can influence attitudes, and

- define the concepts of organizational commitment and job satisfaction and describe their importance to work outcomes in sport organizations.

In order to understand how individuals work in an organization, we must understand personality, emotions, attitudes, and motivations. Of course, we can train individuals to use many skills in order to succeed in the sport industry—for example, managing a budget, using software to handle ticket sales or video editing, and performing facility maintenance. But success on the job is also affected by factors that are unique to each person—elements that we each bring to an organization that will not change dramatically regardless of any training we receive. To help understand these stable aspects of who we are, consider how you would reply to some the following statements:

I have a vivid imagination.

I am comfortable around new people.

I am not polite when I don't want to be.

I tend to procrastinate.

I feel like I'm on an emotional roller coaster.

I see myself as someone who is sometimes shy or inhibited.

Such statements are found in many readily available personality assessments. Your replies can help you understand who you are and how you would work in a particular position in a sport organization. The sport industry offers many types of work in many settings. For example, consider the work skills—as well as the personality traits, attitudes, and motivation—necessary to be succeed in the following positions:

- Inside ticket sales representative for an NHL team
- Youth programming coordinator for a municipal recreation department
- Compliance coordinator for a university athletic department
- Director of event operations for a minor league baseball team

Here are some answers: For an inside ticket sales position, the ideal employee is competitive, willing to talk to strangers, and comfortable with failure (at least some of the time). A youth programming coordinator should be creative, outgoing, and patient with children. A good compliance coordinator will bring strong attention to detail, be willing to engage in disagreements (and perhaps conflict) if faced with the prospect of an NCAA violation, and be comfortable with working alone at times. And a director of event operations needs to be comfortable with making changes and adjustments quickly, be patient with customers, and be able to pay close attention to details.

When you understand the various aspects of your personality and know what motivates you to do your best, you are able to seek out positions that provide the best fit for you. At the same time, sport organizations want to hire individuals who have personality traits and motivational profiles that fit the organization and align with the needs of the job (see chapter 8 for more information about how individuals are socialized into sport organizations and chapter 14 for more information on individuals' contributions to and support of organizational culture). At this point, you may be thinking that you have a pretty good sense of your personality and attitudes, but can you learn more? A good first step is to look for resources at your college or university. Most campuses include a center for career services or career development that is happy to provide you with tools (online or in person) to help you assess your personality traits, attitudes, and motivations.

INTELLIGENCE

Intelligence is one of the unique, stable aspects of a person that affects his or her work outcomes. Intelligence, or innate cognitive ability, is also referred to as *general mental ability* (GMA). It has been proven to serve as a reliable predictor of a person's occupational level and performance at work (Schmidt & Hunter, 2004). However, even though GMA is closely linked to work outcomes, measures of intelligence continue to be controversial, and some scholars question whether such measures accurately capture an individual's level of intelligence. For example, the player evaluation process associated with the NFL draft uses a popular measure of intelligence known as the Wonderlic Personnel Test (WPT). The test has been touted as an important part of evaluating a player's potential for success in the league. However, research has found that WPT scores are unrelated to future performance and number of games started in the NFL (Lyons, Hoffman, & Michel, 2009).

UNDERSTANDING PERSONALITY

What makes a person behave in relatively consistent ways in different situations? We can begin to answer this question by developing an understanding of personality. Formally, personality can be defined as a "relatively stable set of characteristics that influence an individual's behavior" (Nelson & Quick, 2013, p. 84). There is some debate about what determines an individual's personality, but it is generally believed to depend both on one's heredity and on the environment to which one is exposed. Key

IN THE BOARDROOM
Using the Wonderlic in Sport

The Wonderlic Personnel Test (WPT) has been used in the NFL since the 1970s, and its popularity has been attributed to Hall of Fame coach Tom Landry, who viewed it as an important measure of player potential. Here are some sample questions: "A package of gift cards has a length of 8 inches, a width of 4 inches, and a volume of 64 inches cubed. What is the height of the box?" "The eighth month of the year is?" "What is the mathematical average of the number of feet in a yard, seconds in a minute, and months in a year? Enter a numerical value only." Intelligence testing constitutes only one part of the evaluation process for a player's potential success in the NFL, which hinges on many other attributes as well. In fact, the WPT does not appear to be a strong predictor of NFL success, and some of the most successful players have scored below average for their positions, including MVP quarterback and Super Bowl champion Brett Favre (Nieves, 2016). Thus, although the Wonderlic test may be able to predict something about a person's level of intelligence, it fails to accurately predict the intellectual qualities needed for success in football. As a result, in 2013, a new measure was introduced. Known as the Player Assessment Tool, it was designed specifically for football and measures various mental abilities, motivation, learning style, and other psychological attributes (Krupat, 2017). If it is found to predict NFL success with reasonable accuracy, it may replace the WPT.

aspects of an individual's environment include family, education, and culture.

One way of studying personality is to use a trait approach that understands personality by categorizing behavior into sets of observable traits. One of the most popular trait approaches is the Big Five personality model (De Raad, 2000), which, as shown in figure 4.1, focuses on extroversion, agreeableness, conscientiousness, emotional stability, and openness to experience (McCrae & John, 1992).

Extroversion

Extroversion is defined as the degree to which an individual is "outgoing and derives energy from being around other people" (Hitt, Miller, & Colella, 2015, p. 142). Individuals who are extroverted or outgoing tend to be sociable and more assertive than those who are less extroverted. In a group, they tend to be the talkative members who are willing to take charge. Extroverted people are often drawn to positions in sales and development because they are able to connect with different types of people, comfortable with talking and socializing in order to cultivate sales, and inclined to seek the challenge associated with such positions. Overall, extroverted individuals tend to have higher levels of job satisfaction (Judge, Heller, & Mount, 2002), though this relationship has not been tested specifically in sport organizations.

Agreeableness

People with a personality viewed as agreeable tend to be cooperative, tolerant, warm, easygoing, and sensitive to the needs of others. They also exhibit humility, tend to presume honesty in others, and are more likely to yield in cases of conflict (Hitt et al., 2015). Agreeable people may not fit

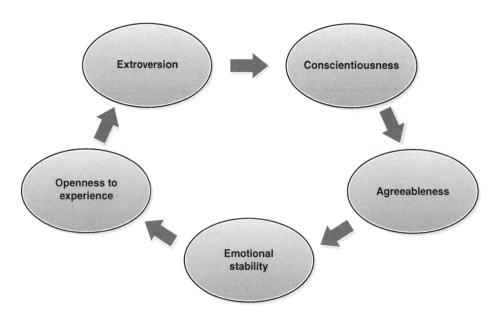

Figure 4.1   The Big Five personality traits.

better than other people into any certain type of position in a sport organization, but agreeableness can be a very favorable attribute when managing or leading a group or team. For example, consider the roles and responsibilities assigned to the director of a local recreation organization, then think about the variety of stakeholders with whom the director interacts. An agreeable personality can be beneficial, for instance, as the director works to address the needs of all members of the community—from children to senior citizens—or works with local elected officials in managing a facility budget. At the same time, having too many people in an organization with an agreeable personality can be detrimental to group functioning, because debate and disagreement sometimes help people resolve issues or meet challenges, thus producing better outcomes for the organization.

Conscientiousness

Conscientiousness is defined as the degree to which "a person focuses on goals and works toward them in a disciplined way"

(Hitt et al., 2015). Individuals considered to be conscientious are reliable, organized, and inclined to follow through on assignments. Moreover, people who rate high in conscientiousness tend to perceive themselves as capable, possess a drive for success, and think before acting (Hitt et al., 2015). As you might expect, conscientiousness is a beneficial personality trait for individuals who work in an organization (sport or otherwise) and relates strongly to job satisfaction (Judge, Heller, & Mount, 2002). Conscientious individuals are particularly suited to perform work that requires strong organization skills and attention to detail. Good jobs for such people include athletic administration positions with a focus on NCAA compliance and positions focused on drafting and reviewing contracts in an athlete representation firm.

Emotional Stability

Emotional stability is evidenced by how easily an individual handles stressful situations and heavy demands; a person with high emotional stability will be calm, self-confident, and relaxed. Other aspects of emotional stability include being slow to anger and rarely discouraged or embarrassed. Because such individuals tend to be relatively free of anxiety and hostility, they tend to be better at meeting performance standards and more likely to experience high levels of job satisfaction (Hitt et al., 2015). In addition, individuals who combine emotional stability with extroversion and conscientiousness are more likely to exhibit potential for team leadership (Gajendran & Joshi, 2012). Emotional stability is a positive personality trait for all employees in sport organizations, especially in the professional and high-level intercollegiate ranks, which tend to operate under heavy scrutiny in fast-paced environments.

Openness to Experience

Individuals are considered high in openness to experience if they tend to seek out new experiences and think creatively about the future (Hitt et al., 2015). Other aspects of openness include curiosity, insightfulness, and a wide range of interests. Individuals with high levels of openness can be well suited for creative and inventive positions—for example, marketing and promotions, sport media, sport product development, and new sport ventures (i.e., development of new sporting events, such as those seen in adventure racing).

Thus the Big Five personality traits offer considerable potential benefits, but they can also be associated with potential detriments. In fact, an extremely high level of any given trait can be detrimental in a work context. For instance, extremely high conscientiousness can lead an individual to pay too much attention to insignificant details that detract from achieving overall job goals. Here's an example: Working in a sport communication department may require a person to submit daily press briefings for members of the local media. In this position, a person with

extremely high conscientiousness might spend a great deal of time editing and rewriting a briefing in order to make it "perfect" before releasing it. However, timeliness is as important as attention to detail in writing press briefings, and paying too much attention to detail can reduce timeliness. In another example, extremely high emotional stability may lead an individual to over-control emotions, which can be counterproductive to the development of social relationships in the workplace (Nelson & Quick, 2013). For instance, an athletic director who over-controls his or her emotions may have a difficult time demonstrating empathy and support for coaches and student-athletes, which could give the impression of not caring about their emotional or physical well-being.

PERSONALITY AND EMOTIONAL INTELLIGENCE

At this point, you may wonder where emotional intelligence (EI) fits into the discussion of personality. The concept was popularized in 1985 by Daniel Goleman's best-selling book *Emotional Intelligence*. In psychology literature, it has been defined in two ways: ability-based EI and mixed EI. Ability-based emotional intelligence is defined as "the ability to carry out accurate reasoning about emotions and . . . to use emotions and emotional knowledge to enhance thought" (Mayer, Roberts, & Barsade, 2008, p. 511). The more common understanding of emotional intelligence—mixed EI, as described by Goleman—deploys a more general concept that includes personality traits, perceived abilities, and individual affect. Mixed EI, which has been more closely linked to positive work performance than has ability-based EI (Joseph & Newman, 2010), is less a type of intelligence and more a mix of certain personality traits: conscientiousness, extroversion, and aspects of self-efficacy (Joseph, Jin, Newman, O'Boyle, 2015).

Emotional intelligence is relevant to organizational behavior because it influences how individuals engage with others and perform work in organizations, including sport organizations. Individuals with higher levels of mixed EI tend to use their emotions to better manage challenges in the workplace while maintaining a positive mood; they are also good at motivating people around them to work toward a common goal (Wan, Downey, & Stough, 2014). Emotional intelligence also exerts a positive influence on counterproductive work behavior (CWB), which is defined as "deliberate behavior of employees that violates significant organizational policies and norms . . . [and] thereby damages the well-being of the organization and/or its employees" (Keskin, Akgün, Ayar, & Kayman, 2016, p. 283). Examples include being late for work, working slowly, skipping work, engaging in verbal abuse, bullying, and harassing (Keskin et al., 2016). CWBs and other negative behaviors are less likely to be exhibited by persons with higher EI (Jung & Yoon, 2012).

More specifically, when considering the challenges of college coaching, emotional intelligence has been shown to help coaches handle emotional stressors in their work. In one study, coaches with higher EI were better equipped than those with lower EI to handle the emotional exhaustion associated with coaching (Y.H. Lee & Chelladurai, 2016).

COGNITIVE CONCEPTS IN PERSONALITY

Cognitive concepts describe "properties of individuals' perceptual and thought processes that affect how they typically process information" (Hitt et al., 2015, p. 146). You are likely familiar with some cognitive concepts related to personality, which include locus of control, authoritarianism, and self-monitoring.

Locus of Control

Locus of control reflects whether one believes that control resides internally (within oneself) or externally (in other persons or in circumstances). People who have a high *internal* locus of control believe in their ability to control what happens to them and to affect the world around them. In contrast, those with a high *external* locus of control feel that they have little or no control over what happens to them and may even believe that they have no option but to follow what is imposed on them. In comparing these two groups, research has found that people with a high internal locus of control believe that if they work hard they can succeed, even at difficult tasks; moreover, they experience more positive social and work-based personal interactions and greater job motivation (Ng, Sorensen, & Eby, 2006).

Authoritarianism

Authoritarianism has been defined as "the degree to which an individual believes in conventional values, obedience to authority, and legitimacy of power differences in society" (Hitt et al., 2015, p. 147). People who subscribe to authoritarianism tend to believe that the use of status and power is necessary and appropriate in organizations and tend to be more submissive to people in positions of power. They are also more likely to engage in or support unethical behavior at work (Son Hing, Bobocel, Zanna, & McBride, 2007). This pattern is concerning when considered in the context of sport organizations, which, as discussed in chapter 3, continue to face considerable ethical challenges. Authoritarianism has been examined in sport participation, but research is lacking in the context of organizational behavior. Accordingly, in a review of research on leadership in sport organizations, Welty Peachey and colleagues (2015) called for more attention to the "darker side" of personality attributes, including the influence of authoritarianism on leadership behavior.

Self-Monitoring

Self-monitoring reflects the degree to which one's behavior is guided by one's true self. As a concept, it helps us understand how consistent a person's behavior is across different situations. People who are high in self-monitoring tend to adapt their behavior to particular circumstances and may be described as "chameleon like." In contrast, people who are low in self-monitoring stay closer to their true selves regardless of situation. Overall, low self-monitors are guided more by internal cues regardless of situation, whereas high self-monitors are more likely to use situational or external cues (e.g., social norms, others' expectations) to guide their behavior (Oh, Charlier, Mount, & Berry, 2014). At work, high self-monitors tend to receive more favorable performance evaluations and to emerge as leaders in their organizations (Day & Schleicher, 2006). However, they may also have lower levels of commitment to the organization and tend to be opportunistic by taking a better position if one becomes available (Oh et al., 2014).

MOTIVATIONAL CONCEPTS IN PERSONALITY

Achievement motivation consists of a person's desire to succeed or to perform to a certain level of excellence in a competitive situation. If you have studied sport psychology, you may recognize this term and recall the application of achievement goal theory (Duda & Hall, 2001) in understanding sport performance. Achievement motivation helps explain a person's aspiration, effort, and persistence in tasks where performance is evaluated against a standard of excellence. In the context of work, individuals with high achievement motivation, or high need for achievement, seek out tasks that require skill and effort, are moderately challenging, and provide clear feedback on

 IN THE BOARDROOM

Importance of Personality for Successful Teams

When we consider the composition of successful teams—whether sports teams or work teams in sport organizations—we often focus on the functional skills required for success. For instance, we think of a successful basketball team as one with a high shooting percentage, strong defensive capability, and various specific basketball skills. In order to put together a successful team, however, we need to think about more than functional skills. We also need to consider personality types and psychological roles, such as being pragmatic, being results oriented or relationship focused, being a process and rule follower, and being an innovative or disruptive thinker. You can learn more about psychological roles through both free and paid services. For instance, free testing is available on the 123test website, which allows you to select from word pairs (e.g., scientific/impulsive, ambitious/harmonious, sober/emotional) to help you understand the psychological roles you may best fulfill. And remember, when putting together a team (whether work based or sport based), consider both functional roles and psychological roles to position your team for success.

performance (C.J. Collins, Hanges, & Locke, 2004). Achievement motivation has been linked to career choice and has also been shown to be an important characteristic for individuals working in entrepreneurial careers. In particular, "individuals high in achievement motivation are more likely to be attracted to occupations that offer high degrees of control over outcomes, personal responsibility, feedback on performance, and moderate degree of risk" (C.J. Collins et al., 2004, p. 112).

INTERACTIONAL APPROACH

Up to this point, we have discussed how individual behavior is shaped by personality, but it is also influenced by context—that is, by the situations in which people act and interact. This idea forms the basis of interactional psychology, which challenges us to understand human behavior by examining both the person and the situation (Terborg, 1981). Interactional psychology includes four main components:

1. Human behavior is a continuous process with multidirectional feedback between the individual and the situation.
2. The individual is active in the process and is both changing the situation and changed by it.
3. Behavior is influenced by learning, motivation, and ability.
4. Behavior is determined in major ways by the psychological meaning attached to the situation and by the person's behavior potential in the situation.

First, human behavior is a continuous process of multidirectional feedback between the person and the situation. Imagine, for instance, that you are spending the summer as an intern for a minor league baseball team. As part of your game-day duties, you are assigned the job of selecting fans to participate in on-field promotions. During your first game, you decide to select fans who are wearing the team's jersey. During this process you have many interactions with different types of fans (e.g., including several who were wearing a team jersey but refused your invitation).

The second component holds that the person is active in the process and is both changing the situation and changed by it. In the example of the baseball internship, you realize during several interactions with fans that the most enthusiastic fans, not only those who are wearing team jerseys, are responding favorably to your request. Third, behavior is influenced by learning, motivation, and ability. Using the baseball example, you recognize that fans refuse your requests if you ask later than the fifth inning so you change your strategy to ask for participants during the first five innings.

Finally, behavior is determined in major ways by the psychological meaning attached to the situation and by the person's behavior potential in the situation (Terborg, 1981). For example, as the baseball season progresses, you become close with your co-workers who develop the promotions. This closeness motivates you to be sure that you find the best fans to participate, thus making your co-workers' promotional ideas fun and successful (in addition to working well for the fans, the team, and the promotional sponsors).

To recap, as we consider the interactional perspective, we must consider not only personality traits but also cognitive (learning) and motivational attributes. We must also consider the situation in the context of organizational behavior, which includes the sport organization, specific work groups, job characteristics, personal life situations, and environmental influences (Nelson & Quick, 2013).

ATTRIBUTIONS IN ORGANIZATIONAL BEHAVIOR

In order to understand why people behave in different ways in different situations, we must also consider attributions, or inferred causes. Attribution theory can help us understand the causes of our own behavior and the behaviors of other people. Attributions for behavior can be directed to an internal set of causes that lie within the person's control (e.g., preparation for a project) or to an external set of causes that lie outside of the person's control (e.g., a chaotic workplace).

For instance, in the context of organizational behavior in sport, you might make external attributions for your success in meeting ticket sales goals by focusing on how easy the task was to complete (e.g., low number of sales needed to meet your goal) or on good luck (e.g., team winning streak). However, you could also attribute your success internally based on your development of sales skills and your experience in selling. Such attributions influence motivation and can help explain why a person persists in working to meet a goal. If, in the ticket sales scenario, you attribute your success to an external cause such as a winning streak, then you may be less motivated to meet your next sales goal because you have characterized your success as lying beyond your own control. However, if you attribute your success to an internal cause such as your skills, then you are likely to be motivated to work toward your next goal.

Our attributions for our behavior can be subject to two common errors—fundamental attribution error and self-serving bias—that carry powerful implications for behavior in sport organizations. Fundamental attribution error occurs when we make internal attributions for someone else's behavior. For example, if we notice that a co-worker is having difficulty with a new type of software, we may attribute that difficulty to a lack of understanding of computers rather than a failure on the director's part to properly train the person. Self-serving bias, on the other hand, occurs when we make internal attributions for our own success but external attributions for our failures. In other words, we take credit for our successes but blame others for our failures. Self-serving bias is a human error that occurs across cultures and in people of all ages (Mezulis, Abramson, Hyde, & Hankin, 2004).

Attributions are particularly important in the process of evaluating employees. Those who conduct evaluations should be mindful of how employees make attributions about their own performance and that of others. Evaluators should also keep in mind the possibility of fundamental attribution error and self-serving bias in order to minimize distortion in the evaluation process.

ATTITUDE

You have likely heard the word *attitude* used as a way to describe a person; in fact, you may have used it in describing someone you know. Phrases such as "he has a bad attitude or "she has a positive attitude" are often used to describe a person's tendency to feel and behave in an unfavorable or favorable way toward a specific person, idea, or object. Like personality, attitudes tend to be relatively stable unless a person is provided with information that changes his or her perspective. For example, if you strongly prefer college basketball to the NBA, you are likely to continue holding that preference unless you are provided with important information that changes your preference.

Attitudes are directed toward a particular object, person, or idea. Therefore, if you have a negative attitude toward your internship in event operations, that attitude will not necessarily influence your positive attitude toward college basketball. It will, however, influence your behavior. For instance, if you prefer college basketball (attitude), you will watch it on TV or attend games in person (behavior).

In the context of working in an organization, people behave in ways that are consistent with their attitudes. This consistency can be problematic if an employee holds a negative attitude toward a co-worker; for instance, that employee (let's call her

Sarah) may not cooperate with the co-worker (Greg) on a shared project. However, if a manager works to change Sarah's attitude toward Greg, then her behavior toward him may improve. In addition, attitudes can be change by behaviors. For example, if Sarah has to work with Greg, she may realize after spending time with him that he cares a lot about his work and is committed to doing a good job. This realization may lead Sarah to develop a more positive attitude toward Greg.

IMPORTANT ATTITUDES IN SPORT ORGANIZATION WORKPLACES

Having described attitudes in general terms, we focus now on two important measures of attitude that are specific to working in an organization: organizational commitment and job satisfaction. Organizational commitment helps us understand how connected an employee feels to the organization and how he or she values being part of it. Job satisfaction, on the other hand, consists of the level of fulfillment that an employee derives from working for the organization. Both of these attitudes have been the subject of significant scholarship in sport management.

Organizational Commitment

Organizational commitment consists of a person's overall attitude toward the organization, including how much the person identifies with the organization and values being associated with it. Strong organizational commitment involves adopting the organization's view as one's own, placing value on being a member of the organization, and being willing to work to help the organization achieve its stated goals (Meyer & Allen, 1991). This kind of commitment matters because it has been linked to reduced interest in seeking another job (i.e., low turnover intention), increased work attendance, and positive behaviors

directed toward other members of the organization (e.g., willingness to help a colleague or stay after work to help finish a project) (Vandenberghe, Bentein, & Stinglhamber, 2004).

Organizational commitment has been studied in various areas of sport, including among coaches, volunteers, and interns. In one study, when U.S. collegiate coaches indicated low commitment to their occupation, they were more likely to want to leave the profession (Turner & Chelladurai, 2005). In another example, organizational commitment demonstrated by volunteers in sport organizations was linked to job satisfaction (Costa, Chalip, Green, & Simes, 2006), job performance (Stephens, Dawley, & Stephens, 2004), willingness to be trained (Kim & Chelladurai, 2008), and intention to continue as a volunteer (Park, 2010). Another study found that interns at sport organizations needed to be provided with challenging job roles in order to develop a high level of commitment to the organization (Dixon, Cunningham, Sagas, Turner, & Kent, 2005).

Job Satisfaction

Job satisfaction consists of one's general attitude toward one's job. It is important in terms of organizational behavior because, as you might expect, a person with higher job satisfaction is more likely to stay in his or her current position (Chelladurai & Ogasawara, 2003). Job satisfaction also exerts a moderately positive influence on an individual's job motivation (Kinick, McKee-Ryan, Schriesheim, & Carson, 2002) and is moderately and positively related to job performance (Judge, Thoresen, Bono, & Patton, 2001). Because job satisfaction is so important to organizational behavior in sport, we have dedicated chapter 6 to exploring it.

SUMMARY

The factors that make each of us unique exert a strong influence on which jobs we seek out in sport organizations. More spe-

CASE STUDY

Importance of Personality in Supporting Volunteer Work Teams

As director of community outreach for a major professional sport team, you have been asked to put together a 20-person team of staff members and community volunteers to work on a service project in a local elementary school. After meeting with the school principal, you recognize that the project will be quite extensive. Specifically, your team has been asked to repaint the hallway leading to the gymnasium, help repair and repaint the boys' and girls' locker rooms, and, if weather permits, help landscape the outdoor playground. In total, the project will likely require your team to work at least three 10-hour days. Because it is a service project, all members of the staff will be volunteering their time on nonwork days, which means that both the staff members and the community volunteers will be giving up personal time on weekends.

Given the scope of the project—and based on your understanding of personality, attitudes, and motivation—you know that you will need to be thoughtful in selecting staff members to volunteer for this work. You are also a bit concerned about the fact that you won't meet the volunteers from the community until the first day of the project. You decide that in order for the project to succeed, you need to meet with your staff volunteers beforehand to go over project tasks and logistics. You also want to help your staff volunteers understand the importance of personality, attitudes, and motivation in order to enable a positive experience for both them and the community volunteers while meeting the project objectives. To facilitate the meeting, you decide to start it off with a presentation, and in order to develop a presentation outline you must address the following questions.

Case Study Questions

1. Will you introduce aspects of personality during this meeting? Why, or why not? If yes, what specifics will you discuss?

2. You know that the cognitive concepts of personality are important when forming a team. Describe them and explain why it will be important to recognize them when supervising your volunteer team during the community service project.

3. What information would you look for during the first day of the project in order to determine whether you need to make changes in your volunteer work teams?

cifically, both intelligence and personality traits can determine the types of work we seek and whether we excel in our jobs. Understanding intelligence and personality can also help employers and managers as they identify, select, and train people for specific positions.

We must also consider cognitive aspects of personality, which include locus of control, authoritarianism, and self-monitoring. These aspects influence how people behave and work in sport organizations and the ways in which we can best manage and support people in their work.

Achievement motivation helps us understand a person's aspirations, efforts, and persistence in tasks where performance is evaluated against a standard of excellence. Managers can use the concept of achievement to determine how to provide appropriate tasks for employees and appropriate feedback to best support employees.

Attributions are inferred causes that help us understand our own behavior and that of others. We must recognize that we are all susceptible to fundamental attribution error—the tendency to make internal attributions when focusing on someone else's behavior. We must also guard against self-serving bias, in which we make internal attributions for our successes but external attributions for our failures; in other words, we are more likely to take credit for our successes and to blame others for our failures.

Finally, the concept of attitude helps us understand a person's tendency to feel and behave in either an unfavorable or a favorable manner toward a specific person, idea, or object. A person's attitudes influence his or her behavior and tend to be relatively stable unless the person is provided with compelling information that leads to a change in perspective. Two major measures of attitude in organizational behavior are organizational commitment and job satisfaction. Organizational commitment consists of a person's overall attitude toward the organization, including how much the person identifies with the organization and values being associated with it. Job satisfaction is a measure of one's general attitude toward one's work. Both of these factors influence work-related outcomes, including intention to remain in or leave a job.

DISCUSSION QUESTIONS

1. What services are offered in the career resources center at your college or university that could help you understand how your personality and interests best align with certain careers?

2. Do a Google search for "personality testing" to find information about the Big Five personality traits. Next, locate a relevant online assessment that can be used free of charge and work through it. Do the findings of the assessment align with your understanding of your personality? If you feel comfortable doing so, share the findings with people close to you and ask for their thoughts, then summarize the insights you gain from the resulting conversations.

3. Describe a time when you committed a fundamental attribution error in a work or school scenario. Now that you know about this kind of error, how will you try to avoid committing it in the future?

4. Why is it so important for managers in sport organizations to understand organizational commitment?

5. Identify a job you have now or used to have (it can be an internship, summer job, or part-time position). Describe your level of job satisfaction in this work and the reasons for having that level. What do your answers tell you about the concept of job satisfaction?

Chapter 5

Learning, Motivation, Training, and Development

Chapter Objectives

After studying this chapter, you will be able to

- describe principles of learning and how they can be applied in sport organizations,

- describe learning through association and how to appropriately use reinforcement in the learning process,

- apply principles of social learning theory to training and development in sport organizations,

- describe the concept of motivation and how it influences learning and performance in organizational behavior in sport,

- explain performance in the context of organizational behavior and describe how goal setting and reinforcement are used to enhance performance, and

- determine which training and development programs will best support improved employee performance in a sport organization.

Learning, motivation, training, and development are critical components in the process of supporting individuals' work in sport organizations. If you think about the skills and knowledge that you have acquired as a postsecondary student—including content specific to sport management—then you know that you are well on your way to becoming a successful employee in a sport organization. You probably also realize that you still have a lot to learn about the various types of jobs available in sport. For example, you may have taken a course in sport marketing and may even have interned as a game-day promotion assistant at your university, but do you know how to use graphics software to design weekly game announcements and other promotional materials? Do you know how best to work with coaches from various sports in order to promote their teams? These and other skills are crucial to success in the marketing arm of an collegiate athletic department, and you will probably have to learn them while training for a position (in the case of using graphics software) or on the job (in the case of working with coaches). Training can help you develop and enhance your command of such skills and work behaviors, in order to succeed in the workplace.

The quality of your learning, training, and work in an organization depend in large part on your motivation to be the best you can be in your position. Therefore, this chapter describes various ways to motivate individuals and, more specifically, how to use motivation to enhance learning and performance in sport organizations. It also addresses the concept of training and how to develop effective training programs for employees.

LEARNING IN SPORT ORGANIZATIONS

Learning is the process by which an individual acquires new skills, knowledge, and behaviors through interactions with the environment (Taylor, Doherty, & McGraw, 2015). In fact, learning itself is a behavior—one that is unique to each individual and is critical in supporting a person's training and development. Learning always occurs in a context, or environment, and certain people may learn best by performing in certain environments. Others may experience learning more as a mental activity that involves making meaning by connecting what is being learned (i.e., new knowledge) with what is already known (i.e., existing knowledge). If you prefer to learn in a certain context, you likely appreciate learning by performing the work in an experiential learning setting, such as an internships. If you prefer to learn through mental activity, then you likely appreciate having concepts explained to you and then being provided with follow-up assignments to demonstrate your understanding. Some people also prefer collaborative learning, which involves working with and gaining new perspectives from others; thus collaborative learners appreciate the chance to engage in group projects. And still others learn best when given opportunities to reflect critically on their actions and the ensuing outcomes (Taylor et al., 2015); these learners appreciate the chance to consider what they have learned and how they have applied that learning—for example, through reflective journaling after a training session.

Learning has been explained through three recognized theories, which can help managers best support the training and development of employees in sport organizations: the behavioral approach, the cognitive approach, and the constructivist approach. The behavioral approach to learning focuses on providing the individual with feedback based on observable behavior. Depending on the type of behavior exhibited, the feedback may take the form of either positive or negative reinforcement. For example, a marketing director might train a new team member by providing positive feedback after seeing the employee devote extra time and attention to detail (i.e., desired behaviors) to enhance the pictures in a promotional flier to be distributed campus-wide. As the employee becomes more familiar with the graphics software, the director might provide further positive feedback when the employee demonstrates expertise in using the software. The reinforcement of learning is addressed in more detail later in this chapter.

A second way to understand or explain learning is through the cognitive approach, which focuses on mental processes. This approach "suggests that learning occurs when information is mentally processed and the result is a change in the structure of the learner's knowledge" (Taylor et al., 2015, p. 96). A cognitive approach to learning takes into account how individuals perceive, interpret, and consider the environmental events they experience in a manner that allows them to make quick adjustments to their own behavior. In the marketing example, the director could provide specific feedback to the employee about his or her use of the graphics software while the employee is designing the promotional flier.

In contrast, the constructivist approach describes learning as an interpretive process. This approach views learning as an intentional and conscious activity on the part of the learner that results in a relatively permanent change in the person's knowledge or behavior. In the marketing example, the new employee could seek out activities that support learning the new software, engage in learning the new software by using it, and then reflect on those activities. The constructivist approach focuses on three major characteristics of learning (Taylor et al., 2015):

1. The duration of the change is long term.
2. The change involves the content and structure of knowledge in memory or in behavior of the learner.
3. The cause of the change is based on the learner's experience in the environment.

Constructivist learning requires shared responsibility on the part of the employee and the sport organization. The employee needs to pursue opportunities to acquire new skills and knowledge that will support job performance, and the manager (on behalf of the organization) needs to provide training opportunities that support the employee's learning. Sport organizations that explicitly encourage and support the learning process as a strategic objective are considered to be "learning organizations" (Taylor et al., 2015).

In the section that follows, three different types of learning are described. Learning through association can be understood through the cognitive approach to learning. The process of learning through reinforcement, punishment, and extinction applies a constructive orientation toward learning. The process of learning described by social learning theory applies both the behavioral and constructivist theories of learning.

Learning Through Association

Classical conditioning, or learning through association, was described by the famous Russian physiologist Ivan Pavlov, who conditioned dogs to salivate at the ring of a bell. Initially, the dogs would salivate when they were provided with food, and they began to associate the presentation of food with the sound of a bell that Pavlov rang when feeding them. After carrying out this process multiple times, Pavlov then rang the bell without providing food, and the dogs salivated anyway because they had come to associate the food with the bell. Thus the key to learning through association in classical conditioning is to develop a conditioned stimulus—that is, something that incites an action and develops a response. To develop a conditioned stimulus, one must link a neutral stimulus (e.g., the ringing bell) to another stimulus that already influences behavior (e.g., food).

Here is an example of how classical conditioning could occur in a sport organization. A marketing director often calls employees into her office to talk about work issues (neutral stimulus). However, when she addresses a discipline issue, which can result in termination of employment, she often closes the door (conditioned stimulus). Thus, the conditioned stimulus of being called into the director's office and having her close the door could lead employees to worry that they are about to be disciplined and possibly fired.

Learning Through Reinforcement, Punishment, and Extinction

Operant conditioning is the process of modifying behavior through positive and negative reinforcement of specific behaviors. Negative reinforcement involves the use of punishment and extinction in order to modify or diminish undesirable behavior. Negative consequences for undesirable behavior consist of outcomes that are unattractive (aversive) to the individual, such as a negative performance evaluation, a demotion, or other disciplinary action by a supervisor. Positive reinforcement provides positive consequences for desirable behavior, including resource-based rewards that are attractive to the individual demonstrating the behavior—for example, a pay increase, a promotion, or a day off. Reinforcement of desirable behavior could go beyond mere resource-based rewards; for example, it might include training and development opportunities (e.g., leadership development programs), equity (i.e., stock) in the company, or getaway weekends or weeklong personal trips with spouses and families. In sport organizations, nonmonetary rewards might include opportunities to attend high-profile games (e.g., NCAA Final Four), access to a sponsor's suite at a major professional sport event (e.g., U.S. Open), or a chance to attend an awards show (e.g., ESPN's Espy Awards).

In order to support desirable behavior, managers and trainers can begin with continuous positive reinforcement and then move to intermittent reinforcement as the individual becomes more competent or consistent in the desired behavior. Continuous reinforcement, which is provided each time a person demonstrates the desired behavior, tends to bring forth desired behavior more quickly than does intermittent reinforcement. However, the behavior may stop when the reinforcement is no longer present. In contrast, when behavior is acquired under intermittent reinforcement, it is more likely to continue even after the reinforcement is removed. Intermittent reinforcement can be implemented on four types of schedules:

1. *Variable schedules* reward behavior at random times. Examples include surprise bonuses and lunches to reward high-performing teams or individual employees.
2. *Fixed-ratio schedules* provide rewards when the desired behavior has occurred a certain number of times. For example, an employee might be provided with free tickets to a concert or sport event after making a thousand cold calls to sell season tickets.
3. *Fixed-interval schedules* reward behavior after a given amount of time has elapsed—for instance, an end-of-quarter sales bonus for employees who meet sponsorship sales goals.
4. *Variable-interval schedules* provide rewards after a random number of occurrences of the desired behavior—for instance, providing a surprise bonus or lunch to reward the highest-performing team at random times during a sales quarter.

In general, variable reinforcement schedules result in more consistent patterns of desired behavior than do fixed reinforcement schedules (Uhl-Bien, Schermerhorn, & Osborn, 2014).

When managers seek to reduce or eliminate unwanted or undesirable behaviors by employees, they can use punishment in two ways: applying negative consequences and withholding positive consequences. For example, if a new marketing employee fails to show up for a scheduled meeting with a coach, the marketing director could give the employee a negative consequence by issuing a formal, written warning that is placed in his or her personnel file. Alternatively, the director could punish the employee by withholding a positive item such as a monthly salary bonus.

Using punishment as a way to reduce or eliminate unwanted behavior comes with challenges because punishment is experienced differently by different people. Specifically, for some people, punishment can be psychologically damaging and result in negative emotional or behavioral consequences; in such cases, it is detrimental as an option for eliminating or reducing undesirable behavior. Therefore, managers must note very clearly the specific behavior that has led to the punishment; in other words, the employee must understand—and the manager must make crystal clear—that the punishment is a response to the behavior, not to the person as a whole.

In addition, only significantly detrimental behaviors should result in punishment. For instance, most athletic departments will provide volunteers or interns with athletic department apparel to be worn when carrying out duties for the department. An example of this would be an intern for event operations who is given a warm jacket by the department to wear during a late season soccer match. The intern may be required to return the jacket at the end of the event. If the intern accidently wears the jacket home for the weekend instead of returning it after the event, that behavior (forgetting to return the jacket after the event but returning it on Monday) would not be appropriate behavior warranting punishment (e.g., prohibiting the intern from working with the athletic department in the future).

One alternative to punishment is another form of reinforcement known as extinction. In this approach, the undesirable behavior is not punished but is simply ignored. Extinction may be most effective in reducing undesirable behavior when it is coupled with the application of positive consequences for desirable behavior—that is when positive behavior is rewarded but negative behavior is ignored. For example, if the new marketing employee is consistently late for work but co-workers cover the tasks missed by the new employee, then the tardiness will continue. However, the marketing director could ask the co-workers to stop covering the missed work for the new employee (i.e., to apply the extinction strategy), thus withdrawing the positive consequence (i.e., completing the missed work) received by the tardy employee for being late. However, to reward on-time behavior, the marketing director could provide coffee and bagels to employees as they arrive at the office each morning.

Reinforcement is an important way to foster learning; however, it comes with both positives and negatives. One signifi-

cant criticism holds that the reinforcement approach can be demeaning to employees (Kreitner, 1982). Others contend that the use of rewards and punishments to reinforce learning creates opportunities for managers to abuse their power and exert undue control over individuals in the organization (Uhl-Bein et al., 2014). Those who support the reinforcement approach note that control of employee behavior is a legitimate aspect of a manager's job and argue that the key is for the organization to use reinforcement strategies constructively (Gray, 1979). When reinforcement is used constructively, employees recognize that desired behaviors are supported at work; similarly, when punishment is used appropriately, it provides employees with clear indications of what is wrong (Uhl-Bein et al., 2014).

Social Learning Theory

Social learning theory describes learning that occurs when an individual observes behavior by others and is then reinforced and encouraged for modeling the observed behavior. The theory was developed by Albert Bandura (1986), who posited that "virtually all learning phenomena, resulting from direct experience, can occur vicariously by observing other people's behaviors and the consequences for them" (p. 19). For example, the director of community relations for a Major League Baseball team could model behaviors expected of interns in the department, such as wearing professional attire, preparing effectively for community outreach events, and engaging in friendly and positive interactions with people who attend the events. According to social learning theory, the interns are likely to follow the director's lead by modeling his or her behaviors when they work at community relations events. The director would then reinforce the modeled behavior by supporting and encouraging the interns.

Social learning theory also employs the concept of self-efficacy, which consists of one's belief in one's ability to successfully perform tasks. Individuals with high self-efficacy believe that they are capable of performing tasks, putting in the required effort to get the task done, and overcoming any challenges or obstacles they may encounter. General self-efficacy influences both job performance and job satisfaction (Judge & Bono, 2001). More specifically, self-efficacy has been found to predict performance in tasks of lower complexity but to be less effective in predicting performance for more complex tasks (Judge, Jackson, Shaw, Scott, & Rich, 2007). Therefore, when deciding how to help individuals develop new skills, we should consider helping them improve self-efficacy for less complex tasks, but more support and development will be required in order to help individuals become competent and successful when learning more complex tasks.

The development of self-efficacy depends in part on social reinforcement, which, along with rewards, can exert a significant influence on behavior in the workplace. Self-efficacy is developed through

1. previous experiences,
2. behavior modeled by others who successfully perform the task,
3. positive persuasion from other people, and
4. the individual's assessment of his or her current emotional and physical capabilities. (Bandura, 1989)

One way to help new employees (and interns and volunteers) develop self-efficacy for specific functions is to provide opportunities for them to role-play key behaviors. Returning to the MLB community relations example, the director could provide opportunities for new employees to role-play meeting with members of a community organization to discuss potential partnerships or programming. Employees could also role-play interacting with local youth during a team-based community outreach program.

MOTIVATION THROUGH GOAL SETTING

Another approach to supporting individual learning and performance in an organization falls within the broad psychological construct of motivation, which addresses an individual's "inner desire to make an effort" (Mitchell & Daniels, 2003, p. 226). Understanding an individual's motivation or "drive to engage in a particular behavior" (Taylor et al., 2015, p. 132) is considered critical to understanding his or her performance in an organization.

One motivation theory used in support of development and performance is goal-setting theory. Goal setting is the process of identifying "desired results that guide and direct behavior" (Nelson & Quick, 2013, p. 204). Of course, goals can be defined at both the individual level and the organizational level. One popular method for setting performance and learning goals uses the acronym SMART to indicate key characteristics of effective goals (see figure 5.1). In a sport organization, SMART goals can be used to support not only entry-level employees as they develop needed skills but also all employees as they work to help the organization achieve its goals.

PERFORMANCE IN SPORT ORGANIZATIONS

Effective performance in an organization is defined as the accomplishment of a work-related task. For example, the director of an athletic development department might measure staff performance in terms of the number of new prospective donors identified within a specific time period. Work performance is often multidimensional and therefore must be clearly defined and understood in order for employees to perform well in their jobs. For instance, identifying new prospective donors requires interpersonal skills, attention to detail, and effective time management. This multidimensionality of work means that managers must detail the required skills and behaviors for successful performance of each job in the organization.

To help enhance performance in a sport organization, managers first need to accurately measure and evaluate performance and then, based on that evaluation, provide feedback to help employees improve their performance. Performance appraisal is the process of evaluating "a person's actual performance based upon the defined performance requirements of the job" (Nelson & Quick, 2013, p. 210). By accurately appraising employee performance, managers can support employee development and growth while also providing input about how each employee is fulfilling his or her role in the organization. The purposes of performance appraisal are to provide employees with feedback on performance, identify developmental needs, make decisions about rewards and promotions, and evaluate whether demotion or termination is necessary (Nelson & Quick, 2013).

As we have discussed, goal setting is an effective way to increase an individual's motivation and effort and, in turn, improve her performance. In order to use goal setting as a means for performance improvement, we must be mindful of the relationship between goal difficulty and task performance. This relationship follows a curvilinear path (figure 5.2), which shows that as the goal difficulty increases, the individual puts forth more effort in order to accomplish the goal. However, when the difficulty of the goal reaches a certain point—the point at which the person believes that he lacks the capability to achieve the goal—effort sharply declines.

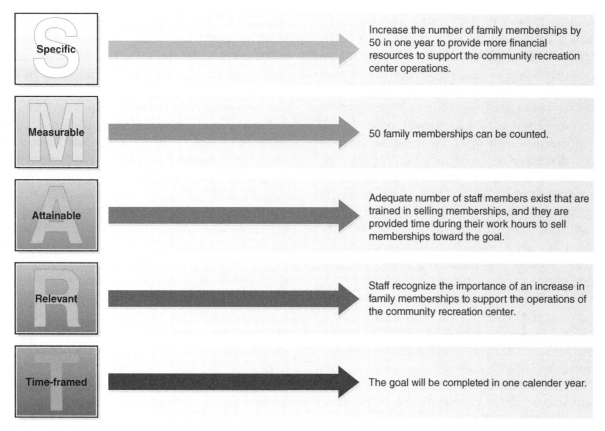

Figure 5.1 Example of SMART goals related to increasing family memberships at a community-based recreation center.

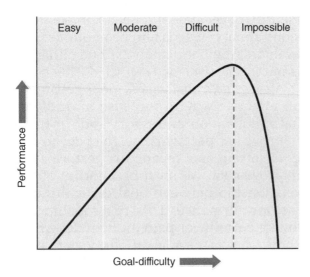

Figure 5.2 Relationship between performance and goal difficulty.

Given this relationship, the manager must understand the individual's task capabilities and work to establish goals that will maximize task effort. Using the example shown in figure 5.1, if a manager establishes a goal of selling 250 new family membership in one year (five times the original goal), employees might perceive the goal as unattainable and therefore choose not to increase their effort in pursuit of it.

Managers can also use goal setting to help increase self-efficacy, which, as discussed earlier, supports individual learning and development. By setting realistic yet challenging goals—that is, goals that employees are able to accomplish—managers enable employees to improve their self-efficacy by meeting those goals. For instance, if employees meet the goal shown in figure 5.1, they will likely develop increased self-efficacy regarding their ability to sell memberships and increased confidence in meeting future goals for membership sales.

When using goal setting to motivate individual performance, three important behaviors should be considered (Nelson & Quick, 2013):

1. Employee participation
2. Supervisor (manager) commitment
3. Helpful performance feedback

When employees participate in the goal-setting process, they are more likely to accept the goals that are eventually established, which is a critical component in developing effective goals. Commitment is also needed from managers and the organization as a whole, and this commitment includes providing employees with the support and training they need in order achieve the goals.

As employees work to accomplish the established goals, managers also play an important role by providing them with feedback. Goals that are specific (as in figure 5.1) allow managers to provide targeted feedback to help employees reach the goals. Specific goals can also help improve employee performance when intermittent feedback is provided by managers (Locke, Shaw, Saari, & Latham, 1981). As part of intermittent feedback, both positive and negative feedback can positively influence employee performance in meeting goals (Fedor, Davis, Maslyn, & Mathieson, 2001). Consider our example of the goal for 50 new family memberships by the end of the calendar year. If by June the membership support division has sold 25 new memberships (halfway to their goal), supervisors can provide feedback indicating that the division will fail to meet its stated goal because previous research has indicated the percentage of membership sales drop significantly during the summer and into the start of the academic school year. Therefore, the division must recognize it will need to adjust its sales tactics to meet the stated goal. Feedback by managers is most helpful when it is useful to the employee (e.g., sharing leads for potential new family memberships) and timely (e.g., provided at the midpoint of the sales period) to help employees meet the stated goal (Nelson & Quick, 2013).

After providing appropriate performance feedback, managers can help employees improve their performance through the process of performance management on the basis of models developed by organizational behavior scholars. One model, OB Mod (Luthans & Kreitner, 1985), describes how task performance by employees can be improved using both positive reinforcement and extinction. First, it is necessary to identify desirable and undesirable work behaviors in the organization and recognize which employees are demonstrating those behaviors. Next, managers decide on reinforcements to support and encourage the desired behaviors while also determining what reinforcements (negative or extinction) are required in order to reduce or eliminate undesirable behaviors. Managers then observe whether and how the chosen reinforcements alter employee behavior and apply those lessons to continue helping employees improve their performance. To fully evaluate the success of OB Mod, managers must also use job indicators to assess whether changes in employee behavior are positively influencing work-based performance.

TRAINING AND DEVELOPMENT TO ENHANCE INDIVIDUAL PERFORMANCE

The process of training and developing employees is supported by the processes of learning and setting goals in order to improve performance. Training focuses on developing and enhancing the employee's job-related skills and abilities. Examples include learning a new software program for processing ticket applications, getting oriented to event management policies and procedures, and learning the HR processes for selecting new interns. Development, on the other hand, focuses on improving the employee's overall capabilities through processes such as attitude and behavior changes as well as skill building

IN THE BOARDROOM
Selling More Season Tickets

Although ticket sales are critically important to the success of all professional sport organizations, selling season tickets (i.e., packages of tickets for all of a team's home games) is such a challenging task that some teams have stopped trying. Even so, there are some ways to make season ticket sales more manageable, according to Bob Hamer (2017), president of Sports Business Solutions. First, do not try to sell the season ticket package during the first conversation with the potential buyer (fan). Because season ticket packages can be expensive—2017 packages for the Boston Red Sox started at about $7,000—buyers need time to consider the investment. Therefore, Hamer recommends setting up a personal appointment for a follow-up discussion about season tickets. He also recommends inviting potential buyers to the stadium or arena, showing them around the facility, and reminding them of the value of a season ticket. Finally, he encourages sales teams to pitch season tickets with conviction and belief in their value.

(Taylor et al., 2015). Examples include programs to enhance leadership skills and abilities, introduce best practices for recruiting and hiring new employees, or develop advanced emergency preparedness among event managers.

The training and development process is most effective when it is supported by five key steps. First, managers must identify the behaviors to be learned. Second, if the new behaviors are complex, then the training must chunk them into smaller, logically arranged segments. Third, managers and supervisors should model the new behaviors (see the discussion of self-efficacy earlier in the chapter). Fourth, employees should practice and demonstrate the new behaviors in the presence of a trainer. And, finally, managers can use rewards (discussed earlier in the chapter) to support the employee's attempts to replicate the manager's behaviors (Hitt, Miller, & Colella, 2015).

Organizations use many methods for training employees, including on-the-job orientation programs, organizational socialization (see chapter 8), apprenticeship training, coaching by managers, formal mentoring programs, job rotation (i.e., trying multiple jobs in the organization), career development activities (e.g., leadership or management training), and technology-based training. In addition, off-site training methods may include instructor-led classrooms, video conferences, corporate institutes, and virtual-reality simulators (Hitt et al., 2015). To consider one example in the sport industry, ESPN provides its employees with the following learning and development opportunities: mentoring and training programs that use more than 10,000 online reference materials and resources, management and leadership development opportunities, professional development programs, business immersion programs, and individual

career development opportunities (ESPN, "Learning & Development," n.d.).

Training and developmental activities that help employees develop their skills and abilities provide two major benefits: supporting employees' personal career growth and helping the organization retain employees and meet its strategic goals (Taylor et al., 2015). For example, in community-based sports, clubs formed by local residents—such as a youth lacrosse league or senior running group—rely on volunteers to help them meet their objectives. In such cases, research has found that training and development of volunteers and coaches is critical to club success (Doherty, Misener, & Cuskelly, 2014). For instance, training (or lack thereof) was identified as one reason that basketball referees left their positions. Specifically, they viewed their training, which focused only on rules and enforcement, as inadequate and felt that they would have been better served by training focused on helping them establish better communication with coaches, players, and spectators (Warner, Tingle, & Kellett, 2013).

Another study in this area (Popp, Simmons, & McEvoy, 2017) examined training related to sport ticket sales. This research revealed a significant lack of sales training for employees working in ticket sales despite the positive relationship between amount of time spent in certain types of training and attainment of sales goals. Those who were most successful in sales in their organizations spent more time in training (both initial and ongoing) and found that using a variety of training methods were most effective.

SUMMARY

Learning is a critical component of both individual and organizational success. We

IN THE BOARDROOM
Training and Development in Ticket Sales

As intercollegiate athletic programs continue to seek opportunities to increase revenue generation to support operations, departments are partnering with private organizations to support operational areas including marketing and ticket sales. One such group, the Aspire Group, has established partnerships with several colleges (e.g., UConn, UMass, and Ohio State University) and conducts training and development programs for employees. For example, the Raise Your Game Executive Development Program helps train and develop employees to perform at their best while recognizing and advancing those who want to become leaders in the industry. The program consists of 24 two-hour training sessions on topics such as ticket sales, sales management, sport business, sales and service, and life skills. Employees who complete all 24 sessions receive credits toward completion of a master's degree at their employing institution. When you search for an internship or entry-level position in sport, look for organizations that will provide you with opportunities to learn and develop new skills.

must understand how we learn in order to construct and implement appropriate training and development programs that lead to success. Learning can occur through classical conditioning, operant conditioning (positive and negative reinforcement), and social learning. Each of these types of learning can be used to support individuals working in a sport organization. The question of which learning approach will work best depends both on the needs of the individual and on what is appropriate in the context of a particular sport organization.

Individual development and successful performance are also influenced by motivation. One common motivational theory used in organizational behavior and in various sport contexts is goal-setting theory. Goal setting is the process of identifying a desired outcome in order to guide and direct behavior. We can establish effective goals at the individual and organizational levels by using the SMART approach to ensure that goals are challenging but realistic. If a goal is too easy to achieve, it will not increase motivation; if it is too difficult to achieve, it may even decrease motivation. The process of setting challenging but realistic goals can be facilitated by involving the affected individuals in the goal-setting process.

The chapter also addressed the training and development of employees in a manner that is supported by learning processes and goal setting to improve performance. To best support training and development, we can take three key steps: identifying what new behaviors need to be learned, providing appropriate training for complex new behaviors, and having managers support the learning process by modeling desired new behaviors. Employees can then practice and demonstrate the new behaviors, and managers can provide contingent rewards as appropriate.

CASE STUDY
Developing Employees in Intercollegiate Athletics

First, here is some key background information for this case study. An athletic development department is responsible for raising funds in the form of contributions by supporters of the college or university. Therefore, people who work in athletic development must be able to cultivate positive relationships with potential donors. Mastering this complex skill requires experience. Potential donors to athletic programs include very wealthy individuals, and new employees face a daunting task in deciding how to approach them and then develop a relationship that leads to a significant donation. Such gifts can be enormous. For example, Nike founder Phil Knight and his wife Penny Knight donated some $300 million to the University of Oregon's athletic department (Peter, 2014). Although the Knights' contribution was larger than average, donors to college athletic departments generally serve as a sizable and growing source of revenue (Wolverton & Kambhampati, 2016); therefore, great pressure is exerted on athletic development officers to help cultivate and support this important source of revenue. As a result, the tasks of initiating and cultivating donor relationships are critical to the employee's and the department's long-term success, and managers must foster self-efficacy in these tasks when developing new employees.

Now we can look at the case study itself, in which an associate athletic director for athletic development has hired three entry-level employees. He recognizes that it will take some time for these new employees to develop the skills and behaviors they need in order to cultivate relationships with donors. For example, one skill that the employees must develop sooner rather than later is the ability to recognize ways in which potential donors feel most connected to the university as a whole and to the athletic department in particular. Doing so requires staff members to get to know donors and ask tactful questions that prompt them to articulate their preferred ways of connecting.

To help these employees develop self-efficacy in regard to such tasks, the associate athletic director begins by having them shadow him as he meets with prospective new donors. During these meetings, he asks the employees to take notes about the kinds of questions asked by donors and the follow-up responses he provides. He then asks the new employees to role-play various scenarios in which they act out meetings with potential donors. After shadowing several meetings and conducting multiple role-playing scenarios, the new employees can begin scheduling their own meetings with potential donors who are interested in giving relatively small gifts (i.e., less than $5,000) to the athletic department.

Case Study Questions

1. Based on the concepts of social learning theory, what should the associate athletic director do to ensure that his new employees are in fact learning how to develop donor relationships during the meetings in which they shadow him?

2. How would role-playing activities help the new employees develop task-specific self-efficacy?

3. Based on the concepts of social learning theory, why would the associate athletic director have new employees conduct their first solo meetings with potential donors who are interested in making relatively small donations?

DISCUSSION QUESTIONS

1. What type of reinforcement would you use to address the behavior of an intern who is using social media for personal purposes while working as an event operations assistant during a basketball game? Provide support for your answer.

2. Develop a SMART goal that supports the objective of obtaining an internship in a sport organization.

3. Explain why a supervisor might use intermittent feedback to help an employee reach a performance objective. How can this type of feedback best support an employee in reaching the goal?

4. Research a training program intended to support employee development in one of your favorite sport organizations. Discuss who the training is designed to support and how it is implemented.

Chapter 6

Job Satisfaction and Design

Chapter Objectives

After studying this chapter, you will be able to

- define the concept of job satisfaction,
- differentiate between job satisfaction and job dissatisfaction,
- understand how people may behave when they are dissatisfied with their work,
- determine ways in which management can enrich employees' jobs and increase their job satisfaction, and
- appreciate the similarities and differences between various sport stakeholders.

Work is an integral part of our everyday lives; in fact, we are likely to spend more than half of our lives working, whether in part-time jobs, temporary full-time positions, or career-oriented work. Therefore, it is vitally important that we find work in which we can experience job satisfaction, which is among the most researched—and most discussed—areas of organizational behavior (OB). Generally speaking, job satisfaction derives from appraisals of one's job (or job experiences) that result in pleasurable or positive emotional states (Locke, 1976). More specifically, research has linked job satisfaction to subjective evaluations of working conditions, task variety, communication, and working with others (Dormann & Zapf, 2001). Job satisfaction has also been connected to other management focuses in sport settings, including job commitment, motivation, turnover intention, and performance (e.g., Bang, Ross, & Reio, 2012; MacIntosh & Walker,

2012). Thus job satisfaction depends both on one's own judgment or evaluation of one's work and on the environment and context in which that work is performed (McShane & Steen, 2012). Its importance has been demonstrated by a body of research in the organizational sciences, which has also documented the need for managers to monitor employees' attitudes toward their work and their work environment (Dormann & Zapf, 2001; McShane & Steen, 2012; Robbins & Judge, 2008).

Understanding what satisfies people who work in sport organizations—whether as employees, volunteers, coaches, athletes, or administrators—is a critical building block that intersects with other OB topics included in this text, such as personality, emotions, attitudes, motivation, and job stress. Later in the chapter, we discuss some of the sport management research on satisfaction in volunteers, coaches, and athletes.

UNDERSTANDING JOB SATISFACTION AND JOB DISSATISFACTION

In order to fully understand job satisfaction, we must appreciate both what it is and what it is not. In the simplest form, job satisfaction involves one's attitudes toward one's job, one's assessment of the job, and one's values and beliefs related to work (Locke, 1976). Job dissatisfaction, on the other hand, relates specifically to aspects of work that are often not motivational, such as company policies and supervision.

For management scholars, understanding the various factors involved in job satisfaction can expose discrepancies between employees' and managers' ways of thinking about the job and about the context or environment in which the work is performed. In practical terms, it is helpful to understand the factors that contribute to one's assessment of one's job, and of the work environment, because many of these factors can be managed or changed.

Some of the seminal research conducted on job satisfaction was developed by Herzberg and colleagues, who advocated separating our understanding of what motivates and satisfies people at work from our understanding of what leaves people dissatisfied. For instance, Herzberg, Mausner, and Snyderman's (1959) research was inspired in part by the desire to understand what causes various attitudes and what consequences those attitudes might bring in terms of a person's job. This research highlighted two distinct factors: on one hand, happy feelings and good attitudes that were task related, and on the other hand, feelings of unhappiness and bad attitudes that were not task related. The idea was that a person's unhappy or bad feelings derived from various conditions around the job. This important research, popularized as *motivation-hygiene theory*, argued that people are motivated by job factors (motivators) such as recognition,

achievement, growth, responsibility, advancement, and the work itself. In contrast, a worker's feelings of unhappiness relate to aspects (hygiene factors) that are either absent or insufficient—for example, salary, company policies, interpersonal relationships (with peers, supervisors, or subordinates), working conditions, quality of the administration, job security, status, and personal factors.

Perhaps the easiest way to understand motivation-hygiene theory is to say that these various factors are either satisfying or dissatisfying. Ultimately, the presence of motivators can create job satisfaction, but their mere absence does not indicate dissatisfaction. Instead, dissatisfaction is caused by the hygiene factors, but, as with motivators, their mere absence does not indicate satisfaction. Motivation-hygiene theory postulates simply that a person's higher-order needs are influential in determining satisfaction and that managers who want to increase employees' levels of satisfaction should focus on these motivators as antecedents. However, as Wilson (2010) articulated, fitting motivation-hygiene theory into two distinct boxes of intrinsic contribution to job satisfaction and extrinsic contribution to dissatisfaction misses the key idea that certain hygienes (e.g., company policy or level of supervision) can affect a worker's interest and success in a job.

Thus, despite the wide appeal of motivation-hygiene theory, its binary (two-factor) nature caused it to be challenged by other researchers. For instance, Locke (1976) suggested a need to distinguish a person's values from the person's needs because values have more in common with goals than needs do. Locke argued that job satisfaction is a positive and pleasurable "emotional state resulting from the perception of one's job as fulfilling or allowing the fulfillment of one's important job values, providing [that] the values are compatible with one's needs" (Locke, 1976, p. 1304). The essential premise here is that one's level of satisfaction depends on the perceived discrepancy between intended and actual performance, or the degree to which one's performance is discrepant with one's set of values. Essentially, the smaller the difference is—that is, the greater the achievement of one's values—the higher the yield of satisfaction. Consequently, although motivation-hygiene theory provided insight into various aspects of work that could contribute to job satisfaction and job dissatisfaction, Locke's contention further determined that a person's values are unique and that they shape the person's perceptions of work itself and of the work environment.

These and other studies helped us develop our understanding of the antecedents of satisfaction and dissatisfaction. Yet one commonly held belief persisted—that people who are more satisfied at work perform better—even as it was debated in much of the literature (Wilson, 2010). Some research has demonstrated that higher levels of satisfaction lead to lower levels of absenteeism and turnover (MacIntosh & Walker, 2012; Tett & Meyer, 1993), but the link to achievement and performance is not nearly as clear. For one thing, as noted by Wilson (2010), job satisfaction and motivation are difficult to study due to disagreement about how to define and measure them for different people in different contexts. In addition, general attitudes do not always predict specific behaviors. For example, McShane and Steen (2012) noted that an attitude of dissatisfaction about work may lead to leaving, complaining, or just patiently waiting for change to occur rather than to a definite reduction in performance. Moreover, many dissatisfied employees are reluctant to reveal their true feelings in the form of a direct statement or behavioral act. As a result, feelings of dissatisfaction may linger for some time in an employee and may cause a variety of negative organizational outcomes.

Thus employees may respond to dissatisfaction with their work in various ways.

One tool for understanding this range of possibilities is known as the Exit, Voice, Loyalty, and Neglect model (EVLN; Withy & Cooper, 1989). Exit, of course, means deciding to get out, whether by leaving the organization, transferring to another department, or otherwise removing oneself from the dissatisfying situation. Voice refers to any attempt to change, rather than escape from, the dissatisfying situation. It may be handled in either a positive or a negative manner, depending on how the person articulates the problem and to whom; in this case, effective communication is critical (for more on communication, see chapter 13). In the third option, loyalty to the organization leads the dissatisfied employee to suffer in silence rather than exiting or voicing dissatisfaction. Finally, neglect involves a noticeable reduction in work effort, as well as reduced attention to quality of work, both of which carry obvious negative consequences for the organization.

One of the challenges in managing an employee is understanding the employee's true feelings as they relate to work. Can you easily discern the employee's satisfaction or dissatisfaction? Do you have confidence that the employee will let you know when there is a problem? Such questions point toward the difficulty in assessing job satisfaction, and of course, in determining whether job satisfaction is leading to job performance (or vice versa). Management must also consider the important role of incentivizing employees and rewarding them for desirable behavior and good performance outcomes. Granted, research on motivation teaches us that people perform better overall when they have a sense of internal motivation than when they are incentivized through an external reward (Deci, Koestner, & Ryan, 1999). Yet we also know that external rewards can help produce both motivation and satisfaction. Consequently, managers still need to ensure that rewards play a role in their management system.

IN THE BOARDROOM
Making Rewards Meaningful

Although it is nice to offer rewards based on a person's performance—for example, rewarding a person for reaching a targeted number of season ticket sales—managers must ensure that the rewards provided are both meaningful and motivating for the individual. In order to do so, managers must develop a sense of what constitutes a meaningful reward to a given employee by understanding their personnel and considering staff members' needs and wants. To put it in terms of a simple example, some people may value a new set of steak knives, whereas others are vegetarian. If a reward itself holds little value for the recipient, it will not enhance motivation or satisfaction.

Research shows that job satisfaction is influenced by both situational factors of the job and personal characteristics and desires of the employee (Davar & Bala, 2012). Situational factors include influences such as budget and resource constraints, company policies, and external competition. In recent years, for example, many collegiate athletic departments in North America have experienced budget cuts, which have likely reduced job satisfaction for many staff members. Such realities mean that job satisfaction is context specific, and the challenge is compounded by the fact that each person holds a unique set of values and beliefs and brings a different set of needs and desires to fulfill. For instance, a seasoned veteran of an athletic department may take a different view of budget reductions than a newer employee does. These two individuals may have different levels of interest in the work they are asked to do, as well as different motivations and varying degrees of commitment to the department.

There is some agreement in the literature that job satisfaction is an important predictor of turnover and intention to leave (MacIntosh & Walker, 2012; Tett & Meyer, 1993) and, within the service sector, that employees who are satisfied with their work can enhance customer satisfaction (Morrison, 1996; Namasivayam, 2005). Therefore, collegiate athletic managers need to ensure that their employees are satisfied with their individual and collective work. Most often, this process requires a case-by-case approach to understanding job satisfaction.

ENHANCING JOB SATISFACTION

It is important for managers to consider the various ways in which they can enhance an employee's job satisfaction through, for example, job design (Chelladurai, 2014). In discussing the earlier work of Herzberg (e.g., 1966, 1967), Chelladurai (2014) noted that the process of job enrichment involves practical application of motivation-hygiene theory. Thus, when managers consider, for example, vertical loading—redesigning a job to satisfy a person's higher-order needs—they may be able to enrich that person's job and increase the level of felt satisfaction. Chelladurai (2014) noted that this process can be implemented by assigning people more responsibility and letting them make decisions about how and when work will be done. This approach is premised on the idea that a person will experience an increased level of motivation, which will result in personal growth and higher performance. Thus a manager's ability to tap into a person's internal motivation is a key element of effective management.

Research on self-determination theory by Deci et al. (2001) posits three universal psychological needs—competence, autonomy, and relatedness—which suggests that the work climate has the potential to produce need satisfaction and increase employee wellness. Competence hinges on succeeding at optimally challenging tasks; autonomy requires experiencing choice in one's own actions; and relatedness involves a sense of respect, caring, and reliance on others. These three components certainly constitute part of a manager's repertoire in designing and enhancing a person's job. In particular, autonomy—which managers can provide by giving employees opportunities to work unsupervised and make decisions about how to organize, plan, and lead their own tasks—seems to be critical in producing both motivation and satisfaction.

We can see the value of autonomy when we consider it in terms of the job characteristics model (JCM; Hackman & Oldham, 1980), which indicates that various motivational properties of a job can influence both individual and organizational outcomes (see figure 6.1). More specifically, the JCM examines a number of core characteristics that influence a person's psychological state and are purported to influence important outcomes such as growth and general satisfaction. The model also holds that managers need to consider individual differences when determining job characteristics and outcomes. Ultimately, the model suggests that by understanding the five core job characteristics—skill variety, task identity, task significance, autonomy, and feedback—managers may be able to affect a person's feelings related to work, which in turn can facilitate desired outcomes. This sequence is evident when we look at the purported links from autonomy to responsibility to general satisfaction, which highlight the importance that people attach to having a say in how they go about their work. For

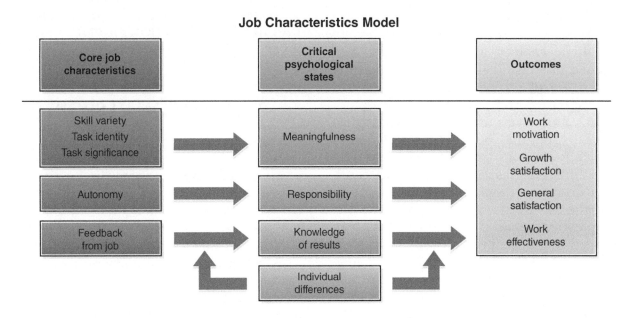

Figure 6.1   Determining job design for positive outcomes.

Reprinted by permission from J.R. Hackman and G.R. Oldham, *Work Redesign* (Upper Saddle River, NJ: Pearson Education Inc., 1980), 90.

instance, Namasivayam (2005) remarked that high levels of autonomy can produce feelings of responsibility to complete the task, which is appealing; this assertion has also been advanced by Deci et al. (2001).

Alongside these benefits, we must also acknowledge that people sometimes take advantage of autonomy. A person who is granted a very high level of autonomy to perform work but receives no monitoring, supervision, or feedback could take advantage of the organization's managerial leniency; this overstepping might take the form of misbehavior such as cheating, fraud, theft, or lying. For this reason, management should never adopt a laissez-faire leadership style (see more in chapter 9). Unfortunately, there are all too many examples in sport in which excessive autonomy has resulted in negligence and corruption—for instance, construction contracts awarded to friends or family members, bribery (e.g., the FIFA corruption case), and vote-rigging and pay-for-play scandals. Thus, although it is important to provide autonomy in light of its association with employee satisfaction and motivation, too much autonomy can be problematic.

The JCM suggests that when jobs are depressive in nature—for instance, involving little variety, low significance, and inadequate task identity (completing only a portion of the work and not seeing it through until completion)—people do not attach high levels of value or meaningfulness to what they do and therefore do not typically exhibit high degrees of motivation and growth satisfaction. Again, there is a constant need for management to engage in various types of feedback with employees (recall the need to allow and encourage employee voice, as discussed earlier). Feedback is important because it lets employees know the value of their performance, the aspects in which they are doing well, and where improvement can be made; it also allows management to understand how best to enrich employees' jobs.

Chelladurai (2014) noted that sport managers should consider tweaking jobs when they recognize employee dissonance or dissatisfaction. They can do so through job enlargement (adding more tasks), job enrichment (giving employees more responsibility to schedule and coordinate their own work), and job rotation (moving employees from one job to another). These human resource management strategies may produce greater feelings of employee meaningfulness in work. The same is true for managers of two other distinct and critical groups—sport volunteers and interns. Managers must appreciate the need to avoid boredom among volunteers and interns by creating enriching and interesting experiences for these important sport stakeholders. Interns in particular are looking to develop a skill set that will help them with future employment; therefore, they value work characterized by a sufficient level of challenge. Overall, then, managers must approach the jobs performed by employees and the responsibilities assigned to volunteers and interns with an eye toward key aspects, such as task significance and experienced meaningfulness. By minimizing tasks that are repeated, mundane, and perceived as unimportant, management can create a more satisfying workplace.

STAKEHOLDER SATISFACTION IN SPORT

Various stakeholders in sport organizations may have very different levels of responsibility and autonomy in their work, roles, and tasks. For example, research on job satisfaction has been conducted to help us understand each of the following stakeholders: coach, volunteer, and athlete. This research points up several facets of management-related work that are in some cases consistent and in other cases variable across these important stakeholders.

The role of the coach is crucial to both player and team satisfaction and perfor-

IN THE BOARDROOM
Creating Meaningful Work for Employees

Managers must understand that an employee's work can be enhanced both by paying attention to the general working environment and—perhaps even more important—by implementing techniques such as job rotation, enlargement, and enrichment. For example, the director of a national volleyball team might benefit from evaluating the work environment for employees in order to determine their levels of satisfaction and motivation. If the results indicate a need for improvement, the director can either redesign jobs or create a better workplace atmosphere in which employees feel welcomed, appreciated, and sufficiently challenged. When a redesign is needed, management can look for ways to enhance core job characteristics, such as providing employees with more significant tasks. For instance, an employee could be asked to communicate with national team representatives to ensure that athletes' needs are met during an upcoming indoor tournament. This work might also help the employee develop a new skill set that he or she desires, which might enhance both motivation and job satisfaction. In order to be aware of employees' desires, as well as their strengths and interests, managers can engage in ongoing communication and feedback; this effort will be repaid in their increased ability to enhance employees' growth satisfaction.

mance; therefore, the coach's role, and satisfaction in that role, have been viewed as topics of great importance in sport management. The evidence points to several features of coach satisfaction, as well as variations depending on factors such as the country where the person coaches and the person's level of experience in the coaching role. For example, Chelladurai & Ogasawara (2003) found that Japanese coaches expressed lower levels of satisfaction than did U.S. coaches in several facets of their work, including supervision, autonomy, security, and relations with co-workers. In addition, U.S. coaches were more committed to their occupation, whereas Japanese coaches were more committed to their organizations. Thus, here again, we see the significance of differences in context, values, needs, and wants. Differences in satisfaction also appear when we look at experience. For example, as compared with a veteran coach, a new coach may have a lower expectation of work-hour flexibility

and therefore express less dissatisfaction when asked to hold office hours or make reports to a supervisor. The more established coach, on the other hand, may expect more control over schedule and decisions and therefore express extreme dissatisfaction with the same request.

Thus it appears that the relationships between various job features and both satisfaction and dissatisfaction are not static but are both time and context specific (Dixon & Warner, 2010). Furthermore, it has been demonstrated that the need for recognition, in a coaching context, is a particularly influential factor and that receiving recognition increases job satisfaction (Dixon & Warner, 2010; Matzler, Fuchs, & Schubert, 2004). When job expectations are not met, it becomes increasingly likely that the employee will express dissatisfaction and experience increased intention to leave the role (Dixon & Warner, 2010). Therefore, understanding the coach's needs and wants can help sport managers identify job elements that may need to change. As a result, managers need to acknowledge and recognize the importance of monitoring satisfaction on a regular basis—not simply at the end of the season via the commonly held end-of-year evaluation or when a person decides to quit or leave the organization altogether and an exit interview is conducted. In order to optimize performance, management must make a conscientious effort to engage in dialogue with coaches throughout the playing season (Martensen & Gronholdt, 2001).

Ideally, management has at its disposal both a general knowledge of the conditions that can produce satisfaction and the resources necessary to enhance satisfaction regardless of position (e.g., coach, volunteer, or athlete). In reality of course, needed resources (e.g., money) are not always available. To consider an example, a manager who cannot provide everything that employees need in order to be satisfied with their jobs (e.g., performance bonuses) might focus instead on job flexibility and control, program-building opportunities, and relationships with colleagues—all of which are among the biggest factors contributing to satisfaction and job performance (Sagas & Cunningham, 2005). Other options include providing employees with meaningful recognition, which can promote a sense of accomplishment, and enabling them to develop their own interests, skills, and desires in their work. To provide recognition, managers should consider recognizing a person's achievement and excellence in front of immediate peers or even in more public formats (such as in front of the media). Managers should also look for ways to allow people to achieve more in their job in order to enhance personal growth. In many sport organizations, an abundance of financial rewards is not available, and skilled sport managers must find ways to empower their employees and volunteers by creating more fulfilling roles.

Sport also relies heavily on volunteers, from the grassroots level to high-performance systems in countries around the world (Taylor & Morgan, 2017). Given that volunteers play key roles related to planning, organizing, and operating sport events, understanding volunteer satisfaction is a critical task for management (Doherty, 2009). In this vein, Bang (2015) found that job satisfaction encourages retention of an older volunteer base and that, as a result, managers who want to retain volunteers must enhance volunteers' satisfaction in the work they perform. We know that when a person is dissatisfied with the workplace, it is likely to manifest in resistance to management and in a reduced quality of customer service (Townsend, 2004); indeed, the translation of satisfaction from service-industry employees to customers is well established (e.g., Allen, 2006; Hom & Kinicki, 2001; Namasivayam, 2005) in a variety of settings.

Given that sport programs and sport systems rely on both employees and volunteers, managers must achieve higher levels of job satisfaction among individuals in the various roles required for the organization to operate. Although monetary incentives may not always be possible, management can often afford individuals the flexibility to create their own time for work. For instance, modern technology often makes it possible for both employees and volunteers to work remotely, and it is becoming more common for an organization to be characterized by geographical spread. Other factors to consider include allowing both employees and volunteers room for personal challenge and growth, thus again suggesting that money is not everything when it comes to satisfaction.

In more specific research about volunteers, one study (Rogalsky, Doherty, & Paradis, 2016) noted that role performance and role satisfaction were predictive of a volunteer's overall level of satisfaction with a multisport competition. In addition, as with employees (c.f., MacIntosh & Walker,

2012), the volunteer's overall satisfaction was predictive of intention to continue with the organization. Other research (Elstad, 1996) on sport volunteers has found that overall satisfaction is related to controllable features of the event (e.g., food, transportation) and job factors (e.g., task overload). Another study (Kim, Kim, & Odio, 2010) noted that the pride associated with being involved in a particular event motivates volunteers to become involved and to return. Research has also shown that the experience itself influences the level of job satisfaction and that the types of duties, feedback, and rewards provided can influence satisfaction (Kim, Kim, & Odio, 2010). Other research has found that an individual's feelings of satisfaction and accomplishment are influenced by organizational support, empowerment, group integration, the nature of the work, and personal communication with the supervisor (Aisbett & Hoye, 2015; Hoeber, Doherty, Hoeber, & Wolfe, 2015; Silverberg, Marshall, & Ellis, 2001).

At this point, we have considered the employee, the coach, and the volunteer but have yet to address one of the key stakeholders in sport—the athlete, who of course benefits from the work performed by these other individuals but also acts as the prime producer of entertainment in sport. Maier, Woratschek, Strobel, and Popp (2016) noted that it is important for sport organizations to provide various types of support for athletes, including assistance when an athlete experiences a personal problem. Given the very public nature of sport, athletes need protection when they face personal or family issues that may be exposed through the media. Maier et al. went on to argue that nonmonetary incentives should be part of the sport manager's toolkit because they can help improve job satisfaction; these researchers also suggested the need to provide athletes with second-career support in that the transition out of sport and into another career requires some guid-

ance and mentorship including knowledge exchange and friendly advice. Their results showed that higher job satisfaction improved performance among athletes in elite team sports but that monetary incentives held relatively low importance for these athletes; therefore, managers should consider other ways in which to increase athlete satisfaction in elite team sport. In a similar vein, MacIntosh and Parent (2017) found that athlete satisfaction at the Commonwealth Games was influenced by many of the event's controllable aspects, such as social factors, service, and communication. For example, the researchers noted that the quality of interaction through social and cultural opportunities contributed to athlete satisfaction by helping to make the Games special and memorable for them.

Overall, the research on coaches, volunteers, and athletes provides a compendium of ways to increase satisfaction levels among these stakeholders. Even when we remove money and winning from the picture, we find that many controllable features of sport management exert significant influence as antecedents of satisfaction for these groups.

SUMMARY

Job satisfaction continues to be one of the most discussed topics in organizational behavior research and practice. It is critical for managers to understand what job satisfaction is; what it is not; and how it is linked to motivation, commitment, turnover, and performance.

Management must consider not only what creates job satisfaction but also what creates job dissatisfaction. The key here is that individual employees each bring their own predispositions, interests, and values to the work environment; therefore, what satisfies one person may not work as well with another person. Job satisfaction also relates to a person's attitudes and beliefs, which of course can influence the person's behaviors. This individuality

CASE STUDY
Creating Successful Internship Environments

For many students, one of the most important experiences they gain from their degree work is that of taking part in an internship. The excitement of working for a sport organization is something most students anticipate even before entering their degree-granting institution. Sometimes, however, expectations go unmet and the student is left feeling unfulfilled in an internship, which can negatively affect job satisfaction. Such problems often derive from underemployment; that is, the student does not have enough work to do and is left feeling unchallenged, bored, or unmotivated. This situation can even lead to a low sense of worth for the internship, which of course can negatively influence job satisfaction. Indeed, it is not uncommon for students to divulge to a professor that they feel under challenged in an internship and that their assigned tasks are too easy for them. Many students also complain about being assigned repetitive and mundane tasks that, over time, lead them to question the value of the work they are performing. Unsurprisingly, these conditions, coupled with the fact that many internships are unpaid, often leave students feeling dissatisfied and unmotivated to fulfill their obligations.

In such scenarios, it is important for students to find ways to grow their skill sets and advance their knowledge (e.g., technical competence). Although this process requires some self-leadership and initiative from the student, it is equally important for the internship supervisor to establish an environment in which the student is challenged and feels that the work is important, compelling, and valued. Designing an internship environment that is motivating and contributes to student job satisfaction depends in part on effectively communicating assigned roles and responsibilities. As we discuss in chapters 8 and 13, clear expectations are crucial to effective management. Students also need to be aware of their own expectations for personal growth; communicate those expectations to the supervisor; and discuss work-related opportunities, autonomy, and responsibility early on in the process. Students must also understand the available resources and seek—and be provided with—opportunities to be creative in their work in order to grow personally and enjoy a sense of personal worth in the work they perform. The supervisor can contribute to this process by providing tasks and responsibilities that enhance the intern's feeling of worth. Of course, repetitive and mundane tasks may also be required at times, particularly when things must be done quickly and with small funding. However, the internship environment must offer the student more than that, and it is up to both parties to invest in the success of the experience.

Case Study Questions

1. Many amateur sport organizations have limited financial resources to offer to their interns. How can such an organization create internship experiences that are meaningful for students?
2. What types of work might be motivating and satisfying for a student intern to complete?
3. How can a manager help an intern feel a sense of worth in the work?
4. How is feedback important in an internship environment?

makes the study of satisfaction both interesting and difficult to agree on in the research community. As Locke (1976) indicated, the intensity of a person's values and goals need to be factored into considerations of what makes work satisfying; moreover, given that values are unique to the individual, managers must get to know each employee in order to determine the rewards most suitable for that person.

A person's level of satisfaction is related to many basic job dimensions, such as opportunity to learn and grow, recognition and praise for accomplishments, the company of colleagues, and autonomy. Of course, more bottom-line aspects also matter—for example, pay, bonuses, and promotional opportunities—depending on both job context and individual motivations for work.

Ultimately, leaders and managers must strike a balance between focusing on the employee's performance of job-related tasks and focusing on the relationship— that is, on getting to know the employee as a person. At the same time, the employee must communicate to the manager his or her particular work-related needs and desires. When both parties express clear expectations, they can create a better working environment and work that is more meaningful and motivating for the employee.

DISCUSSION QUESTIONS

1. Identify three factors that influence job satisfaction and three that influence job dissatisfaction.
2. In your opinion, what are some of the most challenging factors that sport managers must overcome in order to facilitate employee satisfaction?
3. Why might employee satisfaction influence customer satisfaction?
4. From your perspective, how might your own values, beliefs, and attitudes be influential in finding a job that you would be satisfied to perform?
5. What might a sport volunteer and a sport coach have in common when it comes to reasons for job satisfaction?

Chapter 7

Stress and Well-Being

Chapter Objectives

After studying this chapter, you will be able to

- explain the various causes of stress;
- explain the ways in which people show stress;
- define eustress;
- describe how a manager can recognize stress in an employee or colleague;
- recognize the ways in which stress is present in higher-performance sport, including posttraumatic stress disorder;
- discuss how a manager can help prevent stress from becoming a problem in the workplace; and
- define job burnout.

Stress is a major issue in all organizations, and sport is not immune to the variety of pressures that operate in a workplace environment. Whether running a sport event, creating a marketing campaign, or scheduling an intramural season, people who work in sport face a range of job demands, interpersonal situations, and external organizational pressures that can create stress.

As a result, stress affects all people at some point in their careers, either through personal challenges, professional obligations and tasks, or a combination of these factors. People can feel stressed for any of numerous reasons, some of them deeply personal (e.g., family problems, illness, feelings of inadequacy) and others resulting from the workplace environment itself (e.g., difficulty with job task, too many job demands, minimal resources to complete work properly, poor leadership, harassment, incivility, office politics). These organizational issues can be compounded when people experience non-work demands (e.g., becoming a parent, caring for an aging parent), which can increase the tension experienced by the person at work. Fortunately, when managers understand the antecedents of stress in the workforce, they can minimize some of the negative consequences that result from a stressful environment.

Both stress and the subsequent stress response can come in several forms, including physiological, psychological, social, and behavioral. Physiological stress can manifest in many ways, including elevated blood pressure, red or bloodshot eyes, muscle tension, digestive issues, and constant headaches, to name only a few. Psychological symptoms can include moodiness, agitation, poor judgment, diminished memory, signs of anxiety, over-worrying, and depression. Social signs can be observed when people avoid situations, isolate themselves from others, appear overly busy, or fail to engage with others. And behavioral consequence of stress can include changes in sleep and eating patterns or the use of alcohol or drugs as a coping mechanism. These examples cover only a few of the ways in which a person may experience stress.

Stress has been described as an unconscious preparation to fight or flee that is experienced when a person is faced with a demand (Nelson, Quick, Armstrong, & Condie, 2015). When a person is unable to cope with the stress, the various responses just noted may begin to manifest in observable features of the person's behavior. Stress can be set off by any of various triggers, and each person has a different capacity to handle stress, which may vary depending on personality (see chapter 4), the level of support provided at work, and the person's social circles. For example, in a sport setting, some athletes may be able to handle an increased training demand based on their physical strength, ability to recover quickly, or their learning from prior experiences, whereas others may experience the same increase in training as a stressor. Those who see the added training as a burden may accumulate an increasing level of stress, both physiologically and psychologically.

Although the preceding example is drawn from competitive sport, parallels exist in office and boardroom settings. Here again, some people perceive certain situations quite differently than others do; in other words, some people cope readily, whereas others find it harder to navigate stressful situations. Consequently, stress in the workplace—and its causes, as well as each person's reactions and coping mechanisms—depend on a variety of personal and organizational factors. In addition,

prolonged exposure to stress can produce serious effects, including posttraumatic stress disorder (PTSD).

This chapter examines various types of stress experienced in the world of sport management, including pressure on the job, stress among coaches and competitive athletes, and stress experienced by various stakeholders as a result of organizational factors. The chapter also discusses the potential consequences of stress in a person's life, including examples of PTSD in sport.

CAUSES OF STRESS

One reason that stress often plagues work life is that it can derive from so many causes. One of the biggest causes lies in the fact that people need to work with and through other people in order to get their work done. These interactions can be a breeding ground for both interpersonal (relationship) and task (focus on the issue) conflict. For example, it can be very personally upsetting—and stress inducing—when a person experiences harassment or poor leadership or is ridiculed publically by a colleague or manager.

Other causes of stress on the job include work (task) demands, job insecurity, role ambiguity, and work (task) overload, to name only a few. For instance, when a person tends to have low task-related control (i.e., low autonomy) and to face demanding deadlines, the person is often placed in situations in which his or her work must be done both correctly and fast. There is not necessarily anything wrong with this scenario—after all, work must get done—but problems can arise if the person has an inadequate skill set or if lines of communication are poor.

Managers can alleviate role ambiguity for employees by clearly articulating job descriptions and desired outcomes and establishing an environment that provides adequate resources to complete the job as expected. It is critical to set the employee up for success, not failure. Poor management and poor leadership result in a depressing work environment for employees that adds stress to their jobs. Managers must clearly state their expectations and fulfill their obligation to provide employees with the necessary support to do their work.

In one study (Fletcher, Rumbold, Tester, & Coombes, 2011), stress among sport psychologists was found to be associated with occupational aspects including relationships, interpersonal demands, role in the organization, career and performance development issues, organizational structure, and the climate of the profession. Many of these same causes of stress are part of the general working environment in sport organizations. Thus it is clear that managers need to better understand the sources of stress in the workplace and find ways to help prevent the buildup of stress among employees.

NEGATIVE AND POSITIVE TYPES OF STRESS

Research has shown that job stress consistently ranks among the top 10 work-related health problems and leads to many detrimental effects, both on individuals and on organizations' ability to achieve their objectives (Sharif, 2000). In fact, stress costs organizations billions of dollars annually due to consequences such as higher levels of absenteeism, lower productivity, and even disability (Sharif, 2000). More specifically, when negative stress, known as *distress*, is maintained over a long period of time, it can have several deleterious effects on a person's physical and mental health and emotional disposition (e.g., undesirable weight loss or gain, anxiety, depression). Thus it is crucial for managers to recognize signs of stress and distress and to understand that there are ways to prevent employees from experiencing negative consequences.

At the same time, it is also possible for stressful events to produce healthy, positive, and constructive outcomes for

a person (McShane & Steen, 2012). This type of stress is referred to as *eustress*. If a person perceives a stressful situation to be a challenge—one in which the person can learn and grow—then the situation can be motivating and the person may use preparative mechanisms to promote a sense of achievement in the experience. For example, some people are reluctant to engage in public speaking but know that it is an area where they can improve and realize benefits by overcoming their initial reluctance. When a person adopts a mind-set of improvement and learning, he or she creates an opportunity to grow a useful skill set in a valued area. The same is true for other job-related areas that may initially elicit reluctance but can produce feelings of eustress because they provide an opportunity to develop skills and aptitudes. Examples include taking on a supervisory role for the first time (e.g., leading a team of employees and volunteers in planning a sport event on campus) and engaging in a new business opportunity with a reputable person or organization (e.g., pitching a sport sponsorship opportunity). In summary, stress can be empowering if it is perceived as a growth opportunity. Thus one's perception of stress and of one's ability to handle stressful scenarios has a great deal to do with how one copes and activates or uses the resources in the surrounding environment to resolve stressful situations.

STRESS IN THE COMPETITIVE SPORT ENVIRONMENT

In the world of competitive and high-performance sport—whether amateur or professional—managers, athletes, and coaches face a number of stressors due in part to the premise that winning is everything. For instance, stress in the high-performance world can derive from factors such as increased training demands, heavy travel schedules, time away from loved ones, public performance, and fear of failure. For some seasoned stakeholders in sport, their prior experience with various triggers may aid them in their coping behaviors. For instance, though the rigors of training camp are demanding for anyone, they do not come as a surprise to someone who has experienced them before; in other words, the camp is less difficult if the person has experienced the same expectations and demands in prior seasons. For example, the camp veteran may have a deep understanding of the importance of proper nutrition, rest, and mental imaging. The new player, on the other hand, may be unprepared to cope with the physical and mental exhaustion that comes with training camp. Physical stressors can have deleterious consequences on the body that may be compounded by psychological stressors (e.g., pressure to perform, feelings of inadequacy or failure).

At the same time, relevant experience does not necessarily make the veteran immune to stress. In fact, athletes nearing the end of their athletic career often experience stress related to postcareer decisions. Faced with the daunting task of fashioning a postcareer identity, athletes may struggle with anxiety about the unknown. Thus, in recent years, many amateur sport organizations have taken on the task of helping athletes transition into the next phase of their lives. See, for example, the Canadian Olympic Committee program known as Game Plan, which helps athletes phase out of sport and into a postathletic career.

The competitive nature of sport presents a constant challenge for many primary stakeholders, such as administrators, athletes, coaches, and officials. In addition to the demand to perform well, the challenge is heightened by the fact that high-performance sport plays out under scrutiny from the public eye. Thus a number of researchers have argued that the demands placed on athletes should be carefully considered by management (e.g., coaches, administrators), who should help athletes prepare for and implement intervention strategies to manage the competitive stress they face (Fletcher & Hanton, 2003; Mellalieu, Neil,

Hanton, & Fletcher, 2009; MacIntosh & Nicol, 2012).

More specifically, research on the elite athlete experience has demonstrated the importance of a well-thought-out competition environment, in which stress can be alleviated through proper handling of factors such as adequate sleeping quarters, food, medical services, transportation, security, and communication (e.g., Hanton, Fletcher, & Coughlan, 2005; MacIntosh & Parent, 2017; Parent, Kristiansen, & MacIntosh, 2014; Woodman & Hardy, 2001). Furthermore, stress is also likely to be caused by the logistics of training and from the demands of competition schedules. Thus event managers must provide top-quality venues for training and competition, as well as a variety of services that support athletes' preparation and well-being (MacIntosh & Parent, 2017). If the event environment does not support high performers' needs related to sport and to adequate living conditions, then it is likely to produce unnecessary stress for both rookies and seasoned athletes.

In a competitive multisport environment such as the Olympic Games or the Pan and Parapan American Games, stressors are also prominent for the staff members, volunteers, and interns. These stressors derive in part from the fact that the Games are time bound (with a fixed start date and end date) and take place under intense scrutiny from the media and the public (Parent & MacIntosh, 2013). It is common for these individuals to put in very long hours in multitasking roles both before and during the Games while also working with a variety of other stakeholders (e.g., athletes, dignitaries, government officials, coaches, family members, members of the media).

Stress can also arise in sport situations in the form of social stress—that is, difficulty in balancing sport and life. This type of stress is observable at various levels of the sport industry, from high school and college to the high-performance amateur and professional ranks. Consider, for instance, the difficulty faced by younger athletes as they try to balance school achievement with sport participation; they must often make a difficult choice between continuing to pursue their sport or leaving it due to the pressure to become employable and earn a living. This choice is made necessary in part by the fact that many sports do not enable competitors at the highest levels to earn a comfortable living—for example, lawn bowling, archery, and hurdling. Moreover, even in sports that offer lucrative deals, there is no guarantee that a given athlete will make a decent living in the midst of intense competition for jobs in the sport; examples include American football, soccer, and hockey.

For younger athletes in particular, the decision to continue pursuing a high-performance sport can be difficult and stressful. For those who do continue and experience success, the sudden fame may itself become a stressor for which they are unprepared (Kristiansen & Roberts, 2011). Consequently, it is crucial that younger athletes recognize the stressful environment they face and acknowledge that coaches and support staff have a role to play in encouraging rest and recovery (Kristiansen & Parent, 2014). More generally, as research on athletes has demonstrated, a number of organizationally controlled factors can become stressors for both younger and more mature athletes if they are poorly conceived or improperly managed by event organizers; examples include the training environment, accommodations, travel logistics, and security (Hanton et al., 2005; Parent, Kristiansen, & MacIntosh, 2014; Woodman & Hardy, 2001).

TRAUMA AND STRESS IN SPORT

The competitive world of sport is often filled with physical and sometimes psychological trauma, and the nature of sport as public spectacle can be stressful for stakeholders, including athletes, coaches, and even members of management. Consider, for example, a sport event in which physical trauma such as a gruesome injury is evident. What happens immediately afterward—and what happens later (e.g., physical rehabilitation)—may be documented, but what about the repetitive experience of remembering the event and the potential for a psychological wound that affects the individual severely? In this vein, one area that has received scant attention in sport is trauma in the form of posttraumatic stress disorder (PTSD). Studies have been done on PTSD among military personnel and first responders, but no such discussion has been conducted in sport management.

The following examples provide anecdotal evidence that PTSD does indeed occur in sport. For starters, in the last decade, sport events have been targeted by violent extremists (e.g., ISIS). In one case, during a friendly soccer game between France and Germany at the Stade de France in November 2015, a suicide bomber was blocked from entering the stadium, but areas around the venue experienced a horrifying loss of life from automatic gunfire. The players and coaches were feared to be targets—particularly the German team, whose bus could easily be identified. This event, and the threat of similar attacks around Europe, created an air of fear and anxiety for sport organizations and their stakeholders, and the PTSD that results from such events can lead to detrimental social changes (e.g., people shying away public spaces). It is not hard to find other examples in the history of various sports.

Another area that can marked by trauma is that of sexual abuse—for example, the infamous Penn State case that involved abuses committed by a coach and covered up by others. It is often very difficult for victims to come forward and speak the truth, due to fear of how others may perceive them or fear of challenging a powerful person (such as a head coach) and perhaps getting cut or kicked out of their sport altogether. Many victims of abuse report feeling shame and not knowing how (or to whom) to report their experiences. One victim, former NHL player Theoren Fleury, suffered sexual abuse by his junior hockey coach, Graham Jones—a trauma that Fleury indicated had led to his own abuse of illicit substances and alcohol. In Fleury's postplaying career, he told his story of abuse in his book, *Playing with Fire*, in which he discussed being a victim of sexual abuse as a young amateur-level hockey player. He filed a criminal complaint against Jones, who pleaded guilty. Now, Fleury continues to serve as a leading advocate for people affected by relational trauma. He lamented his behaviors with alcohol and drugs as attempts to cope with the mental anguish and trauma he suffered from the sexual abuse. Many times, he said, he felt at a loss, without positive coping mechanisms and support from his team and league—issues that he has repeatedly raised and that still need to be dealt with on a systematic level in hockey (from the grass roots to the professional ranks).

Psychological trauma can also result from major injuries, sometimes well after the injury has been treated physiologically. For example, one of the most gruesome injuries ever suffered in sport occurred in 1989 when NHL goalie Clint Malarchuk nearly died on the ice after an artery in his neck was severed by a skate blade. The injury required 300 stitches to save Malarchuk's life, and he experienced years of psychological turmoil in its aftermath. Like Fleury, Malarchuk became addicted to alcohol, which, as we have discussed, is a negative behavioral response to stress. Malarchuk also reported attempting suicide on two occasions as he suffered from depression and undiagnosed PTSD and felt that there was no source of help. Eventually, with the assistance of a psychiatrist, he received the support and advice that he needed in order to become well. Today, he advocates for finding ways to cope with psychological trauma.

These examples are only a few among many that have occurred in the realm of sport, and they raise the following question: What should leagues and teams do in such scenarios? In the search for answers, perhaps PTSD should be treated as an area of concern in sport management circles when it comes to both practice and research. In fact, some research is now being done in this area. For example, Caddick and Smith (2014) found that sport and physical activity are excellent coping mechanisms for people experiencing PTSD. More specifically, they noted that for military veterans, engagement in sport and physical activity enhanced feelings of well-being, reduced PTSD symptoms, and enhanced quality of life. The authors also noted that participating in sport and physical activity can help people enhance their motivation to continue living. Thus, given that sport and physical activity can serve as coping mechanisms for stress and PTSD, management must find ways to encourage employees to engage in these healthy behaviors. Organizational leaders must also create safe spaces for participating in various stress releases (e.g., yoga) and advocate for treatment when it is needed.

One noteworthy program in this regard is Bell Let's Talk Day. Started in 2010, the campaign gets people talking more openly about eradicating the stigma often attached to people who feel the need for mental wellness support. The initiative highlights the fact that many people experience various forms of psychological health issues (e.g., depression, anxiety) and that there is a real need to provide room for healthy support from the people and the organizations where they work. The initiative has featured several notable sport figures who act as advocates for creating healthier environments in sport and at work. Examples include Clara Hughes, Olympic champion cyclist and speed skater, and TSN broadcaster Michael Landsberg. For more information about the program, you can visit http://letstalk .bell.ca/en.

Over time, through initiatives like this one, sport organizations can find ways to support employee health and wellness that go beyond merely treating physical symptoms. It is time for sport leaders to get involved in creating programs that implement preventive measures to care for psychological well-being and other support programs as needed.

DEALING WITH STRESS

Whether you are experiencing stress or trying to make things less stressful for people with whom you work, certain well-known and proven techniques can help. Examples include deep breathing exercises, progressive muscle relaxation, and various types of meditation (Godbey & Courage, 1999). In addition, the meditative practice known as *mindfulness*, which is the psychological process of bringing one's attention to experiences occurring in the present moment, has been shown to be negatively related to burnout in athletes (Gustafsson, Skoog, Davis, Kentta, & Haberl, 2015). Engaging in mindfulness can provide various benefits, such as helping people become more relaxed and emotionally well-balanced, which helps to improve their general disposition. Another study found that symptoms of job stress can be addressed in part through increasing one's amount of daily exercise and consuming a well-balanced, nutritious diet (Godbey & Courage, 1999). By taking steps to help employees manage stress—through exercise, mindfulness training, counseling, meditation, and the availability of personal time—management can keep the work environment from becoming overly stressful. As a result, more organizations are providing employees with flextime; covering part of or all of the cost of gym memberships; offering relaxation therapy sessions in the office; and encouraging people to engage in various forms of activity to help reduce, modify, or eliminate stressors (Nelson et al., 2015).

At the same time, it is rather common knowledge that even though many people know how to prevent stress, stress levels remain high in many organizations. This paradox reflects the fact that knowing doesn't necessarily translate into doing. But why, in this case? Perhaps one explanation is that people avoid or disengage from positive behavior because they have a tendency to put other people's needs before their own—for example, to take on more and more responsibility, even when they are already overloaded, in an effort to prove themselves or get ahead in their careers.

Another possible reason that stress continues to plague people and organizations alike is that it continues to be stigmatized. The stigma says that experiencing psychological or emotional stress is a sign of weakness, and most people do not want to appear weak or incapable of handling their own business. Therefore, they may not want to acknowledge that they need some time away or make an effort to get what they need in order to be well. This avoidance is particularly evident in the world of sport, where competition, winning, performance, and success lie at the core of the endeavor. In such cases, the people who are close to the individual experiencing stress (distress) can provide support in the form of friendship, stress-relieving social activities, exercise, active listening, shared laughs, and so on. Thus family members, peers, colleagues, and management all have an important role to play in supporting a person who is stressed. In addition, the affected person can also seek help directly, particularly if he or she feels the need to engage a source of support outside of the immediate family or peer or work group—for instance, a counselor, support group, or therapy animal.

Even if a person is aware that his or her stress level is high, it is not always easy to identify and implement positive coping mechanisms. For instance, Sonnentag and Jelden (2009) found that after a stressful day of work, when people particularly needed a positive stress-relieving activity (e.g., sport participation or other physical activity), they engaged in less of that activity. This finding is alarming but perhaps not surprising given that it is often easier to take the lazy route and fall into poor habits (e.g., TV watching, alcohol consumption). The authors also noted a paradox in that "people perceive sport activities as more recovering than low-effort activities but generally spend little time on sport activities" (p. 177). They went on to observe that "the more situational constraints . . . [people] encounter at work on a specific day, the more likely it is that they spend more time on low-effort activities and little time on sport activities" (p. 177). The proposition advanced, then, is that when people have low energy for coping, their self-control for making positive decisions and using coping mechanisms is also diminished. Consequently, they avoid or simply do not initiate the stress-reducing potential of sport and physical activity. The authors concluded by stating that "job stressors not only directly affect health and well-being but also make the pursuit of health-promoting behaviors more difficult" (p. 179).

For managers, then, it is important to recognize the signs and symptoms of stress in themselves and in their employees—for example, inability to focus, poor decisions and judgments, and short temper. Managers can reduce stress levels in a variety of ways. One method is simply to be mindful of stress in the workplace and take the needed action to enable positive release and coping. Another way is to set up stress-reduction systems for the organization, such as yoga practice, retreats, and stretching and walking breaks.

Another approach (McShane & Steen, 2012) identifies four major steps for combating stressors:

1. Withdrawing from the stressor
2. Changing stress perceptions
3. Controlling stress consequences
4. Receiving social support

Withdrawing does not mean that one is avoiding the stressor; it simply means stepping away from the stressor in order to focus on an activity that is calming or diverting. Indeed, the worst option that someone could choose is to ignore the stressor, which can be devastating. Thus both employees and employers need to

 IN THE BOARDROOM

Destigmatizing Stress in the Workplace

For managers, it is generally not a good idea to avoid employee problems; it is better to address problems in a professional and respectful manner. Given the prevalence of stress and its deleterious effects on individuals, it is a good idea for managers to initiate various awareness programs and events to help people deal with their feelings. In one heartening example, Toronto Blue Jays pitcher Roberto Osuna publically discussed his anxiety and was treated with dignity and respect by key members of the organization. Specifically, representatives of the organization (e.g., president, GM, manager) indicated that the matter was being handled internally and, out of respect for Osuna, did not go into specifics. Furthermore, they demonstrated public support for Osuna by repeatedly describing his decision to speak out and address his anxiety (first with the local media and then nationally) as a sign of character and strength. The coach and general manager discussed how proud they were of Osuna and the mental strength it took to speak publically about his anxiety. In addition, it is highly likely that the organization provided Osuna with help through professionals in their network—which is a best practice for any sport organization.

know the signs of elevated stress and, more important, how to relieve stress and manage stressors. These situations are highly dynamic, and the exact nature of the intervention—such as devoting more resources to complete the task (e.g., additional time or help from staff with the needed skill set)—depends on the urgency of the task and the context of the work environment. The key is for both the manager and the employee to be open about levels of stress, the individual's adaptability to the environment, and the task itself. Stress and anxiety are slowly becoming more recognized and more-often treated, but they remain all-too-often stigmatized as signs of weakness. We need to eradicate this stigma in organizations and in society as a whole.

PREVENTING STRESS FROM BECOMING BURNOUT

To help us fully understand the negative potential of unmanaged stress, we turn now to the work of Hans Selye (e.g., 1946, 1956). Selye helped advance research on chronic stress and disease, most notably by observing that a person's physiological responses to repeated stress can be understood in terms of three stages, which he referred to collectively as general adaptation syndrome (GAS):

1. Alarm
2. Resistance
3. Exhaustion and collapse

The GAS model explains the body's physiological responses to perceptions or experiences of stress. The model describes the body's attempt to maintain homeostasis, or steady state, despite changes from a stressor (Selye, 1974; see figure 7.1).In the alarm stage, the brain sends messages throughout the body to create physiological responses in preparation for the resistance stage; the alarm stage happens fast and can be automatic (i.e., the fight, flight, or freeze response). The shock of the alarm stage can lower a person's energy level and hinder other coping mechanisms and therefore the person' overall ability to deal with the stress. In the resistance stage, psychological and behavioral responses are activated, thus increasing the individual's resistance to stress. However, with time and repeated exposure to stressful situations, one's ability to cope will diminish. Eventually, this reduction can result in exhaustion and collapse. The individual usually either finds a solution to the stressful situation or withdraws from it before reaching exhaustion; by leaving the situation, the person gains an opportunity to restore energy levels and return with new vitality. However, if the individual is unable to cope

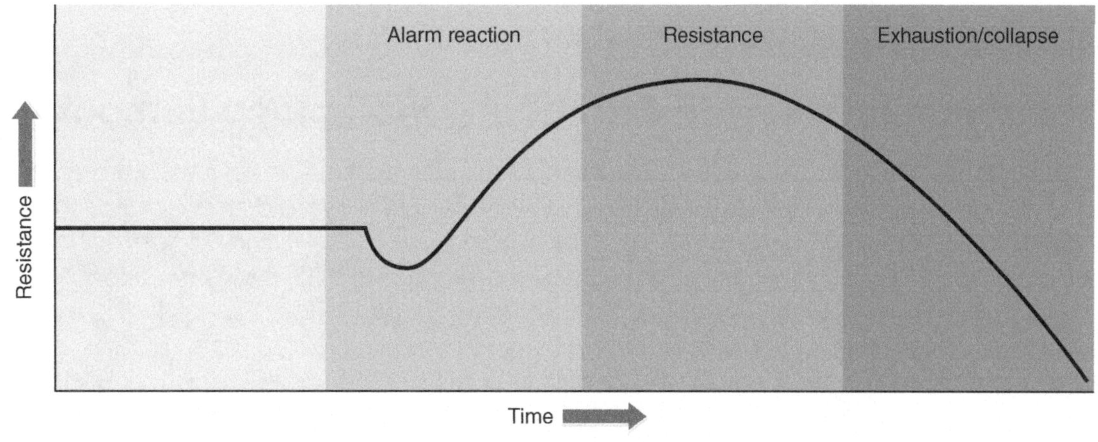

Figure 7.1 The stress response.

and the stress becomes overwhelming, the person's physical health may suffer serious consequences (i.e., sickness).

In summary, then, Selye's body of work (e.g., 1974) highlighted the tendency of the individual to adapt to events and achieve a stable physiological state. However, if the adaptive reaction to the stressor fails, then the person is unable to continue coping; moreover, if the person is unable to either remove the stressor or remove herself from the situation, then exhaustion and burnout are likely to occur. Burnout has been defined as "the process of emotional exhaustion, cynicism, and reduced personal accomplishment that results from prolonged exposure to stressors" (McShane & Steen, 2012, p. 109). Managers can develop better understanding of burnout by using tools such as the Maslach Burnout Inventory (MBI), which lays out a three-part conception of the condition. According to Maslach and Leiter (2008), the first component, exhaustion, involves feelings of being overstretched and depleted, both emotionally and physically. The second component, cynicism or depersonalization, consists of attempts by the individual to put distance between self and work. The third component, reduced efficacy, involves feelings of incompetence and lack of achievement. The MBI was originally developed to assess professional burnout in human services but has been adapted for use with workers in other occupations (Maslach & Leiter, 1997).

Coaches and athletes are not immune to the challenges of stress or to the consequences of prolonged stress and burnout. In fact, their experience in sport can morph from initial attraction and excitement to feelings of entrapment. Over time, athletes and coaches may simply feel obligated to stay involved rather than doing so for love of the game (Raedeke, 1997). Consider why people are attracted to sport in the first place and what might create a feeling of being trapped. In the realm of high-performance sport, many young people form their identity earlier than most people do and envision for themselves a future that is directly associated with their sport. Unfortunately, for many athletes, this sequence can result in becoming unfulfilled in the sport and continuing with it only because they've invested so much in it that walking away would feel like a waste of money and time.

In the highly public world of professional sport, we often see and hear elements of burnout influencing an athlete's decision to step away from the game. Athlete burnout has been conceptualized as a psychophysiological syndrome in which the athlete experiences emotional and physical exhaustion, including a reduced sense of accomplishment and a devaluation of the sport (Gustafsson, Kentta & Hassmen, 2011). For example, soccer star Landon

IN THE BOARDROOM

Management's Role in Combating Workplace Burnout

A workplace environment that continuously places demands on people and denies their need for autonomy, responsibility, and challenge can be detrimental to their well-being and negatively influence their performance. Therefore, management needs to ensure that the work environment provides employees with room to alleviate stress. There is nothing wrong with injecting a little fun into work! In fact, considering the many negative consequences of work-related stress for employees, work groups, and the organization as a whole, management is well advised to consider providing time for employees to engage in nonwork tasks that are revitalizing, such as a 30-minute talk, a stretch break, or a team bonding activity).

Donovan was a member of the U-17 U.S. Men's National Team who went on to play professionally in Germany, enjoy a distinguished MLS career with the LA Galaxy (including five championships), compete at the highest levels (e.g., FIFA World Championships, Olympic Games), and rise to national and international fame through his many accomplishments. Despite all his soccer success, he also experienced a loss of passion for the sport and subsequently decided to take a 21-month break from competitive soccer between the 2014 and 2016 seasons. Many observers in the media speculated that Donovan stepped away because he needed to refresh his energy and that he might one day come back.

The demands of physical performance and public scrutiny are not the only factors that can lead an athlete to feel stressed and burned out. From a purely organizational perspective, research has demonstrated that job demands themselves can cause exhaustion and result in decreased performance; in addition, a deficiency in job resources (which can include support, social factors, or even salary) can also lead to job disengagement (Bakker, Demerouti, & Verbeke, 2004). Still, in today's high-tech and information-rich world, athletes (and coaches) must contend not only with the physiological demands of activity (e.g., training, nutrition, recovery) but also with the dual role of being an athlete (or coach) and a public figure. For the most popular individuals, this mixed role also requires a level of business understanding in order to meet the demands of sponsorships and public appearances. Some individuals find these multiple demands difficult to balance. In addition, now more than ever, athletes and coaches are active in the world of social media and are expected to engage with their fans in ways that reveal personal information.

As summarized by Arnold and Fletcher (2012), sport performers experience a wide range of organizational stressors related to leadership and personnel issues, cultural and team issues, logistical and environmental issues, and performance and personal issues. The combination of such varied responsibilities increases the pressure in the professional and high-performance sport environment. Given these realities, it is vital for managers to understand the causes and consequence of prolonged stress and the reality that burnout is a part of the industry. Perhaps it is time, then, that sport organizations start taking stress factors much more seriously for the sake of their stakeholders and find ways both to prevent stress from building and to support their people with coping mechanisms that work.

SUMMARY

Competition is a basic assumption of the sport industry, and it creates a breeding ground for stressors that can weigh heavily on people if left uncontrolled. Indeed, both physiological and psychological stress are facts of life for student-athletes, leaders of sport organizations, employees, and others involved in sport. Each of these stakeholders acts according to personality, preferences, and the accumulation of experience over the years to enable the stress response and the various coping mechanisms with which they are familiar. Stress at work can be displayed in a variety of ways but is perhaps most noticeable when a person begins to withdraw from activity, exhibits high absenteeism, becomes sick often, or exhibits high levels of anxiety.

Recognizing the signs and symptoms of stress is part of the process of becoming self-aware and helping others by consciously adopting a relationship-centered approach. Therefore, as a current or future sport manager, it behooves you to set up an internal structure and external support mechanisms (e.g., professional counseling) to help people manage excessive stress. Management must play an important role in eradicating the stigma attached to various forms of psychological stress (e.g., anxiety, depression). Finally, even as we make the best efforts that we can in the near term, we are also in desperate need of more research in this area of sport management.

CASE STUDY
The Stress of Coaching in High-Performance Sport

In the world of high-performance sport, the coaching reins often change hands. This major move is usually made in response to lack of success on the field and is timed to avoid disruption immediately before major competition. Neither was the case for the Canadian Women's Hockey Team when it experienced a head coaching change only two months before the start of the 2014 Olympic Games in Sochi. The official line was that Dan Church resigned for personal reasons, but the rationale for the move was (and remains) unclear.

Church was appointed head coach in 2012 due to his success in coaching the youth women's team to numerous medals. He brought a good coaching pedigree and a strong resume—for example, winning the IIHF Women's World Championship in 2012 and earning a silver in the following year. It should come as no surprise that in Canada, success on the international stage is highly desirable not just for Hockey Canada but also for a great many hockey fans. With gold medals at the Olympics in 2002, 2006, and 2010, the team faced tremendous pressure, both from within the organization and beyond, to win again. Thus, although some observers speculated about philosophical differences between Church and Hockey Canada leadership, he may also have been motivated by personal reasons, such as the stress of being away from home, as well as the pressure to meet sky-high expectations. In any case, his resignation came as a surprise to many people, including his athletes, and forced Hockey Canada to fill a critical role shortly before the start of an important competition.

Case Study Questions

1. What job stressors might have contributed to Church's abrupt decision to resign from the head coach position only months before the Olympics?
2. What signs and symptoms of stress might have been exhibited that could have been addressed by Hockey Canada?
3. Provide examples of coaches in other sport leagues who have resigned mid-season. What reasons were reported for their decisions?

DISCUSSION QUESTIONS

1. What are three ways in which a manager can help prevent job-related stress from building in the workplace?
2. What is the difference between job stress and personal stress?
3. Provide some examples of positive coping mechanisms for dealing with stress.
4. What is eustress? Provide an example in the workplace setting.
5. What types of incidents in sport might cause PTSD?
6. What are the signs, symptoms, and consequences of burnout?

Chapter 8

Socialization and Integration

Chapter Objectives

After studying this chapter, you will be able to

- explain strategies to help a new recruit learn a job, fit in, and evaluate organizational expectations;

- explain why the socialization process is important for the new entrant's transition into his or her role in the organization;

- describe the steps of socialization according to Feldman's model;

- apply various techniques that management can use to ensure a good transition for the new recruit; and

- describe differences between socialization plans in enduring organizations and those in temporary organizations.

Socialization is the process through which new members acquire the attitudes, behaviors, and knowledge that they need in order to integrate into an organization and perform well in it (Van Maanen & Schein, 1979). Organizational socialization has been a topic of interest in industrial psychology and management literature (e.g., Allen, 2006; Ostroff, & Kozlowski, 1992) but has received little attention in sport management research (Bravo, Shonk, & Won, 2012). Nonetheless, it is a highly relevant concept for sport managers to understand.

Although the general premise of organizational socialization focuses on the process of hiring an employee and helping him or her transition into the organization, the preceding steps are also critical. Even before an individual is formally offered a role in the organization—whether as coach, athlete, administrator, volunteer, or service provider—the sport manager should work to create positive feelings in the person. Setting the right tone goes beyond making a good first impression; it also elicits lasting and authentic emotions and attitudes that can lead to positive behavior. In today's highly educated and competitive sport marketplace, it is not enough to have important information handy for people to read and digest online. We also need to ensure that it is the right information and is accurate, interesting, and relevant. Even before a would-be recruit becomes familiar with the job you are seeking to fill, you must post online information that accurately depicts life in the organization. This information may serve as a teaching mechanism to help both potential and new members learn about the key values and beliefs that guide behavior in the organization (Taormina, 2009).

Organizational socialization has been linked to many other important topics of organizational behavior addressed in this book, including job satisfaction, commitment, and organizational culture. Clearly, then, it merits careful attention from management (e.g., Adkins, 1995; Jones, 1986; Klein & Weaver, 2000). Morrison (2002) remarked that the socialization of the new employee involves the creation of a new network that carries implications for his or her success in learning about the organization's culture, ascertaining satisfaction with their work, experiencing role clarity, and achieving job mastery—all of which are critical to doing the job well.

When organizational socialization is conducted effectively, it helps people gain necessary knowledge about—and begin to feel comfortable with—the organization, their role in it, and the people with whom they will be working. For both employees and volunteers, these early days present a critical opportunity for management to teach people what is valued in work life and how things are done in the organization. Ultimately, then, the socialization process is about initiating the new person not only into his or her new roles and responsibilities but also into the wider organization. As a result, socialization is both short term, for the purpose of initial integration, and medium and long term, for the purpose of learning about the role, gaining key knowledge for mastering it, and being fully integrated into the organization (Fogarty & Dirsmith, 2001; Ostroff & Kozlowski, 1992).

Despite its important benefits, organizational socialization can be a negative process, either because of a laissez-faire attitude on the part of leadership (discussed in chapter 9) or simply because of poor design or failure to understand the importance of the process. In many instances, negative organizational socialization violates the psychological contract between the new entrant and the organization by neglecting the person's need for integration and leaving his or her expec-tations for the job either inappropriately addressed or unmet. Such an outcome does not necessarily indicate malice on the part of the leadership; it may simply reveal that the entrant's needs (social and psychological) have not been accounted for beyond the assignment of the job and the tasks for which the person was hired. The responsibility here is shared; specifically, management is responsible for socializing the new entrant (e.g., teaching him or her the organization's rules and regulations), and the individual is responsible for asking questions, seeking clarity, and engaging with other people in order to understand work expectations. Thus organizational socialization is a two-way process—that is, an exchange.

For managers, supervisors, and other leaders, it is their job to ensure that the socialization process helps the new person understand the job, the fit, and the working environment. This responsibility extends to the process of bringing in volunteers and interns, who offer important skill sets for the organization and come with their own expectations about the work they will be asked to perform. Irrespective of their specific roles, new entrants must be allowed to learn the values, expected behaviors, and social knowledge required in order to assume and fulfill their roles in the organization (McShane & Steen, 2012). Socialization gives new entrants a "chance to align, or realign, their preconceived expectations about the organization" (Taylor, Doherty, & McGraw, 2008, p. 82). Thus it helps new entrants acquire key aspects of the organization's culture (e.g., values, beliefs) and understand how certain groups can function within the organization (for more on organizational culture, see chapter 14).

PROCESS OF SOCIALIZATION

An important framework for understanding the process of socialization was developed by D.C. Feldman (1976), who posited three phases or stages of organizational socialization: anticipatory socialization, encounter socialization, and role management.

Anticipatory Socialization

As its label suggests, this stage occurs before the individual joins the organization. It encompasses the person's preentry expectations about the organization and lays the groundwork for the psychological contract with the organization. The psychological contract addresses the person's understanding of what he or she owes the organization and can expect from it in return (Taylor et. al., 2008). For example, a new employee in the marketing unit of an intercollegiate athletic department should understand that the work will involve long hours and include attending home events to conduct promotional activities; on the other hand, department leaders allow marketing employees to report to work later on the morning after a game day.

As noted by Rousseau (1989), the psychological contract is based on beliefs about job promises and obligations with a focus on the employee and her perceptions; moreover, it involves a "reciprocal exchange" (p. 123). In the marketing example, the leaders responsible for the new employee play an important role in creating and clearly defining aspects of the job that go beyond the job description itself. Several studies have demonstrated that breaching the contract is negatively related to satisfaction, commitment, and job performance. For a review of relevant studies, see Bravo et al. (2012), who suggest that "the psychological contract in sport organizations can be observed through the lens of the culture in which most sport organizations operate" (p. 208).

In today's wired society, an organization's website provide key information about the organization and the possibilities for someone to become involved as an employee or volunteer. During the anticipatory socialization stage, website information (e.g., organization history, about us section, mission) is absorbed by new recruits (e.g., employees, volunteers, interns) as they form expectations. This is when they begin to form expectations related to the new position, its tasks, and the organization as a whole. For example, an intern may form ideas about what it means to work in a sport organization's marketing department, such as getting involved in game-day promotions and hospitality opportunities with area businesses. The person's developing sense of work responsibilities and opportunities in the organization may—or may not—be congruent with the actual responsibilities and opportunities.

Encounter Socialization

This stage of Feldman's (1976) model is marked by signing the contract (for employees) and learning the specifics of the new role, the assigned job tasks, the other people in the organization, and how the organization operates. Therefore, the new entrant begins to reconcile initial expectations and ideas about how things are done with what she is now learning through observation and involvement. During this stage, the new entrant is formally introduced to her role and tasks, the physical environment, and the people who are part of her group, a well as others in the organization. This is the stage in which the person begins to settle into the job and feel like part of the organization as a contributor. She also begins to form the interpersonal connections that are critical to group integration, teamwork, communication, and, in turn, the achievement of both group and organizational objectives. Over time, the employee masters various job tasks and becomes more comfortable with and integrated into the setting.

Role Management

During this final stage of the model, new recruits master tasks and roles while adjusting to the group's values and norms (Kinicki & Kreitner, 2008). This stage involves fine-tuning one's expectations about the job and the organization and understanding the reciprocal obligations which exist between oneself, one's immediate work groups, and the organization as a whole. Essentially, then, this phase focuses on adjustments, mastery, and clarity as the individual becomes an "insider" in the organization—that is, someone who is very familiar with the organization's internal workings and wields influence on both internal and external stakeholders.

For sport managers, Feldman's (1976) model provides a way to organize thoughts about how to help new entrants transition into the organization. For example, as a manager, you might design a socialization process that accounts for these various phases and includes short-, medium-, and longer-term check-ins with the new entrant. A formalized program for socialization provides the new entrant with the best transitional and learning opportunities to help him integrate into and thrive in the company. Though Feldman's model is simplistic, it does provide a manager with a framework for designing a socialization program. It also provides a basis for the manager to understand organizational socialization as an exchange-based relationship that develops throughout the three phases of socialization, which are critical components for effective management and integration of new entrants. In order to set up a successful program for organizational socialization, managers must understand that new entrants require information about the job and its roles and about the people with whom they will work.

EASING NEW MEMBERS INTO THE WORKFORCE

There are many ways in which a sport manager can help a new person feel welcomed into and valued by the organization; there are also many ways in which a manager can do just the opposite. For this reason,

it is sometimes helpful to learn what *not* to do. Learning from mistakes made by others is a great way to ensure that you do not step on the new person's toes. As an exercise, consider the ways in which you have been integrated into an organization for which you have recently worked:

- What did the manager or leader do well in your experience?
- What did the manager or leader do poorly in your experience?

Here are some good examples of what to do as a manager or leader:

- Be available.
- Provide contact information.
- Create a plan and share it with the new entrant.
- Articulate the job and management expectations.
- Provide opportunities for relational exchanges within the new entrant's immediate work group.
- Provide opportunities to meet other members of the organization.
- Be honest about your expectations.
- After the first month, check in from time to time to ensure that things are still on track.
- Model the way.

And here are some examples of what *not* to do as a manager or leader:

- Don't assume that the new person doesn't want help integrating.
- Don't close your door (i.e., don't be aloof, laissez-faire, or hands-off).
- Don't ridicule new ideas or ways of doing things.
- Don't provide insufficient details about work expectations.
- Don't communicate ambiguously.
- Don't avoid issues that need to be addressed.

In another approach, Van Maanen and Schein (1979) outlined six tactics that can help management design socialization programs to help new entrants understand their roles and how the organization generally wishes to operate. Over time, this approach has been taken up and adapted by a number of researchers (e.g., Ashforth, Saks, & Lee, 1998; Cable & Parsons, 2001; Jones, 1986; MacIntosh, Bravo, & Li, 2012) who have discussed various tactical strategies to aid management in designing organizational socialization processes. Here are some examples.

1. *Collective versus individual.* In collective socialization, a group of new recruits are provided with a common experience through which they learn about the organization, various jobs, and appropriate responses to situations; these elements are instructive right from the beginning. This activity helps reduce uncertainty about roles and can produce a sense of shared values among people in the organization. This socialization tactic is common, for example, during rookie orientation periods, in which all new players participate in camp-style activities and thus develop a set of common experiences. This type of socialization differs radically from the more individualized approach of an apprenticeship or mentor relationship, which is more common when the job is highly specialized.

2. *Formal versus informal.* Formal tactics help provide a consistent and specific message to a new recruit and signal the importance of adapting to the new organization, job, and expectations. This tactic tends to segregate the new person but is intended to help reduce uncertainty about the job. It can help the newcomer become familiar with specific duties, which is crucial when the work is risky to self or others. For example, in sport, field maintenance and gate security require very specific attention to detail in order to prevent harm to stakeholders; therefore, these jobs require the use of formal teaching tactics. Although this approach may institutionalize the status quo to some degree, it also enables awareness of important cultural values in the specific job that reflect the larger organizational culture. In contrast, informal tactics are less intervention oriented; instead, they provide opportunities for trial and error and for learning on the job. Informal socialization processes do not distinguish the newcomer's role specifically.

3. *Sequential versus random.* Sequential tactics provide information about the sequence of learning activities and experiences, which helps reduce uncertainty about job tasks and responsibilities. In other words, sequential tactics teach the newcomer about the preferred routine to be followed. It is thought that this tactic helps the person learn a sense of personal control in the job; thus it can be used to reduce the anxiety and stress associated with adjusting to a new environment and organizational culture. For instance, a person who works in a sport and recreation program would be given the needed reference material for organizing the new season. In contrast, in random socialization, the steps are unknown and the job has an ambiguous character—not ideal when operating a specific sport program, which has many steps that need to be followed in order to ensure safety of operations for patrons.

4. *Fixed versus variable.* Fixed tactics help provide information about the timing of each socialization stage; thus, as with the use of sequential tactics, this approach can reduce anxiety about the job and help newcomers develop a sense of control over their new environment. More specifically, fixed socialization provides clear expectations about the length of time in which the new person is expected to complete the stages of socialization—for example, a schedule for completing coaching level courses in order to advance to the next stage of responsibility in the organization. In contrast, variable tactics do not provide specific time lines. This approach is often associated with organizations facing variables that are unknown or difficult to

control, such as the economy or political environment. For example, a major project such as the development of a new venue requires involvement by various levels of government, which means that the person responsible for permits and regulations may have no specific or fixed schedule for completing a given task.

5. *Serial versus disjunctive.* Serial tactics include using experienced members of the organization as role models or mentors for new recruits. This approach helps the new recruit learn about the job and the organization from someone with inside knowledge of the working environment. It can help the newcomer make sense of the environment and discover resources that will aid job performance while developing a sense of competence and task mastery. Many succession plans in sport use this method—for instance, to teach an assistant GM the roles associated with the GM position or to teach a new trainer the roles involved in serving as head trainer. In contrast, in disjunctive socialization, the new recruit has no role model, does not knowingly follow in the footsteps of those who came before, and is not introduced to regulations and guidelines for fulfilling his or her duties. At times, this situation may result from the proverbial changing of the guard, in which a new person brings in a new agenda. Still, when no role model or mentor is available, disjunctive socialization can result in ambiguity and confusion for the new person.

6. *Investitive versus divestitive.* Investitive tactics provide newcomers with positive social support and feedback about their competencies and skills. This approach can help the recruit develop self-confidence early in the socialization process. It also lets the organization show the new recruit that it values her skills and is open to her ideas about improving the company. For example, many sport organizations today place tremendous value on sport analytics, but this work requires a specialized skill set that is not easy to learn. Thus it is important for organizations to bring in people who possess this ability and can help others acquire information more holistically. In contrast, divestitive socialization asks the new recruit to remove or forget old habits of behavior and learn to resolve problems based on the new organization's expectations.

Adapting these six tactics can help management design effective socialization programs, but it may also create a risk of reproducing the status quo in the organization if the programs go unreviewed and do not change according to the new organizational realities or individuals' specific needs. Consequently, management must thoroughly consider the design of the socialization program and its specific goals. Depending on the specifications of a given job, it may be important to provide the new recruit with informal, unplanned, and random discussions with others in the organization, especially during the early adoption period. This can help the new recruit understand the general roles of others and the general working environment of the organization itself, both aspects that can help him or her transition into the new role.

If used appropriately, the various socialization tactics available for management can help the new entrant fulfill personal needs and wants related to the job, which can increase loyalty and decrease employee turnover (Allen, 2006). Furthermore, when the socialization process makes good use of experienced organizational insiders (e.g., veteran employees)—either as role models or mentors—they can help the new person learn the values and beliefs that guide behavior in the organization. Using a senior-level person who has a wealth of experience in the job and in the organization may also help the new person feel more welcomed.

However, as we discuss later in the book, the socialization process may also involve—and challenge—power relationships, due to factors such as ageism, bigotry, and gender bias. Various forms of power operate in organizational life (see chapter 12), which can at times create conflict, particularly when someone feels challenged or threatened by a new person's skill set or abilities. Thus, with each new hire, it is possible that the socialization process will serve as a stage on which power plays are acted out. It is almost impossible, of course, to ensure that such dynamics never happen; even the best socialization programs cannot totally avoid interpersonal conflict.

The tactics discussed here may work in some organizations but fail in others, depending on the values and beliefs of the organizational culture (see chapter 14). In order to work, a socialization system must be authentic and uncontrived. In addition, the extent to which a sport organization produces a well-conceived socialization plan may depend on the nature of the job and the type of organization—for instance, enduring (e.g., sport team) or temporary (e.g., sport event). Among the many factors that can shape a new entrant's socialization process, one that deserves close attention is that of organizational context (Wang, Kammeyer-Mueller, Liu, & Li, 2015).

SOCIALIZATION CONTEXTS

Wang et al. (2015) identified the following features that affect the context in which a new person joins an organization: formal organizational practices, organizational climate, and socialization agents. The formal practices are institutionalized and can be controlled through the human resources department. Many of the tactics such as scheduling time to meet other employees during the work-day and learn about part of their job responsibilities were described earlier in this chapter in the discussion of Van Maanen and Schein's six-tactic typology work. In addition, Wang et al. suggest that a manager must consider the organizational climate in relation to the new recruit's need to understand the general atmosphere surrounding daily work life expectations, which can help them make sense about how to go about or approach their work related responsibilities. Understanding the organizational climate should help foster employee development related to their job tasks and provide further opportunities to acquire

IN THE BOARDROOM
Room for Personal Growth

One of the pitfalls of working in the service-related industries (e.g., fitness, retail) is that they are notorious for high employee turnover. This factor presents a real management challenge in that for every employee who leaves, a new person must be recruited and trained. One way to reduce turnover is to ensure good understanding of the expectations held by each party (organization and employee), such as the types of personal growth desired by the employee and the opportunities for personal growth offered by the organization. For example, younger employees may want to gain responsibility and autonomy by taking on new challenges or by taking courses to increase their knowledge base in particular subject areas (e.g., video journalism, interviewing). Millennial workers often seek to enhance their base of experience in order to qualify for a promotion, snag an important job interview, grow their knowledge, or increase a skill set. More generally, employees have a role to play in ensuring that management understands their career objectives; therefore, they should be readily able to communicate about those objectives both through informal dialogue and in the context of performance reviews.

and exchange knowledge important to performing their job. The individual's socialization can also be aided by various socialization agents, including leaders, coworkers, and clients. Wang et al. note that these agents help the new person acquire two types of resources: tangible (e.g., financial rewards, office materials) and intangible (e.g., feedback, advice, social support). However, this research is more relevant to the enduring type of organization (which is more commonly associated with socialization theory in the business literature) and does not typically account for the temporary organizations that are prevalent in sport.

TEMPORARY VERSUS ENDURING ORGANIZATIONS

For the most part, research about organizational socialization and the various tactics involved has focused on enduring organizations (e.g., sport retailers, professional sport teams, university athletic departments). By their nature, enduring organizations seek longer-term involvement in their business operations. In the world of sport management, however, many organizations are temporary—for example, organizing committees for sport events such as the Olympic Games, which operate on a fixed schedule with clear starting and ending dates. Thus the nature of the workforce for such events differs from

that of an enduring organization, and the temporary nature of these jobs requires a different kind of socialization process. For instance, temporary organizations such as sport event hosts operate on compressed schedules that create a need to quickly gel work groups (Parent & MacIntosh, 2013; see figure 8.1). These organizations have an urgent need to equip new entrants (whether employees or volunteers) with constructive expectations about work life and to infuse guiding principles and values that will govern work. These steps will be critical to the ongoing negotiations and interactions among the people affected by the management process.

As you can see, the various ways to design a socialization system are highly dependent on the type of sport organization (e.g., enduring versus temporary) and the type of job (e.g., long-term skilled work versus short-term labor). In the world of sport, the design also depends on the type of hire (e.g., short-term rental player, long-term finance department member, rookie, veteran, volunteer). Unlike a temporary organization, a professional sport team or league relies on keeping employees for (ideally) longer periods of time. With that need in mind, enduring organizations such as the NHL have created a variety of programs, and used a range of tactics, to help their players transition into new roles and then eventually into their postcareer lives.

In addition, for both teams and leagues, the specialization of player roles requires

IN THE BOARDROOM
NHL Core Development Program

The NHL has taken strides to help players become professional in their attitude and behavior, both on and off the ice, through its Core Development Program. The program is intended not only to help players transition into the professional realm of North American hockey but also to help them prepare for postcareer life. It offers a variety of educational activities, helps players build networks, and addresses financial and philanthropic goals. Most teams, if not all, also offer assistance in the form of mentorship to help new players learn their way around the league.

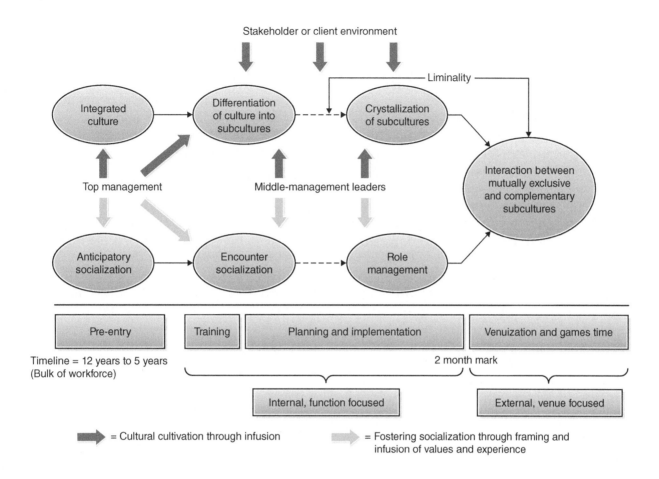

Figure 8.1 Organizational socialization and evolution of culture in a temporary organization.

Reprinted by permission from M. Parent and E. MacIntosh, "Organizational Culture Evolution in Temporary Organizations: The Case of the 2010 Olympic Winter Games," *Canadian Journal of Administrative Sciences* 30, no 4 (2013): 223-237.

these organizations to continually replenish the system with younger talent, whether through the draft, the development of young players in a farm system, or trades. Of course, younger players are often less mature, which creates a need to help them integrate into a new and sometimes very different way of life. For an example, see this chapter's case study (Socialization in Professional Basketball: The Rookie Transition Program).

Given the vastness of the sport industry and its wide range of jobs (e.g., service versus product), these differences must be accounted for when designing a socialization system. There is no magic formula or recipe that can work in every type of sport

organization; to the contrary, each socialization process needs to be context specific. For instance, enduring organizations can use probationary periods with new entrants in order to determine whether they are able to, interested in, and willing to continue in the assigned role. Enduring organizations also have the luxury of using job learning tactics such as job shadowing, training the trainer, mentoring, and other forms of personal interaction that can take several weeks or even longer. For temporary organizations, however, these strategies may be less feasible due to restrictive time constraints, such as critical start dates that can be very difficult to shift. Thus, a new entrant must demonstrate competence more quickly than in an enduring sport organization.

INTERNATIONALIZATION OF SPORT

In recent years, much of professional sport in North America (e.g., NBA, MLB, NHL) and around the world (e.g., English Premier League) has experienced considerable internationalization in the ranks of players, coaches, and administrators. This trend, which can be referred to as the internationalization of sport (c.f., MacIntosh & Harris, 2017), is now becoming more prominent in the collegiate sport system as well, both in the United States and in Canada. As a result, organizational socialization programs must now address the presence of cultural differences among athletes and the increasingly diverse composition of teams. Both professional and collegiate programs should attend to the differences in attitude and expectations that may be found both among players from their own country and among new entrants or recruits from other countries. For instance, the presence of players from various countries has created a need for interpreters to help athletes conduct interviews; thus a new and critical role has appeared in many sport organizations. In addition, players who leave their home country must understand that the working environment may differ from what they are used to; therefore, they have an important responsibility to learn not only a new language but also new rules and expectations associated with professionalism by their new team or league.

One way to help a person integrate from a different country is to try to understand the person's cultural preferences. For this purpose, research on the dimensions of cultural difference (e.g., individual versus collective, masculine versus feminine) has been used in several fields to aid understanding of the ways in which cultural differences are important when managing people (c.f., Hofstede, Neuijen, Ohayv, & Sanders, 1990). Although this research can be helpful in integrating new players into a team, it is very nationalistic and is based on generalizations that do not always accurately account for a person's individual preferences and expectations; nor is it based in sport. Indeed, as of now, the literature in sport management offers little treatment of issues related to international diversity among players and coaches in a team-based environment.

In one nonsport study, Grøgaard and Colman (2016) suggest that local context and perceptions help provide frames for interpretation. Specifically, they note that espoused values are influenced by local

IN THE BOARDROOM
International Acquisition

Given the growing practice of acquiring international talent, sport teams must pay attention to the particular needs of a new person joining the team from another country. For example, the player must learn about new tax laws, job benefits, responsibilities to the team, societal norms, and many other aspects of life that may differ greatly from life in the home country. As a result, management must consider both cultural and personal differences that can exist between individuals (e.g., religious practices, foods preferred or avoided) and be sensitive to the practices of the new person while also teaching him or her what is expected and viewed as desirable by the new team.

CASE STUDY

Socialization in Professional Basketball: The Rookie Transition Program

One example of a socialization program for new entrants into a sporting league is the Rookie Transition Program developed by the NBA and the National Basketball Players Association (NBPA). Of all the professional sport leagues in North America, the NBA is arguably the most international in terms of player demographics. Given the prominent role of internationalization in the NBA's strategic plan, the league and the NBPA collaborated to create a series of seminars and workshops that help younger players (from both within and outside of the United States) adapt to the challenges inherent in their new profession, both on and off the court. The program was born of former players' concerns regarding the ability of new entrants to cope with the stress of NBA life and the pressure of public performance.

The mandatory program takes the form of a crash course that occurs over a three- or four-day period (Kennedy, 2016), during which new recruits and players learn about important aspects of attending to their physical and mental health, professionalism in the league, financial management strategies, ethics, respect and inclusion, sponsorship and personal branding, community involvement, and stress management techniques (Kennedy, 2016; Remme, n.d.). In addition, special sessions are offered for players who are 20 years of age or younger and for international players facing the unique challenges of entering a new country. Young players are taught how to be on their own for the first time and how to understand their role on the team. Foreign players learn about cultural adaptation, overcoming the language barrier, and acclimating to the style of play in the NBA. Ultimately, the program helps players move successfully through the encounter phase of socialization and increase their understanding of the business and their role in it, both for their team and for the league as a whole. The NBA and NBPA also offer a 24-hour support system in collaboration with social workers, former players, and other experts (Remme, n.d.).

The Rookie Transition Program is administered by the player development departments of the NBA and NBPA and is viewed as an important step in the life of an NBA player. It also provides an example of good practice in helping people transition into a new role (in this case, that of professional player). Of course, it is up to the individual's team to ensure that the transitional period is marked by opportunities for the young athlete to ask questions and get to know the internal workings of the franchise.

Case Study Questions

1. In what ways does the Rookie Transition Program address the needs of younger athletes as they enter into large professional contracts?
2. What information do you think is most valuable to convey in this type of program?
3. What might have motivated the NBA and NBPA to implement this initiative?

embeddedness and by perceptions of the organization's national office or headquarters. For example, the authors noted that although espoused values of the organization "were perceived by . . . [headquarters] to be universal or geocentric in the formulation, i.e., reflecting values that are recognizable and appreciated across countries and continents, our data show that they were interpreted differently in the subsidiaries" (p.181). Although the study focused on multinational enterprises, it raises important questions about how people learn and interpret values and carries implications for internationally diverse groups who work together in sport. For instance, a new entrant from another country may have many needs and interpret everyday norms in many ways that differ from the norm in the new society.

As Grøgaard and Colman (2016) discuss, interpretive frames can either impede or facilitate socialization. Therefore, sport organizations should consider, for example, establishing open lines of communication as early as possible and enlisting the help of a translator when needed. They should also offer support in such matters as travel documentation and work visa requirements, provide knowledge of taxation and regulatory issues, and, per- haps most important, help the new person understand the customs and norms of both professional and personal life in the new country.

SUMMARY

Organizational socialization is critical to effective management. A well-thought-out program for new entrants can ease the transition, instill confidence, and facilitate acceptance in the new role and organization. Sport managers must consider the various tactics available for designing a program that accounts for the new person's needs and skills and provides social opportunities that are authentic to the culture of the organization. Doing so helps increase loyalty and decrease turnover—two obvious antecedents of effective management and strong organizational performance. Investing in the organization's people early on promotes good will, as does continued investment in fulfilling employees' needs and wants beyond the early stages of socialization. In both enduring and temporary sport organizations, the process of organizational socialization can benefit both the newcomer and the organization in terms of both affective and behavioral outcomes.

DISCUSSION QUESTIONS

1. What are the stages in Feldman's socialization process?
2. Discuss three socialization tactics that a sport manager could employ to help a rookie athlete entering his or her first professional contract.
3. Identify some likely differences in approach between enduring and temporary sport organizations in designing a socialization plan.
4. What is the psychological contract, and why is it important?
5. Identify some differences between good socialization plans and bad ones.

PART III
MANAGING THE GROUP

Part I laid out what we believe to be the fundamental components of organizational success, and part II detailed some of the individual considerations that affect a person's well-being at work. In part III, we examine the integration of the individual into group settings and describe the managerial implications of groups that perform well.

Chapter 9 discusses classical and contemporary views of leadership and introduces several characteristics that are important for leaders to consider in regard to employee tasks and relationships with colleagues and supervisors. The chapter also discusses the nature of authentic leadership and the importance of leadership development in sport organizations.

Decision making pervades all aspects of work in a sport organization. Some decisions are routine and can be made on the basis of policies and procedures, but others require engaging in a concerted process. Chapter 10 examines various models for understanding decision making, including the rational model, the administrative model, and the garbage can model. The chapter also examines group decision making and its potential benefits (e.g., creativity, increased support for decisions) and challenges (e.g., groupthink).

Chapter 11 describes teamwork, which, in the context of organizational behavior, can be defined as a group of people working together based on specific skill sets or abilities to accomplish a specific task or function. The chapter covers various types of teams: cross-functional, problem-solving, employee involvement, self-managing, and top-management. It also describes the process of team development, which includes forming, storming, norming, performing, and adjourning. The chapter then describes cohesion—a type of social glue that enables teammates to become attached to one another and work together as a unit. Finally, it explores how teamwork can be undercut by social loafing.

Chapter 12 addresses conflict, negotiation, and power. Conflict permeates all levels of sport and can be positive or constructive; of course, it can also be negative or destructive when not managed properly. Conflict can often be reduced or resolved through negotiation, which is the process of making joint decisions when the parties involved prefer different outcomes. When fully successful, negotiation achieves both substance goals and relationship goals. Power is understood as the ability to influence individuals or groups in order to change their behaviors, actions, or attitudes. In sport organizations, it is most often associated with control over needed resources such as money, information, decisions, and work assignments.

Chapter 9

Leadership and Development

Chapter Objectives

After studying this chapter, you will be able to

- identify the stages of leadership research and development,
- discuss contemporary views of leadership research in sport management,
- elaborate on the importance of leadership to sport organizations, and
- explain the concept of leadership development.

The topic of leadership is a classical area of study that continues to draw much interest in today's organizations, including those in the world of sport. The typical image of a leader connotes power, influence, and charisma. But what does it really mean to be a leader? Does everyone have the capacity to lead? Why do some people exhibit forms of leadership to a greater degree than others? What is the difference between leadership and management? These questions continue to permeate the landscape of leadership research and practice.

The discourse about leadership and its great importance to effective organizations sometimes takes on an urgency akin to the fact that people need oxygen in order to stay alive. If that seems overdone, imagine an organization without leadership. It is hard to envision! In both business and sport, we hear about the importance of people "walking the talk," the need for our leaders to be honest and accountable for their efforts, and the importance of being forward looking and even visionary. Certainly, in the sport industry, the idea of leadership (or lack thereof) is intimately associated with our notions of a manager, coach, or player. Thus leadership is a key topic for sport organizations and the people who we work in them on a daily basis.

The many attitudes, characteristics, and behaviors exhibited by people in the world of sport are often telling in terms of what it means to be a leader. Sometimes, in fact, it is easiest to discern what good leadership is when we see the opposite—that is, ineffective or bad leadership. As we will see, the sport industry is rife with examples of both positive and negative leadership.

In the broadest sense, leadership is an influential process, occurring within a social system, through which leaders create a vision and work hard to realize its goals and objectives, whether for a group or for an entire organization (Yukl, 2008). As part of this process, leadership involves creating a clear, strong culture with the ability to produce both affective and effective change (Schein, 1990). In the world of sport, leadership can occur in various settings, including on the field, behind the scenes, in public-facing formats (e.g., media conference), and in the daily activities that people perform in order to achieve goals. Thus leadership is not one thing—it is many!

The topic of leadership has received considerable attention in both business and sport literature due to its importance in directing people's behavior at work and enabling organizational success. Formal leadership is exercised from an officially titled position in an organization—for instance, team captain or general manager—and thus provides a level of accountability. In this regard, the sport environment provides an obvious and compelling arena in which to examine leadership.

At the same time, a formal title is not always necessary in order for leadership to be exhibited in sport; to the contrary, everyone has the ability to lead informally. Indeed, volumes have been written on the subject of exhibiting leadership characteristics and qualities regardless of one's title or position (e.g., Bass, 1985; Bennis & Nanus, 1985; J.C. Collins, 2001; Conger, 1998; Conger & Kanunga, 1998; Kotter, 1999; Kouzes & Posner, 2002). Key topics in this research have included the characteristics (e.g., confidence, authenticity) that make a leader great and the importance of instilling a vision that inspires others. For example, one researcher described leadership as "the process of influencing others to understand and agree about what needs to be done and how to do it, and the process of facilitating individual and collective efforts to accomplish shared objectives" (Yukl, 2008, p. 8). This short definition helps us understand that a person has the capability to both push and pull people (followers) to accomplish tasks; moreover, it provides us with a simple yet refined understanding of a complex topic that continues to be debated.

Before discussing sport-related research, we need to appreciate some of the theories, both early and more modern, that have been put forth in order to explain leader-

ship. Thus we turn now to a brief account of some key periods in leadership research.

HISTORY OF LEADERSHIP RESEARCH

The earliest research on leadership sought to identify traits of great leaders. This effort stemmed from the notion that people possess certain characteristics and that the capacity to be a leader requires extraordinary qualities that regular folks just don't have. This idea developed into what became known as the "great man theory" (GMT), which assumes that certain people are innately suited to leadership—that is, that they were born with the characteristics of a leader (e.g., gender, ethnicity). Developed in the early 1900s by Eugene Jennings (Edginton, Hudson, & Ford, 1999), GMT suggested that individuals whose families held significant social status or heritage were more likely to have children who grew up to be recognized as leaders in their community or society (Bennis & Nanus, 1985; Edginton et al., 1999). Despite its appeal at the time, GMT came under critique due to the ample evidence suggesting that some people develop into or learn to become a great leader despite a disadvantaged birth.

Ultimately, then, Jennings' GMT was not accepted by the mainstream, but it did propagate research about the characteristics of leaders, including the emergent trait theory. Developed during the 1930s and 1940s, this theory saw researchers studying influential leaders of the time in an attempt to identify certain characteristics (e.g., in terms of height, weight, health, appearance, age) as keys to leadership. During this period, Stogdill (1948) reviewed some 30 years of leadership research in an effort to identify characteristics that were constitutive of leadership. He concluded, however, that no single trait or combination of traits could serve as a predictor of leadership. Indeed, research on leadership must also consider the situation. Leaders face constant and often conflicting demands on their time, and we must understand their various interactions with people and consider their ability to communicate necessary messages amid the various internal and external constraints and realities they face (Yukl, 2008).

In light of these questions about the predictive ability of any given trait or set of traits, leadership research shifted to focus on understanding a person's behaviors and the situations in which they occur. In other words, it shifted toward trying to identify aspects of a person's behavior (rather than character) in order to understand and predict successful leadership. However, in trying to explore various commonalities, differences, and patterns, this research has perhaps provided more new questions than answers. Of the plethora of behavioral characteristics that have been discussed by various researchers (e.g., intelligence, speech fluency, insight), the earliest research on leadership behavior indicated that perhaps success could be predicted by types of leadership—for instance, autocratic, democratic, or laissez-faire. In brief, the democratic style of leadership takes a collaborative and interactive approach with followers, the autocratic style sees the leader directing and controlling through actions that enforce regulations, and in the laissez-faire approach the leader fails to accept responsibility and remains aloof and hands-off. For many people, the democratic and autocratic styles remain part of the business lexicon today.

These and other theories of leadership style led to additional debates about the contexts in which some modes of behavior might be more favorable than others. Consider, for example, a situation in which an urgent response is required. Whereas an authoritarian leader might act quickly, a democratic leader could gather more input from others but would take longer to settle on an agreed-upon course of action. Inevitably, these early concepts created the need to give further consideration to the type of context, the specific situation,

and, in later research, the leader's value system and level of self-awareness. Leaders differ in the extent to which they pursue a human relations approach and try to maintain friendly, supportive relations with their followers. Leaders with a strong concern for human relations are considered to be relations oriented or people centered, whereas those with a strong concern for group goals and the means to achieve them are considered to be task or production oriented.

Classical studies examining people's behavior while acting as leaders were conducted by various researchers and studies at Ohio State University and the University of Michigan. The Ohio State studies (e.g., Fleishman,1953; Hemphill, 1950) were interested in determining the behaviors of effective leaders and were largely responsible for determining two important dimensions of a leader's style—initiating structure and considering the employee—which were further described in the Leadership Behavior Description Questionnaire (Stogdill, 1963). The Michigan studies (e.g., Likert, 1961) denoted that leaders can be production oriented or employee oriented, with these dimensions having an influence on group-level performance with the potential to enhance job satisfaction. Both the Ohio and the Michigan studies were focused on the consequences of the leader's behavior. The approach of measuring how leaders spent their time, or what they did on an average day as a leader, raised many questions about the context of their work and the work environment. These two sets of studies have been credited with ushering in a new era of leadership research that considered humans and their work environment to be related to the leader's style and the atmosphere it helps to produce. In this era of leadership research, two distinct categories were ultimately established: task oriented (autocratic, production focused, concerned with initiating structure) and people or employee oriented (democratic, relations or employee oriented, concerned with considering the employee) (Blake & Mouton, 1964; Yukl, 2008).

From here, contingency theories posited that leadership style is determined based in part on the context or situation. Indeed, many believed that the situation would influence the preferred type of leadership style. For example, Fiedler's (1967) model argued that leadership styles interact with situational realities—specifically, the degree of support offered by followers, the structure of the group's task, and the leader's formal authority—which determine "situational favorableness" (Fiedler, 1967). During this period, a plethora of theories were developed and contested as researchers increasingly came to appreciate the importance of environment and context while also examining the need for a leader to be future oriented and visionary. Examples include Fiedler's contingency theory (1967), the path-goal theory from House (1971), Blake and Mouton's (1964) leadership grid, and Hersey and Blanchard's situational leadership model (1969, 1977). The path-goal theory, for instance, approached leader effectiveness based on the expectancy that motivation would enable followers to set and reach goals. However, as with GMT and trait theory, it was subjected to much criticism on the grounds that behavioral leadership theory was too broad and that contingency theories were difficult to validate and test for reliability.

What emerged next was the notion that leadership could be both transactional and transformational (TF)—that is, both task oriented and people oriented, or having one eye on the job and one eye on the future (Bass 1985; Bass & Stogdill, 1990; Burns, 1978). In transformational leadership, the leader creates a vision, communicates it convincingly, models it, and builds follower commitment to achieving it (Yukl, 2008). Bass' model of transformational leadership has been widely referenced in many types of leadership research. More specifically, the concept of TF leadership has been extremely influential in sport

management research (particularly earlier research) related to coaching and upper administration in collegiate sport. At the same time, one example of transformational leadership in sport can be found in the professional ranks in the person of Billy Beane, vice president the Oakland Athletics baseball club. When Beane changed the way in which the team evaluated and scouted players, he ushered in the era of using sport analytics to evaluate player talent and production. His ideas about player evaluation were initially met with much criticism. However, his vision and persistence in bringing a different approach to the game has helped spawn a new generation of thinking about the use of statistics in sport.

Transactional leadership, on the other hand, is said to motivate followers by appealing to their self-interest through a system of rewards and punishments. According to Bass (1985), it is characterized by four components: contingent reward, active management by exception, passive management by exception, and laissez-faire attitudes. Contingent reward involves establishing contracts and exchanging reward for effort. Active management by exception involves observing subordinates and taking corrective action when they deviate from rules and standards. In contrast, passive management by exception involves intervening only if performance standards are not being met. The laissez-faire approach involves avoiding decision-making processes and relinquishing responsibilities.

Ultimately, it was Bass' model of transformational leadership (1985) that was thought by most leadership scholars to be predictive of effective leadership on the basis of the following key points: attributed charisma, idealized influence, inspirational motivation, intellectual stimulation, and individualized consideration. In this model, attributed charisma relates to the leader's self-confidence and assertiveness, which engender trust and respect from subordinates. Idealized influence concerns the leader's ability to actively promote his or her beliefs and vision. Inspirational motivation is conceived as the leader's ability to convey high expectations for, and confidence in, subordinates. Intellectual stimulation is provided by the leader's encouragement of proactive and creative problem solving. And individualized consideration involves the leader in interpersonal relations with, and the personal development of, each subordinate.

The model of TF leadership is related to the idea of charismatic leadership, developed in part by the works of House (1977), who viewed the leader as possessing charismatic qualities that can provide role modeling for followers. The premise is that followers attribute certain charismatic qualities to a leader with whose values, beliefs, and work approach they identify. According to Yukl (2008), charismatic leaders have the capacity to bring people together because of their dominant and inspiring personality and their commitment to a vision. In fact, some research on charismatic leaders contends that a leader's desirable personality characteristics could provide referent power (see chapter 12) over followers (c.f. McShane & Steen, 2012). Thus it is possible for a charismatic leader who becomes intoxicated or obsessed with power to perform either ethically or unethically. Despite its power, Bass (1985) asserted that although "charisma is a necessary ingredient of transformational leadership . . . [it is not] by itself . . . sufficient to account for the transformational process" that influences followers (p. 31).

The concept of TF leadership still resonates in many ideas of effective leadership today, but other theories have also articulated concepts that remain relevant, including the notion of servant leadership. For example, Robert Greenleafs described the central tenet of leadership as being concerned with serving the followership, including employees, customers, and the community at large (Greenleaf, 2002). Greenleaf's concept of servant leadership

focuses on putting others' needs above one's own, which of course requires the leader to understand the wants and needs of the group. Thus this style of leadership exhibits a strong focus on the person-oriented way of leading.

Another theory that has received considerable attention is that of authentic leadership (AL). As noted by one pair of authors, "leadership has always been more difficult in challenging times, but the unique stressors facing organizations throughout the world today call for a renewed focus on what constitutes genuine leadership" (Avolio & Gardner, 2005, p. 316). AL has been defined as a

> *pattern of leader behavior that draws upon and promotes both positive psychological capacities and a positive ethical climate, to foster greater self-awareness, an internalized moral perspective, balanced processing of information, and relational transparency on the part of leaders working with followers, fostering positive self-development. (Walumbwa, Avolio, Gardner, Wernsing, & Peterson, 2008, p. 94)*

A self-based model of development for authentic leadership and followership has been offered by Gardner, Avolio, Luthans, May, and Walumbwa (2005). The model posits that both leaders and followers require high levels of self-awareness (e.g., about values and emotions) in order to help them regulate their own behavior and arrive at desirable performances and outcomes. The authors note that "authenticity involves both owning one's personal experiences (values, thoughts, emotions, and beliefs) and acting in accordance with one's true self (expressing what you really think and believe and behaving accordingly)" (p. 344).

The premise here is that authentic leaders inspire trust and commitment in others due to their ability to promote optimism, confidence, and hope. The notion that AL can engender follower citizenship and enhance performance and productivity has generated interest in developing leadership training programs. Indeed, the concept of AL is linked to personal development of the leader and the follower through self-awareness practice and a deep appreciation of the context in which one works (Ladkin & Taylor, 2010). Overall, AL is touted as a positive alternative to traditional leadership research:

> *We believe authentic leadership can make a fundamental difference in organizations by helping people find meaning and connection at work through greater self-awareness; by restoring and building optimism, confidence, and hope; by promoting transparent relationships and decision making that builds on trust and commitment among followers; and by fostering inclusive structures and positive ethical climate. (Avolio & Gardner, 2005, p. 331)*

For example, one study (Hutchinson & Bouchet, 2014) examined universities that were de-escalating (i.e., reducing) their commitment to NCAA Division I athletics, either by discontinuing a Division I football program, reclassifying to a lower NCAA division, or restructuring their athletic department operations. The study found that seasoned university presidents exhibited authentic leadership, in the form of care and consideration for the overall health of the university and its students, by making the unpopular decision to de-escalate with no obvious personal benefit to their own careers or personal lives.

AL and other contemporary ideas about leadership have created a burgeoning area of development wherein individuals can explore what makes them tick, examine ways to communicate more efficiently and effectively, learn through experience, and employ a lens of being both self- and follower-directed. In fact, Dalakoura (2010) postulated that modern leadership results

from leader development, which should be considered through two perspectives. The first perspective focuses on leader (singular) development, whereas the second posits a more complex phenomenon that entangles the leader in a certain context (i.e., social or organizational milieu). Thus, here again we see the idea that leadership can occur in a context of both task and person orientation, only now the notions of self-awareness and context awareness have taken on more prominent roles.

Leadership development is a contemporary practice in many organizations that wish to expand their employees' capacity to step into leadership roles. Indeed, developing and retaining talent is an important ingredient in organizational success. Much of work life involves transferable skills (e.g., confident communication) that can be acquired through leadership development; in fact, many aspects of authentic leadership can be developed (e.g., self-awareness, relationship transparency) through workshops and seminar experiences. These skills can also be learned over time through various aspects of individual and team-based projects in a sport organization and in sport through recreational and competitive situations where one can learn as a teammate, captain, or coach from the various players and other stakeholders they meet and communicate with. Crucial factors from the high-performance world of sport—such as hard work, persistence, and discipline—are equally important skills to have in the boardroom.

In the example provided in the Leadership in a Crisis sidebar, imagine the emotional experience that Furlong must have gone through as a leader of the Vancouver Games. His authenticity and resolve were certainly tested as he responded to tragic circumstances while facing a worldwide audience. In formulating his response, Furlong must have engaged in both self-awareness and self-regulation—that is, internalizing the issue and figuring out how to relate to people as transparently as possible.

IN THE BOARDROOM
Leadership in a Crisis

Sometimes in sport, particularly in moments of crisis, a leader's resolve and authenticity are tested in a public setting. For example, in the lead-up to the 2010 Winter Olympic Games in Vancouver, luge athlete Nodar Kumaritashvili died when he was thrown from his sled on a trial run just hours before the festival's opening ceremony. At that point, the urgent need to address the death in the public domain fell to John Furlong, CEO of the Vancouver Olympic Organizing Committee. At such times, when all eyes and ears await a response—mindful of the pain felt by the family and the shock felt by employees, volunteers, other athletes, and viewers around the world—the role of the leader is magnified and the leader's resolve is tested. In these times, leaders must understand and be true to themselves and respond appropriately and professionally to their constituents. For many people, Furlong's calm demeanor and very real human emotions helped ease a feeling of Olympic despair. His profound articulation of remorse was genuine and heartfelt.

Another body of work on leadership has argued that one's emotional intelligence (EI) is predictive of one's ability to be a leader. Goleman (1998, 2004) suggested that individuals with high levels of EI possess skills that enable them to engage, recognize, and manage their own emotions and those of other people and use that information to guide cognition and behavior. In addition, at least one study has reported that leaders with high emotional intelligence (i.e., self-awareness, self-motivation, relationship management ability, and empathy) were more likely to display transformational leadership ability (Sosik & Megerian, 1999). Once again, and perhaps not surprisingly, we see that aspects of awareness, relationship, and communication factor into what makes someone a good leader.

New leadership studies and theories are continuously emerging. Topics currently being explored include, for example, the potential of experiential learning to build leadership skills, the idea that one must know bad leadership in order to determine what good leadership is or might be, possible connections between leadership styles and gender, differences in approach between management and leadership, and possible effects on leadership from various aspects of individual identity (e.g., race, spirituality, age). As you can see, leadership remains a rich field of inquiry!

LEADERSHIP RESEARCH IN SPORT

Early research on leadership in sport management focused principally on coaches and their effectiveness and congruence with the preferences of team members (Chelladurai, 1978; Chelladurai & Saleh, 1980). As the field of sport management developed, it relied largely on quantitative assessments (such as the Multifactor Leadership Questionnaire and the Leadership Scale for Sports) to determine whether transactional or transformational leadership behavior was preferred (Bourner & Weese, 1995; Chelladurai & Riemer, 1998; Doherty & Danylchuk, 1996; Wallace & Weese, 1995; Weese, 1994, 1995). A large portion of this research was conducted in the context of intercollegiate sport—for example, examining the behavior of coaches and athletic directors. Overall, these studies made clear that transformational leadership was preferred and enabled the creation of a stronger culture but was not necessarily linked to organizational effectiveness.

Though much early research focused on collegiate administrative needs related to management skills, leadership qualities, and coaching behaviors (e.g., Danylchuk & Chelladurai, 1999; Doherty, 1997; Scott, 1999) other studies explored leadership in relation to gender (Defrantz, 1998; Doherty, 1997) and organizational culture (e.g., Kent & Weese, 2000; MacIntosh & Doherty, 2005). To no one's surprise, the research was beginning to demonstrate the profound importance of leadership on the people involved in sport organizations. Even so, gaps remained in the literature, including the consideration of gender and differences in leadership preferences and behavior, which have highlighted both the need and the desire for diversity in sport organizations (e.g., Burton, Barr, Fink, & Bruening, 2009; Burton, Grappendorf, & Henderson, 2011). Other studies investigated aspects of the socially constructed nature of leadership, such as varying constructions of leadership by various stake-

holders (Kihl, Leberman, & Schull, 2010); the authors argued that because leadership is socially constructed, it is necessary to understand stakeholders' experiences in context in order to understand how they form opinions and accounts of leadership.

Ultimately, sport management research has found that the traditional leadership styles—such as Bass' (1985) transformational leadership model—are preferred regardless of gender (e.g., Burton & Welty Peachey, 2009; Welty Peachey & Burton, 2011). Furthermore, it is critical to understand stakeholders' views of leadership because these individuals experience, and construct their own meanings for, leadership characteristics and behaviors (Kihl et al., 2010). In addition, leadership is not restricted to an organization's figurehead or titular leader but can come at any time from anywhere in the organization; indeed, "just as sport is not restricted to elite athletes, so leadership is not just the preserve of senior managers" (Burnes & O'Donnell, 2011, p. 24). To the contrary, various capabilities of leadership can emerge from various organizational stakeholders (e.g., athletes, employees)— for instance, being prepared, leading by example, showing respect, and being

IN THE BOARDROOM
Leadership Characteristics Exhibited by Historically Great Sport Leaders

Many historical sporting icons are recognized for their achievements both on and off the field. For example, Billy Jean King, Muhammad Ali, and Jackie Robinson (to name but a few) overcame stereotypes and great odds to break important barriers in sport. Thus, their leadership went well beyond their tremendous athletic talent and performances. Indeed, these individuals exhibited strong character, commitment, and resolve in the face of adversity to help bring about needed changes in society. These leadership qualities continue to be important aspects for today's sport leaders faced with the challenges and opportunities of creating gender equity, organizational diversity, and ethical organizations.

adaptive to circumstances, all of which are important to an organization's success (Burnes & O'Donnell, 2011). Consequently, as noted by Kihl et al. (2010), we must consider both the context in which leadership occurs and the stakeholders' perceptions of that leadership.

More recent research in sport management has addressed the notion of ethical leadership with a focus on intercollegiate sport (e.g., Sagas & Wigley, 2014). For instance, DeSensi (2014) argued that the culture of intercollegiate sport faces a number of social and moral challenges for which strong ethical leadership is required. Such challenges include the use of social media, which intensifies the public interface inherent in collegiate sport, and the ongoing pressure for athletes to be great at their sport while also performing in class. Thus the collegiate environment requires strong leadership at various levels (e.g., administrative, coaching, player, player support). Moreover, as suggested by Burton and Welty Peachey (2013), athletic directors grappling with these issues

would be well served to employ the servant leadership model in their decision making.

As Weese and Beard (2012) wrote, leaders "seek input from other stakeholders, listen attentively to their thoughts and opinions, and engage the leadership team and its stakeholders in shaping, communicating, and realizing the vision" (p. 1). In addition, they point out that effective leaders today see themselves as members of teams, hold a vision and seek input from others, communicate frequently and honestly, learn from success and failure, and are self-aware and reflective. It is imperative that both current and future leaders in sport take the time to acquire and develop these skills and apply them in their sport settings, particularly given the proliferation of unethical leadership that has plagued some of the most influential sport organizations (e.g., FIFA).

Welty Peachy, Zhou, Damon, and Burton's (2015) review of leadership research (see figure 9.1) denotes many outcomes desired in sport that require contributions from a range of organizational stakeholders (e.g.,

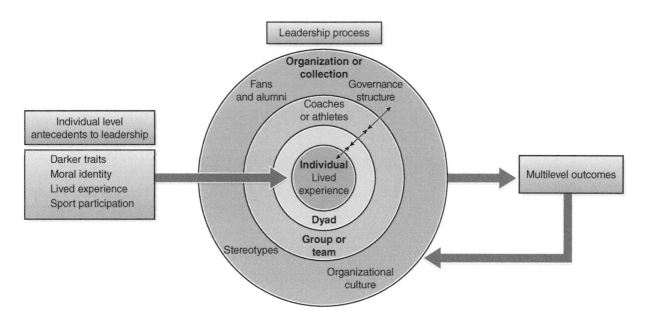

Figure 9.1 Multilevel conceptual model of leadership in sport management.

Adapted by permission from J. Welty Peachey et al., "Forty Years of Leadership Research in Sport Management: A Review, Synthesis, and Conceptual Framework," *Journal of Sport Management* 29, no 5 (2015): 570-587.

CASE STUDY
Leadership and Hindsight

Hindsight often makes it easy to identify poor leadership or lack of leadership in the world of sport. For an example, we need look no further than the rights holder of the world's largest sport event: the FIFA World Cup. Controversies related to the leadership of FIFA have given much cause for concern; in particular, many observers view the scandals associated with former FIFA president Joseph "Sepp" Blatter as constituting a prime example of poor leadership. Blatter's tenure has been criticized for alleged financial mismanagement, vote-rigging scandals, ticket scams, human rights issues, and even bribery related to the selection of World Cup host cities (Russia for 2018 and Qatar for 2022). Blatter's reputation has also been tarnished by his public shaming of referees and his derogatory comments about female players. These issues have damaged FIFA's reputation and left many observers questioning Blatter's suitability to lead in the first place. In addition, many people believe that Blatter wielded too much control and was not only unethical but also overly authoritarian in his approach to running the organization. Leadership theory has taught us that, depending on the situation and context, a leader who involves others in decision making may achieve better results.

Every sport organization needs ethical leadership, transparency, and principled governance. This is particularly the case in large organizations such as FIFA that need to ensure good governance. In some cases, the leader of such an organization generates growth and satisfies corporate sponsors—as Blatter did to some degree—but the path traveled to get there is not revealed until much later. Ultimately, Blatter's leadership will be remembered less for growth of the game than for damage done.

Case Study Questions

1. What type of leadership is needed in order to restore consumer and stakeholder faith in FIFA, and why?
2. Is it fair to evaluate a person's leadership qualities based on public information? Why, or why not?
3. Given what you know of the FIFA situation, what should a new leader learn from this example and carry into the job? What obstacles must now be overcome because of past failures?

fans, alumni, players, coaches). Thus, leadership research needs to examine perceptions and attitudes in order to determine what types of leadership are needed in various circumstances. This work requires a good understanding of the viewpoints and perceptions of leaders themselves regarding their own attitudes and behaviors (antecedents to leadership). Understanding the lived experience of the individual can help reveal his or her relationships with other stakeholders who may or may not share similar desired outcomes. This type of analysis can indicate that certain types of leadership are more suitable to certain contexts or circumstances than others.

SUMMARY

Leadership is a complex topic with a long history of research and ideas about how best to carry it out. Yet despite the advancements made in understanding leadership in sport management, much remains to be learned, and the topic continues to intrigue sport management scholars and practitioners. Judgments about what makes for good leadership can be influenced by many factors; indeed, preferred styles of leadership come with both advantages and disadvantages and are both context and situation specific. In order to understand how leadership can (or cannot) promote successful organizations, we require evidence in the field of sport management. And in practical terms, a person looking to become an effective leader must engage in discussion with a range of stakeholders in order to understand the leadership characteristics they value.

Today, the notion of leadership as a command-and-control phenomenon or autocratic endeavor is typically rebuffed. More than ever, current research and practice acknowledge the criticality of diverse stakeholder groups in getting work done and, therefore, the fact that leadership can come from anywhere and at any time. This reality requires those who hold leadership titles to demonstrate awareness, employ a strong moral compass, take in information from stakeholder groups, and be transparent in the process. Leaders must know that they not only motivate and inspire others to help them achieve great outcomes but also rely on follower groups that are invested in the vision. In this way, leadership research has taught us that the situation itself is a critical feature in understanding what makes people thrive.

The literature has also taught us that leadership is not isolated to a certain set of characteristics or abilities possessed by a person; moreover, though certain characteristics may be held in high regard, there is no single best formula for becoming and behaving like a leader. Instead, leaders can exhibit many qualities (e.g., emotional intelligence, authenticity) that are used in various capacities and called on in various circumstances as appropriate. What someone considers leadership today may not be viewed in the same way 10 years from now. In addition, the external organizational environment can exert great influence on the types of organizational leadership needed in order to succeed and the various competencies required to address a given situation. Considering the major challenges facing sport in the current age, and the need for effective leadership in meeting those challenges, it is fitting that the literature begin building on the concept of leadership development.

DISCUSSION QUESTIONS

1. Name a few current examples of good leadership in sport. What makes them good?
2. Describe three of the historical periods in leadership research.
3. What are the characteristics of an authentic leader?
4. Given the landscape of research on leadership in sport, what areas might you consider for conducting research and why?

Chapter 10

Decision Making

Chapter Objectives

After studying this chapter, you will be able to

- define programmed and nonprogrammed decisions and provide examples in the context of sport organizations;

- describe processes for making decisions in sport organizations, including both the rational and the administrative (bounded rationality) models;

- explain how the decision-making process is influenced by individual differences in gathering information (e.g., sensing versus intuitive approach) and evaluating alternatives (e.g., thinking versus feeling approach);

- explain how confirmation bias and escalation of commitment introduce challenges to the decision-making process;

- describe the benefits of group decision making and indicate when decision making is best done by groups; and

- define groupthink and explain why it may occur during the group decision-making process.

Decision making is a process in which we all engage every day; in fact, we are constantly making decisions, both personal and professional. Consider the number of routine decisions you make during a typical day: when to get up, what to have for breakfast, how to get to class, when to leave for class, what jacket to wear (if any), and so on. And then there are the more significant, and sometimes challenging, decisions you make. What happens if you are chosen for your top two internship sites? Should you pursue a master's degree after college, or is law school a better option? When you go about making a decision, whether regarding how to get to class or whether to go to graduate school, you take steps in a process. As you can see, the decision-making process pervades our everyday lives. It is also a constant in professional life in sport organizations. Consider, for instance, the process engaged in by a college softball coach as she determines who is the higher-priority recruit—a pitching ace or a power hitter. It might be easier to get an ace pitcher who is also a power hitter! Or consider the decisions made by members of an intercollegiate athletic conference regarding expansion of conference membership. Which candidate university would best support the goals of the conference, most enhance competitive and academic excellence, and offer the most beneficial media market?

We begin this chapter by discussing decisions of two kinds: routine (programmed) and nonroutine (nonprogrammed). We then explore a variety of ways in which people go about making decisions—that is, decision-making processes—and how they are affected both by personal characteristics and by aspects of the decision to be made. Then we consider when it is best to make decisions as a group and what benefits and challenges come with group decision making. The more you know about the decision-making process, the more likely you are to make better decisions, both in your own life and when working in a sport organization.

PROGRAMMED VERSUS NONPROGRAMMED DECISIONS

The simple and routine decisions that we face on a daily basis are considered to be programmed decisions. Because they are basic, we do not need to engage in a concerted decision-making process each time we encounter them. In sport organizations, programmed decisions are made quite frequently—for example, scheduling referees for a volleyball match, processing requests for team equipment purchases, and processing ticket orders for a football game. Because these are routine decisions, organizations have developed procedures to address them so that individual employees do not have to engage in a decision-making process.

Imagine, for instance, what might happen if a minor league baseball team did not establish a procedure for addressing the programmed decision of when and how to pull the tarp over the infield during a rain delay. Who would decide that it was necessary to pull the tarp? How would that person find enough employees and interns to pull the tarp? Should fans be asked onto the field to help? Where is the tarp, and how

does one go about "pulling" it? What is the best way to cover the infield? Because rain delays are a common occurrence during baseball season, each team's field maintenance unit establishes procedures for deciding where to store the tarp, when to pull it, who is responsible for coming onto the field to help, and how the tarp is pulled to protect the infield. As a result, when a rain delay occurs, field maintenance crew members do not have to engage in a decision-making process; instead, they immediately implement the procedures established to pull the tarp and cover the infield.

Of course, individuals in sport organizations must also make decisions that are not guided by established procedures. These decisions are considered to be nonprogrammed because they are new, or unique, or require complex or creative solutions. Examples include deciding how best to support increased interest in an aquatics program at a community recreation center, how to market college athletics more effectively to the millennial generation, and how to improve a professional sport organization's relationship with the local community. Decisions like these require us to engage in a purposeful process in order to reach an optimal conclusion.

RATIONAL MODEL OF DECISION MAKING

In general, we define the decision-making process as a series of steps taken to determine a course of action that will address either an opportunity or a problem. At least in theory, a rational decision-making process can be guided by the four assumptions in the following list. Yet, as we describe later in this chapter, decision making is usually more complex and thus fails to meet these assumptions. Even so, it is important to understand the ideal process presented here because it can serve as the foundation for understanding the rational decision-making process. Here are the four assumptions:

1. The outcome will be completely rational.
2. The decision maker is following a consistent set of preferences that are used to choose the best alternative.
3. The decision maker is aware of all possible alternatives.
4. The decision maker can calculate the probability of success for each alternative. (Hitt, Miller, & Colella, 2015)

The first step in the rational decision-making process is to recognize or identify the opportunity or problem; we must identify the real problem or opportunity in order to make a decision that properly addresses it. Second, we must gather information to help us understand exactly why a decision is necessary and what the decision must accomplish. This step is often plagued by three common mistakes (Uhl-Bien, Schermerhorn, & Osborn, 2014):

1. Defining the problem or opportunity too narrowly or too broadly
2. Focusing on the symptoms but not on the causes
3. Focusing on the wrong problem in the first place

The third step in the decision-making process is to identify and analyze possible courses of action for addressing the problem or making use of the opportunity. In this step, we evaluate the potential costs and benefits of the possible actions; in order to do so, it must be clear exactly what we know and what we need to know. Next, we select a preferred course of action on the basis of costs and benefits, effects on organizational stakeholders, and timeliness of results; we must also evaluate the ethical soundness of the choice (Uhl-Bien et al., 2014).

The next step is to implement the selected course of action. Implementation can be problematic if the previous steps have not been followed or if we have not adequately involved stakeholders who need to be part of the process. When the decision-making process involves those who are affected by the decision, their participation can provide us with important information, lead us to creative alternatives and thus better decisions, and encourage participants to commit to successful implementation of the decision. The final step in the process is evaluation, which enables us to determine whether the results of the decision met the expected goals and whether any unexpected or unanticipated consequences appeared.

Thus the rational model of decision making assumes that decision making will follow a logical sequence and that decisions will be made with complete certainty. In practice, this model is unrealistic because decisions are made under time constraints and because decision makers are limited by individual knowledge and information-processing capabilities that may leave them feeling uncertain about the final decision. In addition, decision makers' preferences sometimes change, which can affect the decision-making process. However, even though the rational model is unrealistic, it establishes an ideal for how decision making should occur (Nelson & Quick, 2013).

To get a sense of the challenges involved in using a rational decision-making model, let's consider the example of an athletic director who has an opening for a men's basketball head coach. The rational model assumes that the outcome will be completely rational; however, the athletic director holds his own personal beliefs, assumptions, and biases and will have only a limited amount of time to identify options and make a decision. These limitations will influence the director's decision-making process and thus the final selection itself. The director will also have to consult with influential donors and alumni who hold their own personal assumptions and biases that affect who they would like to see chosen for the position. In addition, the athletic director will be unable to consider all possible candidates who meet the criteria for the position; to the contrary, the process will be limited by the time available for reviewing potential candidates, interviewing them, and making a decision based on that information. Time is further constrained by the fact that the new coach must be hired in a timely fashion in order to keep the recruiting process going and find out whether current players will remain with the team or transfer due to the coaching change. Finally, donors may exert additional pressure on the director to select a top candidate before a rival school swoops in with an offer.

ADMINISTRATIVE MODEL OF DECISION MAKING

The administrative (or bounded rationality) model offers a more realistic approach to decision making by accounting for real-world conditions, such as the fact that decisions are influenced by the decision maker's beliefs, biases, and human inability to process every single bit of information related to a decision. In other words, the model's conception of "rational choice" acknowledges that the decision maker's rationality is bounded by his or her "cognitive limitations" (Simon, 1987, p. 15). The model also recognizes other factors that influence the decision-making process, including limitations on the time

and information available to the decision maker (Slack & Parent, 2006).

In the administrative model, the decision maker selects the first alternative that is satisfactory. This approach, termed *satisficing* (as a combination of *satisfy* and *suffice*) (Simon, 1956), means that when a solution is found, the search for possible better solutions stops. Satisficing is desirable for decision makers because it reduces the time and effort required to review alternatives. The administrative and rational models of decision making are compared in table 10.1.

GARBAGE CAN MODEL OF DECISION MAKING

The rational and administrative models of decision making view the process as both orderly and logical, though in many sport organizations it is neither. In fact, because so many decisions must be made quickly in uncertain conditions, it is unrealistic to think that they could all be made by means of a systematic process. In recognition of this reality, the garbage can model describes the decision-making process as random, unpredictable, and haphazard (Slack & Parent, 2006). In this model, decision making is based on the outcomes of four independent streams of

Table 10.1 Comparison of the Rational and Administrative Models of Decision Making

Rational	Administrative
The decision maker is the person who knows and understands all decision alternatives and their outcomes. This individual is unaffected by factors such as emotions and time constraints.	The decision maker is limited by his or her mental capacity to evaluate all alternatives and outcomes and must also contend with influences such as emotions and time constraints.
All criteria affecting a decision are considered and evaluated according to the sport organization's goals.	A limited number of criteria are identified and used to form a simple model for evaluating the situation.
All possible decision alternatives are considered.	A limited number of decision alternatives are identified that reflect the decision maker's personal preference.
After careful analysis of all alternatives, the most economically viable alternative is selected.	Alternatives are considered until a suitable one is found.

Reprinted by permission from *Understanding Sport Organizations*, 2nd ed., T. Slack and M.M Parent (Champaign, IL: Human Kinetics, 2006), 262.

IN THE BOARDROOM
Executive Search Firms in Athletic Administration

Given the high stakes and potential risks involved in hiring an athletic director or coach for a high-profile, revenue-producing sport (e.g., football, men's or women's basketball), many universities are turning to executive search firms as a way to optimize the search process and land the best candidate. These firms have long been used for hiring leaders in business and academia, but their use in athletic administration is a relatively new (and growing) practice (Heitner, 2013). An executive search firm can serve an important function in a search committee's decision-making process by doing some of the initial legwork, including identifying, interviewing, and following up with potential candidates; it can also conduct background checks and reference checks on potential candidates. Such firms also work with candidates to help them prepare for interviews.

The use of executive search firms in athletic hirings has been the source of some controversy due to both the high cost (average search fee of $70,000; Solomon, 2016b) and the potential for conflicts of interest given that some firms have close ties to the NCAA (Schrotenboer & Axon, 2013). To date, however, the perceived benefits offered by these firms seem to outweigh the negatives, as universities continue to utilize search firms when hiring for high profile positions in athletics (i.e., football and men's basketball coaches, athletic directors).

events: problems (i.e., dissatisfaction with an aspect of organizational performance), choice opportunities (i.e., decisions), participants (i.e., those making the decisions), and potential solutions. When the right participants and the right solutions come together, the optimal decision is reached. Thus, unlike the other decision-making models, the garbage can model draws attention to the role played by chance (Slack & Parent, 2006); accordingly, timing is critical because the right person must find the right solution at the right time.

Another strength of the model is that—unlike the other models, which tend to focus on only one decision at a time—the garbage can approach can account for multiple decisions in the same process. Consider, for example, the challenges of managing game-day operations for a professional football team. Though event operations staff will attempt to plan every aspect of the event down to the minutes

and seconds, unforeseen circumstances are likely to arise, which will require decisions to be made quickly and with limited information. This reality was on display at Super Bowl XLVII, when the Superdome lost power early in the third quarter. The outage lasted 34 minutes, during which operations staff, media, and coaches were faced with uncertainty about what to do while not knowing when power would be restored (Bishop, 2015). During that time, several important decisions had to be made. First and foremost, officials had to determine whether the stadium was safe for everyone or an evacuation was necessary. Once it was determined that the stadium was safe, a number of other decisions had to be made: whether the teams should stay on the field or return to their locker rooms, what messages should be communicated to spectators in the stadium in order to minimize panic, how the broadcasters should convey information to the millions of people watching the game on TV, and countless others. The garbage can model helps us understand that decision making often happens during times of chaos or disorder and therefore that decisions are rarely systematic or logical (Slack & Parent, 2006).

INDIVIDUAL DECISION MAKING

In this section, we explore how decision making is influenced by cognitive styles and individual differences. First, we examine differences in how individuals gather information through the cognitive styles of sensing and intuiting and then use that information to evaluate alternatives through either a thinking style or a feeling style. Then we consider how decision making is influenced by individual differences in comfort with risk and creativity. We also address the challenge posed by cognitive biases, or mental shortcuts, that can negatively affect individual decision making.

Gathering Information

The ways in which we gather information are influenced by individual differences and preferences. Some people prefer information that is readily confirmed by their senses—including information that they can see, hear, or even feel—whereas others prefer more abstract or figurative forms of information when making decisions. Individuals who use information verified by their senses are said to use a sensing style (Hitt et al., 2015) of decision making and to prefer making decisions based on facts that support their decisions. Sensing decision makers see themselves as rational, practical, and realistic and tend to pay close attention to details, concrete examples, and real experiences. Such individuals are well suited, for example, to compliance work in intercollegiate athletics, wherein facts and data must be gathered and decisions must be made on the basis of that information

and the applicable rules and regulations put forward by the NCAA.

In contrast, some people employ a more intuitive style of decision making in which they look to abstractions and figurative examples in order to make decisions; in other words, intuitive decision makers emphasize imagination and possibilities. As compared with sensing decision makers, intuitive decision makers become impatient when they have to go through the process of routine data gathering; indeed, they believe that creativity in the decision-making process is more likely to come from inspiration than from concerted effort (Hitt et al., 2015). Because intuitive decision makers are relatively comfortable with making decisions in the absence of supporting data, they may be better able to respond in a crisis and adapt to changing circumstances. In the world of sport, for example, intuitive decision making may be appropriate for someone who works in athlete representation. Agents need to make certain decisions that benefit from an intuitive approach—for instance, recognizing which team or sponsor is the right "fit" for a client.

Both styles of decision making—sensing and intuitive—can be effective. The degree of effectiveness depends on the context in which the decision is being made.

Evaluating Alternatives

Just as individuals differ in how they gather information for decision making, they also differ in how they evaluate alternatives. Two approaches used to evaluate alternatives are the thinking style and the feeling style. Individuals who use a given type of information gathering—whether sensing or intuiting—are not constrained to a certain type of evaluation; in other words, both sensing and intuitive decision makers may use either a thinking or a feeling evaluation style.

The thinking style of evaluating alternatives takes a rational approach, and individuals who use it tend to be analytical, objective, and logical decision makers. Those who adopt a thinking style are more comfortable when evaluating work and individual behavior but less comfortable when dealing with employees' feelings. These individuals tend to value policies and procedures and, when a policy is violated, they may have no problem with disciplining or firing employees. Though they may appear detached or impersonal, they do not make impulsive decisions; rather, they try to evaluate all necessary information to ensure that their decisions are fair (Hitt et al., 2015). For example, consider a chief financial officer (CFO) for a college athletic department who is responsible for maintaining a fiscally sound program that operates within the department's approved budget. If the CFO adopts a thinking style, he or she is likely will hold all department staff and coaches to the policies and procedures regarding use of the department's fiscal resources; this is generally a good thing for the organization. If a coach asks for funds to support a trip that is not covered by the current policy, then the CFO can decide to refuse the request regardless of the rationale put forward by the coach. In doing so, however, the CFO may upset the coach or others in the department who think that positive opportunities should be considered even when they would cost more than is budgeted.

Those who use a feeling style when evaluating alternatives tend to rely on emotions and personal judgments. Feeling decision makers prefer a harmonious workplace, are uncomfortable with saying harsh or difficult things to employees, and are likely to be influenced by their own or other peoples' personal likes or dislikes. They are also sympathetic and tend to make subjective decisions (Hitt et al., 2015). For example, a head coach who uses a feeling style may be very good at supporting an optimal work environment in which all coaches on the staff feel valued in the decision-making process. However, if an assistant coach is disruptive and causes problems, the head coach may have trouble addressing the issue, which could lead to a negative work environment and potentially affect the performance of the team.

RISK TAKING IN THE DECISION-MAKING PROCESS

Another individual consideration in the decision-making process is the decision maker's willingness to take chances; this factor matters because decision outcomes are never certain. For instance, when hiring a new coach for a high-profile team, an athletic director who is less comfortable with risk may select a coach with a traditional style and a long tenure of adequate success (e.g., several conference championships but no national championship) while overlooking an up-and-coming coach who takes a nontraditional approach and has enjoyed a rapid rise to the top (e.g., lost the national championship game in year two as a head coach).

Individuals with a lower propensity for risk taking may gather more information than is necessary in an effort to minimize risk. This overreaction can slow the decision-making process and may create information overload, which can impede one's ability to make a decision at all. Conversely, individuals with a higher propensity for risk may fail to gather enough information before making a decision. Thus it is important to recognize your level of comfort with risk in order to avoid either delaying decisions by gathering too much information or rushing into decisions based on too little information.

Risk propensity is related to the concept of the reference point, which is a "level of performance used to evaluate one's current standing" (Hitt et al., 2015, p. 318). If a person's performance is below the reference point, then she may be more apt to take a risk to improve it. For instance, if an athletic director recognizes that high-profile teams have performed poorly during her tenure, then she may be more willing to take a chance on an up-and-coming coach in hopes that her style will lead to another chance to play for a national championship. On the other hand, if the athletic director believes that her performance is above the reference point—for instance, because graduation rates have improved for all student-athletes during her tenure—then she may be more averse to risk and decide to hire a more traditional coach.

DECISION-MAKING CHALLENGES

The decision-making process is far from easy, and there are additional challenges that we must address in order to fully understand it. Two of those challenges are confirmation bias and escalation of commitment.

Confirmation bias, or confirmation error, involves our tendency to seek out information that confirms our beliefs or ideas while failing to acknowledge information that goes against or disconfirms them. It can lead decision makers, early in the process, to seek out only information that supports a preferred decision while failing to consider information that may disconfirm beliefs about the decision. This bias can continue to be problematic later in the process as decision makers become more reluctant to go against a decision that is already being carried out. For example, suppose that a director of ticketing decides to switch to a new software system for ticket sales. If the director's information-gathering process consists only of talking with two colleagues who are known to use and like the system—but no one who doesn't like it and no one who uses a different system—then the director is missing potentially crucial information and may not make the best decision. This example illustrates a common occurrence in the decision-making process: We are more likely to seek out information

that agrees with or supports a decision to which we have already committed (Nickerson, 1998).

Decision makers must also work to avoid escalation of commitment. Have you ever wondered why people sometimes stand by a decision that is clearly flawed or simply not working? It may result in part from escalation of commitment—"the tendency to continue a previously chosen course of action even when feedback suggests that it is failing" (Uhl-Bien et al., 2014, p. 203). Decision makers can find it hard to stop putting resources or time into a failing decision when they have already invested much in it. In addition, people in leadership positions may have gotten to those positions by finding ways to save a bad decision. Recall the case of the director of ticketing who decided to invest in new software for ticket sales. Adopting the new software is likely to require significant resources for the purchase itself, the conversion from the old system, and the necessary employee training. If, after one season of using the new software, problems are evident, the director is likely to spend more resources to fix those problems in an effort to make the decision work. This escalation of commitment could continue for several years, as more time and resources are invested into what may have been a bad decision in the first place.

Fortunately, there are steps we can take to avoid or minimize the problems associated with escalating commitment. First, we can set limits on our individual involvement in or commitment to the decision by including involvement of others in the process. Second, we can check that we are making our own decision—not merely following someone else's lead. We can also carefully consider why we are staying with a particular decision; moreover, if there is insufficient reason to continue, we can stop. Finally, we can keep reminding ourselves of the costs associated with continuing the decision and consider whether they justify dis-

IN THE BOARDROOM
Escalating Commitment to Division I Intercollegiate Athletics

Sport management scholars have used the concept of escalating commitment to help explain why some U.S. colleges and universities continue to invest considerable financial and other resources into athletic departments. For example, Hutchinson, Nite, and Bouchet (2015) noted that spending on intercollegiate athletics at the Division I FBS (Football Bowl Subdivision) level increased by 95 percent from 2004 to 2012 even as revenues generated by athletics increased by only 78 percent. Given this disparity, Hutchinson and colleagues were interested in learning why some universities decided to move from a lower Division ranking (e.g., Division II, Division I FCS) to a higher level. To find out, they interviewed key university administrators—such as president, vice president for student services, athletic director, senior associate athletic director—who wielded decision-making authority in the area of athletic oversight. Findings from the study indicated that escalation of commitment to athletics by university administrators was influenced by organizational status (defined by Hutchinson and colleagues [2015] as differences in social rank among organizations that results in unearned, non-merit-based privilege [Washington & Zajac, 2005]), evidence of previous success in athletic programs, and organizational resource interdependence (e.g., contributions from donors, local or state government support, university support through student fees). Thus the study provides some insight into why an organization might commit to—and maintain support for—a decision that may be fiscally unsound.

continuing it (Uhl-Bien et al., 2014). More specifically, in work that examined how to discontinue or de-escalate commitment to a decision at an organizational level—in this case, in intercollegiate athletics—Hutchinson and Bouchet (2014) detailed the processes used by university and athletic administrators to drop or de-escalate their commitment from Division I FBS to Division I FCS, or to eliminate a football program. Their findings, which support the steps described here, indicated that key decision makers (i.e., athletic directors, university administrators) should use evidence-based management to gather support for de-escalation and to limit stakeholder involvement in the process because certain stakeholder groups (e.g., boosters, alumni, fans) may resist the process of de-escalation.

GROUP DECISION MAKING

Thus far, we have focused on individual decision making. However, your career will likely include numerous situations in which you help make decisions as part of a group. In fact, at this point in your academic career, you have probably already taken part in a number of group projects. Along the way, you have probably also become aware of some of the benefits and challenges associated with group-decision making.

When to Involve Groups in the Decision-Making Process

Group decision making is helpful when the leader lacks the necessary expertise to make the decision and requires input from others; it is also useful in cases where implementing the decision will require acceptance and commitment from others. However, group decisions often take more time than do individual or consultative decisions; therefore, in order for the process to be effective, group members must be provided with sufficient time to work together on the decision.

Group decision making occurs in all types of sport organizations. For example, consider the senior leadership team of a sizable collegiate athletic department. In addition to the athletic director, the team typically includes associate athletic directors who lead specific functional areas in the department—for example, marketing, communication, facilities, athletic development, compliance, and academic support. In many cases, the senior leadership team is involved in the majority of decisions made in the department. For example, decisions about capital budgeting projects might include whether to renovate (or replace) a football stadium, resurface an outdoor field, or construct a new ice hockey arena. Such decisions require input from individuals across the department for their expertise in areas such as construction, user needs, and funding sources.

Advantages and Process of Group Decision Making

One of the advantages credited to group decision making is the increase in knowledge and information that results from involving more people in the process. That involvement can also lead to increased understanding and acceptance of the decision and increased commitment to carrying it out.

The process of group decision making mirrors that of individual decision making. Specifically, the group defines the problem that requires a decision, gathers key information to develop alternatives, evaluates those alternatives, chooses the best option, and implements the decision. Though the process is similar, the involvement of

multiple people means that interpersonal dynamics and differing personalities will present some challenges. In addition, some individuals may come to the group having already considered the decision in more detail than others, and some may already have made an individual decision. Strategies for avoiding these challenges include brainstorming, the nominal group technique, the Delphi technique, and the devil's advocacy strategy; these strategies are detailed later in the chapter.

Challenges of Group Decision Making

In addition to the advantages of group decision making, we must also consider the challenges associated with it. These challenges, or potential disadvantages, include pressure to conform to what others in the group decide, domination by one or more powerful group members, and the extended time required to engage in the decision-making process. The following discussion details these challenges, then describes strategies for minimizing them.

Groupthink

Groupthink is one of the most significant challenges associated with group decision making. Pioneering research into groupthink was conducted by Irving Janus (1982), a social psychologist who defined it as a "mode of thinking that people engage in when they are deeply involved in a cohesive in-group, when the members' striving for unanimity overrides their motivation to realistically appraise alternative courses of action" (p. 9). In short, groupthink occurs when a close-knit group of individuals lose their ability to critically analyze decisions and thus fail to function effectively in the decision-making process; therefore, groupthink leads to faulty decision making.

Groupthink can develop as a result of several conditions, and one of the most significant is group cohesion. Members of highly cohesive groups get along well and do not want to criticize one another's ideas,

IN THE BOARDROOM
Groupthink in Penn State Cover-Up

Groupthink can explain one of the most publicized scandals in the history of sport—namely, the cover-up of crimes perpetrated by former Penn State football coach Jerry Sandusky. From the late 1990s through 2012, four senior leaders at Penn State failed in their response to allegations of child sexual abuse committed by Sandusky. Those four are former president Graham Spanier, senior vice president Gary Schultz, athletic director Tim Curley, and football coach Joe Paterno. Instead of reporting the allegations to the police, the group encouraged conformity to opinions that would minimize any negative publicity for the football team, the athletic department, and the university. Multiple conditions for groupthink were present in this tragic example: The four men were part of a small, closed group of powerful individuals. Their decision was viewed as consequential because the university's reputation was closely aligned with that of the football program. Outside opinions were not solicited and in fact were actively avoided; for example, Vicky Triponey, former Penn State vice president, was fired when she tried to shine a light on issues related to abuse of power by the football program.

Ultimately, the group of four senior leaders came to the decision that it was "more 'humane' to cover up the repeated allegations of Sandusky's abuse than to report them to the police; the 'only downside' they saw to this decision was that *they* would be vulnerable if the truth came out" (Cohen & DeBenedet, 2012, n.p.). It appears that the group's decision-making process never considered the humanity and vulnerability of the victims or of potential future victims who were endangered by the group's failure to report Sandusky to the police (Cohen & DeBenedet, 2012). Perhaps if the group members had used strategies to avoid groupthink—including, at the very least, asking for advice from experts among the university's legal and law enforcement staff—they would have reached a different decision, and future victims would have been safe from Sandusky.

which can be problematic in the group decision-making process because the ideas put forward may not adequately address the issue at hand. Groupthink is also more likely to occur when group members enjoy being part of the group and attach positive self-image to group membership, which can prevent individuals from taking issue with other members' ideas for fear of creating division. Perhaps you have experienced such challenges when working with a group of friends on a class project. Though it can be fun to work together, it can also be difficult to challenge ideas put forward by a friend.

When decision-making groups are constituted by individuals in senior leadership positions, groupthink can emerge because members may all share a similar way of thinking. More generally, groupthink is more likely to occur in groups that are less diverse in terms of education, work experience, gender, race, socioeconomic status, or sexual identity (Nelson & Quick, 2013).

Another factor to consider in relation to groupthink is the importance of the decision. When a decision carries powerful implications for members of the decision-making group, individual members may be reluctant to challenge ideas accepted by the rest of the group; alternatively, they may believe that the group "knows better" than one individual group member. In two famous and tragic cases, the deadly space shuttle accidents involving the Challenger in 1986 and the Columbia in 2003 were both attributed to faulty decision making as a result of groupthink.

Groupthink can be recognized by a series of typical symptoms. The first is self-censorship, wherein group members remain quiet despite recognizing flaws in the decision-making process. Self-censorship occurs because group members do not want to cause conflict or upset other members of the group. Second, in an effort to preserve group harmony, pressure is applied to group members who express opinions that run counter to the overall group opinion. Third, as a result of censorship and pressure, an illusion develops that the group has reached unanimity in the decision process. Fourth, in order to minimize warnings against faulty decisions, group members construct a complex rationale for the decision that has been reached. Fifth, group members develop the illusion of being invulnerable and become overly confident in their decision, which can result in taking unnecessary risks and, again, ignoring warnings regarding faulty decisions. Sixth, group members take on the role of "mind-guard," in which they shield other members from important information or criticism in an effort to maintain the illusion of unanimity. Seventh, members of the group believe in the moral authority of the group and therefore in the decisions it has made; this deference can lead to unfortunate ethical lapses in the decision-making process. Finally, stereotypes may influence the group as members develop negative beliefs toward people outside of the group and block opportunities to hear from them (Hitt et al., 2015).

Given the potentially negative and even catastrophic outcomes of groupthink, the following strategies should be implemented when engaging in a group decision-

making process. First, each member of the group should take on the role of critical evaluator and actively voice any objections or doubts that arise during the decision-making process. Second, if the group has a leader, he or she should avoid stating a personal position on the issue before the group reaches its decision. Another strategy is to create several decision-making subgroups that work simultaneously on the decision. The group might also invite an outside expert to evaluate and critique its decision-making processes or appoint one group member to act as a devil's advocate by consistently questioning the group's processes and positions. Finally, once the group has reached consensus, the members should test the group's position by reexamining alternative decisions (Lunenburg, 2012).

Group Polarization

Another challenge that must be faced in group decision making is that of group polarization, in which individuals' initial attitudes toward a decision intensify after discussion by the group. In other words, a member who comes into the group process holding a certain position solidifies that position after the group decision-making process. Group polarization results from biases that occur in both information exchange and information processing by group members (Isenberg, 1986). More specifically, individual members who believe in the correctness of certain positions before entering the group discussion tend to provide more information that supports those positions and less information that counters them. This imbalance leads those individuals to move toward more extreme positions during the decision-making process

Group Decision-Making Strategies

The following subsections address four of the most common strategies for avoiding groupthink: brainstorming, the nominal group technique, the Delphi technique, and devil's advocacy.

Brainstorming

One way to improve the decision-making process is to gather as many decision alternatives as possible. In the group decision-making process, however, if each alternative is evaluated when it is introduced, then individual group members may withhold new alternatives for fear of receiving negative or critical feedback. With this pitfall in mind, brainstorming prompts the sharing of alternatives while avoiding the dampening effect of initial critical discussion. The basic ideas of brainstorming are as follows:

- Creativity is encouraged; no idea is too creative or too different.
- Members are encouraged to build on one another's ideas.
- Ideas are not to be criticized or critiqued.
- Ideas are not evaluated until group members have run out of new ideas.

Nominal Group Technique

This technique is a bit more structured than the brainstorming approach, but the basic concept is the same: to generate as many ideas as possible while reserving judgment until later in the process. The first step in this process is to have all group members silently list their ideas. Second, all ideas are written on a shared chart. Next, each idea is discussed but not criticized. Fourth, a written vote is taken to select the best idea, and the idea that wins the vote becomes the group's decision.

Delphi Technique

The Delphi technique allows groups to work remotely while coming to a decision. In this approach, the group members are typically experts on a particular topic that drives the decision-making process. The experts respond remotely to a survey about the chosen topic, and a coordinator gathers and tabulates the responses. The

results are returned to the experts, who then have another chance to respond; they may or may not choose to alter their responses based on the results they have received. A final decision is reached based on averaging or tabulating the results of the final survey.

Devil's Advocacy

When a group uses a devil's advocate, it assigns an individual or a subgroup of members to argue against or try to expose potential problems in any ideas or alternatives put forward in the group. This strategy helps the group avoid making faulty decisions because it identifies potential problems and alternatives before a final decision is made.

SUMMARY

Decision making is a critical aspect of organizational behavior; indeed, we are faced with a myriad of decisions each day. Some are routine and can be resolved based on policies and procedures, whereas others require us to engage in a concerted decision-making process. The rational decision-making model provides us with a general framework for understanding the process. The first and most important step is to recognize or identify the opportunity or problem that requires a decision to be made. Next, we must identify the available alternatives, then evaluate them and select the best one. The final step is to implement the decision.

Although the rational decision-making model may seem straightforward, it is rarely followed, because the real world often does not align with the model's basic assumptions—that the outcome will be completely rational, that the decision maker follows a consistent set of preferences to choose the best alternative, that the decision maker is aware of all possible alternatives, and that the decision maker can calculate the probability of success for each alternative. Given the disparity between these assumptions and practical

CASE STUDY
Group Decision Making in Hiring Collegiate Coaches

Scholars and advocates have documented the relative scarcity of women (of all races and ethnicities) and of minority men and women in coaching positions in both collegiate and professional sport (Lapchick, 2016; LaVoi, 2017). Data reported by Lapchick (2016) showed that nearly 90 percent of coaches at the Division I level were white and only about 8 percent were African American.

In this context, imagine that you are an athletic director involved in the search for a new head football coach at a Division I FBS school. On one hand, you are seeking to increase the diversity of your coaching staff, which means that you will focus on recruiting and interviewing a representatively diverse mix of potential candidates. At the same time, you understand that the process of selecting a new football coach does not come down to an individual decision that you can make on your own. Instead, it will be made by a search committee that includes senior leaders in the athletic department, the faculty athletics representative (typically a professor on campus), and senior leaders in the university's overall administration.

Based on your understanding of the group decision-making process, you want to avoid the challenges of group decision making while retaining the benefits associated with group-based decisions. You also want to avoid making errors based on confirmation bias. As you prepare for the search committee's first meeting—at which the group will discuss the process for recruiting, interviewing, and selecting the new coach—you provide the members with specific guidelines for reaching an optimal decision.

Case Study Questions

1. Describe how you will reduce confirmation bias among members of the search committee when reviewing resumes from potential coaching candidates.
2. Describe why it is best to use a search committee to make the decision rather than having the athletic director make it alone.
3. How might you reduce groupthink when the search committee reviews resumes from the top candidates?
4. What process would you use to maximize the benefits of group decision making when selecting candidates for interviews? When deciding which candidate to hire?

experience, most decisions instead follow the bounded rationality model, which accounts for making decisions in the real world. The bounded rationality model assumes that the decision maker will select the first alternative that is satisfactory. This practice, known as *satisficing*, is desirable because it minimizes the time and effort needed for reviewing possible alternatives.

Of course, decisions can be made by either individuals or groups. One challenge faced by individual decision makers is that of confirmation bias, which is the tendency to seek out information that confirms one's beliefs or ideas while failing to acknowledge information that counters or disconfirms them. Another challenge is escalation of commitment, which is the tendency to continue a previously chosen decision even when feedback suggests that it is failing.

Group decision making is advantageous when the leader lacks the necessary expertise to make the decision and requires input from others; it is also useful when implementing the decision will require acceptance and commitment from others. However, group decision making also involves challenges that must be addressed, including pressure to conform to what others in the group decide (groupthink), domination by one or more powerful group members, and the extended time required to engage in the decision-making process. Strategies for minimizing these challenges include brainstorming, the nominal group technique, the Delphi technique, and devil's advocacy.

DISCUSSION QUESTIONS

1. Provide an example of a programmed decision in the context of a sport event. Provide an example of a nonprogrammed decision in that same context.

2. Describe what makes the rational decision-making model unrealistic. Support your answer with discussion of an example from professional sport.

3. Would you describe yourself as either thinking or feeling when gathering information as part of the decision-making process? Support your answer with a specific example.

4. Describe examples in either professional or intercollegiate sport that show the negative effect of confirmation bias on decision making.

5. Explain why the Delphi technique is an effective way to reduce groupthink.

Chapter 11

Effective Teamwork

Chapter Objectives

After studying this chapter, you will be able to

- explain the concept of teams in the context of sport organizations,
- describe the different types of teams commonly found in sport organizations,
- recognize the stages of team development and apply them to team development in sport organizations,
- explain team effectiveness and describe ways to best support it,
- define cohesion in the context of teams in sport organizations and identify the benefits and challenges associated with high levels of team cohesion, and
- describe social loafing and how to minimize it in team performance.

When you think of a team in the context of sport organizations, you likely think first of athletes coming together to play a sport. This chapter focuses, however, on teams established to carry out various kinds of work in support of sport organizations. For example, a sports apparel and equipment company might bring together a group of employees to develop a new shoe or racket in order to appeal to an emerging customer group interested in tennis. Or a community recreation center might task its fitness instructors (e.g., yoga, CrossFit, Spinning) with working together to best support the fitness interests of the center's members.

In order to maximize the benefits of working in teams, we must understand various aspects of teamwork, beginning with the basic concept of a team and the roles and tasks supported by teams. We must also explore the types of teams, which include cross-functional, problem-solving,

employee involvement, self-managing, and senior-level or top-management. In addition, we must consider the resources provided to teams, which cannot succeed unless provided with necessary financial, technical, and human wherewithal. A team must also be appropriately sized—small enough to be manageable yet large enough to get the assigned work done—and composed of a mix of members that supports the team's objectives by providing expertise in key functional areas. Team members' ability to work together may also be affected by the team's diversity in terms of race, ethnicity, gender, sexual orientation, and level of education.

A team's ability to realize its goals and objectives also depends heavily on the process of team development, which includes the stages of forming, norming, storming, performing, and adjourning. Teams begin in the forming stage, during which members come together and explore how they will contribute to the team's functioning. As members begin to understand their roles, the team enters the storming phase, during which members may engage in tumultuous behaviors as they explore their power and influence in the group. The team then settles into the norming phase as members begin to know their roles, develop into a more cohesive group, and set norms and expectations for how the team will work. During the performing phase, the team does the bulk of its assigned work and examines ways to improve its functioning. Finally, most teams enter an adjourning phase, wherein the team completes its work and either dissolves or transitions to its next task.

This chapter also examines the phenomena of cohesion and social loafing and their effects on team performance. Cohesion hinges on the sense of connectedness felt by a group's members; teams with high cohesion are usually more effective than teams with low cohesion. In social loafing, individual effort declines when a person works as part of a team. Social loafing can be reduced by holding team members accountable for specific work outputs, reminding them of their contributions to the team, and demonstrating the value of those contributions to the team's ability to meet its goals.

The final section of the chapter discusses some common challenges faced by teams: determining where to start, handling poor individual performance, managing dominant personalities, and addressing conflict between team members that extends beyond the storming phase of team development.

OVERVIEW OF TEAMS AND TEAMWORK

In the context of organizational behavior, a team is defined as a group of people brought together based on specific skill sets or abilities to accomplish a specific task or function. The team pursues a common goal with the expectation that team members will work together to achieve that goal (Taylor, Doherty, & McGraw, 2015). Teams are put in place to achieve work outcomes more efficiently or more effectively than would be possible for individuals working alone. Consider, for example, the challenges involved in developing and supporting a youth sport league or the coordination of skills needed to stage a road race. In both cases, the project can best be completed by a group of people with various skill sets who work together to meet the chosen objectives. For instance, in order for the youth sport league to succeed, you would need some individuals with knowledge of governance and rule development and others with knowledge of coaching and coach development; you would also benefit from involving individuals who possess the necessary technology skills to develop and support a league website.

Such teams are created and designed to address specific work-related objectives and are usually designated formally on an organizational chart. For example, a sports apparel company might coordinate its work through specific functional teams, including a market research team that explores trends and a research and design team that develops new products (e.g., next-generation running shoes, high-performance compression shorts) based on the work of the market research team. The company will also have a sales and business development team that seeks out new customers to buy the company's products. In addition, the company might use temporary formal teams to address specific problems or reach specific short-term organizational objectives. For example, it might put together a temporary formal team to design and produce a special running shoe for athletes performing in the Boston Marathon. In another example, the NCAA might develop a task force that brings together a group of athletic directors to address ways to manage contact with recruits in the age of social media.

Sport organizations are also home to informal groups. Groups are different from teams as teams are developed for specific work-related objectives but groups are developed based on shared interests or experiences of members of sport organizations. For instance, friendship groups often develop among individuals who like each other, enjoy spending time together, and perhaps have shared interests outside of work. These groups may share lunch together, sit next to each other during meetings, and coordinate times to socialize or participate in a sport together after work hours. Shared interests might also include community service events, volunteer coaching, or spending time with other families who have similar-aged children. Informal groups can also form around shared interests that are work related, such as learning new software skills (e.g., web design).

Cross-Functional Teams

Formal teams that are developed to support specific organizational objectives sometimes suffer from lack of communication with other formal teams in the organization. This problem, known as the "functional silo," can appear when teams focus only on their internal needs and functioning while failing to communicate or interact with other formal teams in the organization. As a result, teams "create artificial boundaries, or 'silos,' that discourage rather than encourage interaction with other units" (Uhl-Bien, Schermerhorn, & Osborn, 2014, p. 144). To better understand this challenge, let's return to the example of the sports apparel company. If the market research team gathers information describing a new trend in running shoes but fails to communicate that information, then the research and design team may miss the opportunity to develop a popular new shoe.

One way to address the functional silo problem is to develop cross-functional teams made up of individuals from various work or functional units. In the example of the sports apparel company,

selected members of the market research team, the research and development team, the sales and business development team, and the marketing team could come together to work for a cross-functional team that supports the development of a new running shoe.

Problem-Solving Teams

An organization can also implement a temporary problem-solving team to address a specific work-related issue; this type of team is often referred to as a task force. For instance, a collegiate athletic department might implement a task force to address reports of hazing on one of its teams. The task force would include individuals from the athletic department and other important faculty and staff members at the college. Its purpose would be to understand why the hazing occurred and develop an educational program to reduce the likelihood of another incident. The team might work together for a semester or a year, then issue a report to provide a record of what it accomplished and recommend guidelines for preventing or addressing future problems.

Employee Involvement Teams

Employee involvement teams are developed to address specific workplace issues that affect employees. For example, an employee involvement team might be formed within a Major League Baseball team's front office staff to address the challenges of managing one's personal life during the very long baseball season. The group might develop programs to educate employees about stress management techniques in order to help them through a two-week home stand with no days off. It might also implement a program that brings employees' family members to the ballpark as a way to help integrate family into the employee's day-to-day work activities.

Self-Managing Teams

Teams that do not require outside leadership in order to function are considered self-managing. These teams "are empowered to make decisions to manage themselves in day-to-day work" (Uhl-Bien et al., 2014, p. 145); in other words, they function independently, without oversight from a supervisor or director. Self-managing teams make their own decisions about who carries out specific work-related tasks, when the work will be scheduled, the training and job skills required, the selection of new members, and how to control the quality of the team's work (Uhl-Bien et al., 2014). The size of a self-managing team typically ranges from 5 to 15 members; the team should be large enough to carry out its tasks but small enough to function efficiently. Such teams value employees who possess multiple skill sets because team members are expected to carry out multiple jobs within the team.

For example, imagine a new gym and juice bar that was started by five Cross-Fit friends. Those individuals must now work as a self-managing team to develop, finance, open, and operate the business. Thus each team member should know how to work both as a CrossFit coach and as a sort of juice and smoothie bartender. As for other tasks, the team may decide to delegate marketing to one member, accounting to another, and membership services to a third.

Senior-Level or Top-Management Teams

Sport organizations often maintain a senior-level or top-management team composed of the most senior members of the organization. This team sets the strategic direction of the organization and determines how work can best be carried out by employees. The leader of an organization often relies on members of the top-management team to provide input regarding each functional area of the organization and to raise key ideas,

IN THE BOARDROOM
Self-Managing Teams at W.L. Gore & Associates

You might not think of W.L. Gore & Associates as a sport organization, but the company produces high-performance apparel for runners and bikers. Still, what makes Gore unique is that it does not define itself as belonging to a specific industry; rather, its products cross many industries, including sport, life sciences, mobile technologies, and testing and measurement. In addition, working at Gore is different from working at most companies because it has no formal structure. Instead, the company uses what it calls a "lattice structure" based on interconnections among associates who communicate directly with one another. More specifically, it is composed of self-managed teams of associates who, in the company's words, can "communicate freely to assemble talents and diverse perspectives [in order] to quickly make good decisions and produce quality work that helps us deliver on our promise to our customers" (Gore & Associates, n.d., n.p.).

In addition, Gore gives associates the freedom to create their own self-managed teams. Thus an associate with an idea for a new product can recruit other associates from across the company to form a team, which is provided with the necessary time and resources to develop and test the new product and deliver it to market. This freedom expands the company's boundaries and enables continual innovation. Perhaps it is no surprise, then, that Gore was named by Great Places to Work as 15th on their list of the World's Best Workplaces in 2017.

issues, problems, and opportunities for the team to address. Most college athletic departments have a senior leadership team composed of members who oversee specific areas of the organization, including associate athletic directors for internal operations (e.g., compliance, business office, and event operations) and external operations (e.g., development, sponsorship, promotions, ticketing).

TEAM DEVELOPMENT

Teams of all types go through a staged process of team development, and the stage in which a team is operating at any given time affects its effectiveness and the challenges it faces. The five stages of team development are forming, storming, norming, performing, and adjourning (Tuckman & Jensen, 1977).

Forming

In the first stage of team development, the team comes together. Depending on the nature of the team, this may be the first time that some (or even all) members have met one another. In the example of the problem-solving team (i.e., task force) set up to address college hazing, some members of the college administration may never have worked with or even interacted with some members of the athletic department. In other teams, members may be quite familiar with one another and may even have worked together. Regardless of the level of familiarity, at this stage, all team members are trying to determine their individual roles and contributions to the team, as well as what behaviors are acceptable and how each person will benefit from membership on the team. Thus they may consider questions about the nature of their work, why they were selected, and how much time will be required for them to finish the project. Members may also wonder about group norms, such as whether it's acceptable to be a few minutes late to meetings,

whether it's appropriate to bring food, and whether it's okay to use their computers to take notes (and perhaps check emails). During this stage, then, members are focused largely on determining acceptable behavior by group members and getting to know each other. In later stages, they will engage in the team's assigned work and define their roles as part of the team.

Storming

The storming phase of team development is a tumultuous period marked by tension and, at times, highly emotional behavior. During this phase, team members begin to work toward understanding their roles and their power in the group; as a result, conversations can become heated as members work to establish their influence within the team. In the example of the hazing task force, a faculty member with expertise in workplace bullying might disagree with parameters or restrictions on involvement by student-athletes in anti-hazing programming introduced by a representative of the athletic department. This stage can become particularly contentious if the team faces undue pressure to meet short deadlines or if extra work is added to the group's expectations. For instance, the university president might set a deadline for the hazing task force to finish its work in less than a month, which could be unrealistic during a busy semester or sport season. Despite (or perhaps through) this type of contentiousness, the storming stage allows team members to clarify their expectations and begin understanding each other's needs and how best to support them as the team works to meet its objectives.

The challenges of the storming phase can be addressed through the use of certain strategies. For one thing, team members should accept that conflict is a normal part of the team development process; in fact, trying to avoid conflict will make it difficult for the team to get out of this stage. Thus teams should be responsive to all members' voices and concerns. In the case of the hazing task force, for instance, the faculty member and athletic department representative must discuss their concerns and try to reach agreement on acceptable expectations for student-athlete involvement in anti-hazing training.

The storming stage should not be rushed; it may require several team meetings, and team members should strive to remain positive during this tumultuous time. Moving through this stage in a constructive manner positions the team to conduct its assigned work effectively.

Norming

During the norming stage, the team's work begins in earnest. Members typically feel a sense of relief at having moved through the storming stage and are now ready to tackle the job at hand. During this stage, team members arrive at consensus regarding how to perform their work. As members see the team becoming more cohesive and cooperative, they can begin working together. To do so, they establish ground rules for how to behave as part of the team, define their operating goals, and determine procedures for carrying out their work. At the same time, team members must remember that some tasks, levels of influence, and forms of power may yet shift as the team's work continues.

Performing

In the performing stage, team members accomplish the assigned work of the team in a manner that is interdependent, organized, and well developed. At this stage, team structures are stable, and members are satisfied that their needs are being met. The focus now is on how best to meet the team's goals or objectives. The primary issue is the continued development of relationships among team members.

Adjourning

After completing its assigned work, the team enters the adjourning phase, wherein team members recognize their hard work and celebrate their accomplishments. For permanent teams, these celebrations help the team signal the end of one project and the transition to a new one. For temporary teams (e.g., problem-solving team or task force), this transition can be challenging for members who have developed close bonds as a result of their shared work. All team members should be sensitive to this potential challenge and use the celebration of work accomplished by the team as a way to support each other during the adjourning phase.

As you might imagine, team development does not always follow the linear process described here. For instance, teams sometimes enter the norming phase and then regress to the storming phase because lasting consensus has not been reached about how the team will work together to meet stated goals. It is critical to provide support for teams during the team development process, particularly during the storming phase, which is the most likely to involve dissension and failure. This support should include team-building activities that help members transition into clearly outlined roles. Team outcomes are best achieved when the team establishes a work environment that promotes feelings of togetherness, when team members understand and accept their roles, and when team cohesion and leadership are clearly articulated and exhibited in team members' behavior (Paradis & Martin, 2012). Teams function most effectively when they create an environment where people want to show up, perform their work, and communicate and cooperate on both the interpersonal and group levels.

TEAM ROLES

Individual team members fill particular roles or functions as part of the team's work. When team members understand their roles, and the behaviors necessary to carry them out, the team functions more effectively (Mumford, Van Iddekinge, Morgeson, & Campion, 2008). Team roles can be subdivided into three categories: task, social, and boundary spanning.

Task Roles

Task roles include five subroles: contractor, creator, contributor, completer, and critic (Mumford et al., 2008).

1. The contractor coordinates the team's work, sets up a schedule, and creates time lines to help the team complete its work.
2. The creator evaluates and assesses the team's goals and determines whether they need to be reframed or realigned.
3. The contributor brings information and expertise to the team.
4. The completer puts ideas into action.
5. The critic serves as a check on assumptions made by the team.

Social Roles

The following social roles help ensure that the team operates efficiently: communicator, cooperator, and calibrator. The communicator supports collaboration among team members by modeling good communication, including positive listening skills. The cooperator helps team members with specific expertise work together to meet the team's goals. The calibrator helps keep the team on track and provides suggestions when team processes may need to be adjusted; this person also initiates discussions to address power struggles and other team problems (Mumford et al., 2008).

Boundary-Spanning Roles

These roles—which include coordinator and consul—link the team and its functions to the larger organization (Mumford et al., 2008). Thus they are more externally focused, whereas the task and social roles are more internally focused on the team's own functioning. The boundary-spanning role of coordinator involves engaging with other individuals and teams in order to align the team's work with other work performed in the organization. The consul, on the other hand, gathers information from across the organization to support the work of the team and also communicates to the rest of the organization about the team's goals, objectives, and activities.

TEAM EFFECTIVENESS

Consider a problem-solving team (i.e., task force) formed to help develop a catastrophic response plan (CRP) for a sport event. In order for the CRP team to be effective and meet its stated goals and objectives, it must be designed to provide the resources needed to support its functions. It must also be sized appropriately, and its composition must include members who possess the needed skills, expertise, and experience to carry out the team's work. Finally, the team must appreciate the diversity of its members and understand how that diversity might influence team performance.

Resources

For the CRP team to be effective, it requires appropriate resources—for example, an allocated budget to pay for materials and supplies, access to technology to help develop the plan, and time (perhaps including release time from other work obligations) to support the functions of the team. If the team lacks any of these resources, it could be delayed in developing the plan or fail to produce a complete plan.

Composition and Size

The CRP team will require expertise from personnel in athletic event operations, public safety and security, campus safety and security, and medical emergency response, as well as other athletic administration officials. As with any team, its effectiveness will depend on including team members who possess the requisite skills, expertise, and experience to fulfill team objectives. The CRP team's composition should also take into account the members' personalities and secondary skills. For instance, it would be best to include campus safety and security personnel who have worked specifically with the athletic department, because they will have a better understanding of the unique needs and challenges associate with sport events.

The team's effectiveness will also be affected by its size, which, as with any team, should be based on the type of group and its task goals. Problem-based groups such as the CRP team are most effective when they include 5 to 7 members; most other types of teams function best with about 10 members (Uhl-Bien et al., 2014). Teams with fewer than 5 members may find it difficult to accomplish all of the work required to meet their goals or objectives. At the other end of the scale, when teams have more than 10 members, individuals may have a hard time finding ways to contribute to team tasks and the team may struggle to coordinate members' efforts (Gratton & Erickson, 2007). In addition, if a team will use voting procedures, it should be composed of an odd number of members so that votes cannot end in a tie.

Membership Diversity

Diversity of team membership may take the form of differences in personality,

IN THE BOARDROOM
Problem-Solving Teams in the NCAA

As you are probably aware, the National Collegiate Athletic Association (NCAA) is the main governing body for intercollegiate sport in the United States. It is a member-driven organization, which means that each participating university has voting rights to help establish the rules that determine how sports and championship events are governed. In its role as a governing body, the NCAA develops work teams made up of personnel from university athletic departments (e.g., athletic administrators, coaches, student-athletes) to address specific issues, problems, and opportunities in an effort to improve the college sport experience. One such work team is the Women's Basketball Oversight Committee Ad Hoc Working Group on Recruiting. The objective of this team is to "conduct a comprehensive review of Division I women's basketball recruiting legislation and make recommendations to the NCAA Division I Women's Basketball Oversight Committee" (National Collegiate Athletic Association, n.d., n.p.).

The team's assignment and composition follow the guidelines described in this chapter for team effectiveness. First, the team has been given adequate time (two years) to complete its work. In addition, the team's composition provides expertise in regard to the recruiting rules for women's college basketball; specifically, the team includes women's basketball coaches, conference commissioners, athletic administrators, a senior administrator from the Women's Basketball Coaches Association, and liaisons from the NCAA administrative team. The team is also diverse insofar as it includes coaches from both larger universities (e.g., from the ACC) and smaller colleges (e.g., Ivy League). The team will report its recommendations for changes in recruiting procedures to the NCAA membership, who will then vote on those recommendations.

values, work-related or personal experiences, culture, or demographics (e.g., race, ethnicity, gender, sexual orientation, physical ability). Diversity can be both advantageous and potentially challenging to a team's effectiveness. As compared with more homogeneous teams, diverse teams tend to be more focused on facts and to be more innovative (Rock & Grant, 2016). At the same time, a team's functioning may be challenged by diversity because members may be more likely to have different ideas, thoughts, and ways of completing the team's tasks. These differences can lead to struggles, disagreements, and dissent among members. This mixed effect of diversity—aiding the group's problem-solving ability while possibly making it harder for group members to work together—has been referred to as the diversity–consensus dilemma. This dilemma is most likely to occur in the storming and norming phases of team development (Uhl-Bien et al., 2014). One way to mitigate the potential challenges of team diversity is to highlight its benefits for team effectiveness and encourage members to face their differences and openly consider diverse perspectives while working to achieve team goals (Rock, Grant, & Grey, 2016).

TEAM COHESION

Cohesion can be viewed as a type of social glue, and teams that are cohesive are characterized by members who feel attached to one another and work together as a unit. Highly cohesive teams are generally more effective than less cohesive teams (Beal, Cohen, Burke, & McLendon, 2003). Members of cohesive teams build a collective identity, share a bond with each other, and share a sense of purpose. Members of highly cohesive teams also derive personal satisfaction from membership and feel a strong desire to remain part of the group. This sense of personal satisfaction leads members to work diligently on team activities,

be less likely to miss work or quit the team, and feel personally affected by the team's successes and failures (Uhl-Bien et al., 2014).

Team cohesion is influenced by multiple factors, including size, diversity, time together, teamwork instruction, and satisfaction. Smaller teams tend to be more cohesive than larger teams, and teams that are less diverse (e.g., in terms of gender, race, ethnicity, sexual orientation, level of education, and work experience) tend to be more cohesive than more diverse teams. Cohesion also tends to be stronger for teams that have worked together for longer periods of time and for those that have received instruction or coaching that encourages them to help each other and support the team. Cohesion is also stronger when team members feel more satisfied with the work of the team and with the interactions among team members.

Because team cohesion is related to positive team performance, it makes sense to actively foster it. Cohesion can be fostered by gearing the team's work to meet clearly defined goals that mesh with the organization's broader goals and by clearly defining each team member's expected contribution. In turn, cohesion helps support acceptance of group norms and behaviors—the more cohesive the team, the stronger the acceptance of group norms. This dynamic can backfire, however, if the team develops counterproductive norms, such as working as few hours as possible or spending more time socializing than working. Therefore, when fostering team cohesion, we must establish norms, or productive work behaviors, that support task completion. Cohesion is also fostered by the close physical proximity of team members in an organization and by the development of team rituals (e.g., shared coffee breaks, lunch meetings) to ensure that team members interact regularly.

High cohesion can lead to negative consequences beyond the potential for reinforcing counterproductive norms. For instance, if teams become too cohesive, members may fail to heed advice from individuals outside of the team. They may also be at pains to avoid conflict within the team in order to maintain harmony; although this may sound positive on the surface, it can, as described in chapter 10, lead to the problem of groupthink. Thus, while enjoying the important benefits of a highly cohesive team, members must also be aware of the potential pitfalls.

SOCIAL LOAFING

Effective teamwork can also be undercut by social loafing, which consists of a decrease in effort or work output by individual members when they work in a team setting. The phenomenon was first identified in 1913 by Max Ringelmann and therefore is sometimes known as the Ringelmann effect. Ringelmann studied behavior among a group of male volunteers and noticed (after measuring how hard each volunteer could pull a rope) that the total effort of the group in pulling the rope was less than the sum of the total effort possible for each individual. Ringelmann concluded that the volunteers' levels of individual effort decreased when they were pulling together as a group (Karau & Williams, 1993). Moreover, the degree of social loafing is affected by team size—the larger the team, the greater the likelihood of social loafing (Liden, Wayne, Jaworski, & Bennett, 2004). Social loafing does not indicate that team members are being lazy or lack the desire to put forth effort. Rather, it appears to result from individual team members questioning whether they are making a meaningful contribution to the overall goal and receiving adequate reward for their effort. Social loafing also increases when the team's work involves greater interdependence in work functions among team members (Liden et al., 2004). When each person's individual efforts are necessary to attain the team's objective (interdependence), it will be apparent when one individual is not providing the effort necessary to reach it.

To address social loafing, we can work to ensure that all team members understand that each person must be responsible for an aspect of the team's work in order for the team to succeed. We can also work to assure team members that their individual contributions are valued by the team. In addition, when possible, we can keep the size of the team reasonable for the nature of the team's work; as noted earlier, teams typically function best with 5 to 10 members. Finally, high team cohesion can help guard against social loafing because members of cohesive teams are more committed to each other and to the work of the team.

COMMON TEAM-RELATED CHALLENGES

Teams often face a series of common problems that can diminish their effectiveness. One of the first problems a team may face is that of understanding where to begin; therefore, in taking their first steps as a team, members must clearly establish goals to guide their actions. A second common problem can occur if the team includes one or more members with an overbearing personality that makes it difficult for other team members to get involved. This issue can be addressed by establishing a team rule that requires all members to have equal opportunity for participation in meetings; in addition, team members can hold each other accountable for making constructive contributions.

Another common problem for teams is poor performance by individual team members. If members perceive that a person's low performance derives from lack of effort or low motivation, then they can try to motivate that member to improve performance; if no improvement occurs, they can remove the low-performing member from the team. If, in contrast, poor performance results from an individual's lack of skills or failure to understand the needed work, then team members can help train

CASE STUDY
Development of a
Fitness-Center Work Team

Because the health club industry is so competitive, clubs are always looking for the newest trends in order to stay relevant. As fitness supervisor of a local club, your responsibilities include working with your top personal fitness instructors to generate new ways of keeping club members engaged. To do so, you have gathered a group of your best instructors—referred to as Club Dream Team—and tasked them with putting together a new set of class offerings to ring in the new year. Your hope is that these offerings will encourage members to get back to a regular workout routine after the holiday season ends and New Year's resolutions have been made.

Unfortunately, a month after forming, the team seems to spend more time arguing over who is in charge and how to delegate work than in making progress on the new offerings. In addition, several members of the team have come to you with complaints that one of the instructors is dominating the meetings. You decide to meet with the team in order to remind the members of their goals and encourage them to work together on meeting those goals. After that meeting, the team seems to be making progress on the new class offerings, but a closer look reveals that most of the work is being done by two members while the others slack off and take undeserved credit. As the project deadline approaches, you have doubts about your wisdom in putting together this team; you also wonder why such a great group of fitness instructors have struggled so much. Still, you have not given up, and you return to your organizational behavior notes and textbook to look for ways to better support the team.

Case Study Questions

1. In what stage of team development is Club Dream Team stuck, and why?
2. As fitness supervisor, what could you have done to support the team through the team development process?
3. How might you prevent one member of the team from dominating the group?
4. What should the team do to ensure that all members contribute to the team's work?
5. Given the factors that influence team effectiveness, what do you need to know about the team's makeup in order to support it effectively?

and support that member's development (Jackson & LePine, 2003).

Team effectiveness can also suffer if the group fails to properly address conflict. As described in the discussion of team development, disagreement is a normal part of the storming phase and can also occur during the norming and performing stages. Conflict can present more of a problem, however, if members are unable to work together due to significant personality differences; in such cases, the conflict may never be resolved. When possible, it is best to avoid the situation altogether by keeping the team free of individuals who are known to be adversarial. If that is not possible, then the individuals should be encouraged to agree that they will set aside their difference in order to work together for the benefit of the team.

SUMMARY

In the context of organizational behavior, a team is defined as a group of people brought together based on specific skill sets or abilities in order to accomplish a specific task or function. Teams are put in place to achieve work outcomes more efficiently or more effectively than would be possible if individuals were working alone. Informal groups also develop within sport organizations; these groups are formed not around specific work-related objectives but on the basis of shared interests or experiences.

The types of formal teams described in this chapter include cross-functional, problem-solving, employee involvement, self-managing teams, and top-management teams. Cross-functional teams can be used to address the functional silo problem, in which a team focuses only on its internal needs and functioning while failing to communicate or interact with other teams in the organization. To address this issue, a cross-functional team is made up of individuals drawn from various work or functional units who then work together to achieve organizational objectives. Employee involvement teams are developed to address specific workplace issues that affect employees. Teams that do not require outside leadership in order to function are considered self-managing teams. A top-management team is composed of the most senior members of the organization.

All types of teams go through a five-stage process of team development that includes forming, storming, norming, performing, and adjourning. The stage in which a team is operating affects both its effectiveness and the types of challenges it faces. In the forming stage, the team comes together to determine individual roles and contributions, acceptable behaviors, and personal benefits of team membership. The storming stage is a tumultuous time during which members work toward understanding their roles, their power in the group, and their ability to influence other team members. In the norming stage, team members establish ground rules for behavior on the team and define operating goals and procedures for carrying out their work. By the performing stage, team structures are stable and members are satisfied that their needs are being met; thus the focus is on how best to meet the team's assigned goals. During the adjourning phase, team members celebrate accomplishments and recognize their hard work.

Individual team members fill particular roles or functions of three types: task, social, and boundary spanning. Task roles include contractor, creator, contributor, and completer. Social roles, which help the team to operate efficiently, include communicator, cooperator, and calibrator. Boundary-spanning roles link the team and its functions to the larger organization. These roles, which include coordinator and consul, are more externally focused, whereas the task and social roles are more internally focused on the team's functioning.

For a team to be effective, its design must provide for the necessary resources to support team functions. To be most effective, the size of the team must be appropriate for its objectives. In addition, the team's composition must include members who possess the skills, expertise, and experience necessary to carry out the team's work. The team's design should also consider the diversity of team members and how that diversity will influence team performance.

A team's effectiveness is also influenced by its level of cohesion, which is a type of social glue that enables members to attach to one another and work together as a unit. Highly cohesive teams are generally more effective than less cohesive teams. Members of cohesive teams build a collective identity, share a bond with other members, and enjoy a shared sense of purpose.

Teams must address the challenge posed by social loafing, in which individual effort or work output decreases when people work in a team setting. Social loafing is not about team members being lazy or not wanting to put forth an effort; rather, it derives from team members questioning whether they are making individual contributions to the overall goal and receiving adequate reward for their efforts. To address the issue of social loafing, all team members should understand how their individual efforts contribute to the team's pursuit of its objectives. Each team member must be responsible for an aspect of the team's overall work, and team members should know that their individual contributions are valued by the team.

DISCUSSION QUESTIONS

1. What is the difference between a team and a group when working in a sport organization?
2. What is a cross-functional team, and what problem is it used to address?
3. What are two of the many critical factors to supporting team effectiveness?
4. What factors support development of cohesion in work teams? When can cohesion be problematic in team functioning?
5. What is social loafing? What is one strategy for preventing it?

Chapter 12

Conflict, Negotiation, and Power

Chapter Objectives

After studying this chapter, you will be able to

- explain why conflict can be both positive and negative in the context of sport organizations,

- describe the types of conflict that manifest in sport organizations and detail ways to address them,

- explain the levels of conflict that manifest in sport organizations,

- explain the concept of negotiation and describe negotiation strategies used in sport organizations, and

- detail sources of individual power in sport organizations.

In this chapter, we explore what some consider to be the more challenging aspects of organizational behavior: conflict, negotiation, and power. Because these aspects must be addressed in sport organizations, it is wise to understand them and to know the strategies available for navigating any challenges they present.

Conflict permeates all levels of sport, from a youth baseball umpire facing pressure from overinvolved parents, to a high school athletic director managing competing demands from the boys' and girls' basketball coaches, to a newly hired sport communication director justifying player personnel decisions to local newspaper reporters. In such situations, negotiation is often used as a means to resolve conflict. For instance, the high school athletic direc-

tor will have to work with the basketball coaches in order to reach a solution that can be acceptable to both parties. The coaches may perceive this negotiation to be a process of determining winners and losers—that is, a distributive process—but the athletic director may work to make it an integrative one in which both parties can come away feeling satisfied.

The chapter also explores the concept of power and how individuals hold different forms of power in sport organizations. Some power is held by virtue of a leader's position, such as that of professional team owner, league commissioner, or head coach. However, power is not just about position; to the contrary, expert power is held by individuals who possess specific knowledge or skills. For instance, many organizations seek the expert power of employees with strong IT skills. Two other kinds of power—coercive and reward power—are held by coaches because they get to make decisions regarding who receives playing time. Coaches use these forms of power in differing ways in order to maximize players' performance. Power can also be held in various forms by subunits (e.g., work teams, groups, athletic teams) of a sport organization.

CONFLICT

Conflict has been defined as a "process in which one party perceives that its interests are being opposed or negatively affected by another party" (Wall & Callister, 1995, p. 517). Other definitions include elements of emotion—asserting, for example, that "disagreements exist in a social situation over issues of substance, or whenever emotional antagonisms create frictions between individuals or groups" (Uhl-Bien, Schermerhorn, & Osborn, 2014, p. 214). In fact, there are many ways to define conflict, but they all share some common elements. First, the conflict must involve two or more parties. Second, the involved parties must perceive that a conflict exists. Third, at least one party must be involved in blocking at least one other party from achieving its goals. Fourth, this blocking behavior must result in anger, frustration, or some other emotional response (Slack & Parent, 2006).

Conflict can be either dysfunctional (destructive) or functional (constructive). Dysfunctional conflict impedes or interferes with performance and can be detrimental to the organization if not resolved. For example, a head volleyball coach and a head soccer coach from the same university are engaged in dysfunctional conflict if they argue over access to the weight room and the strength and conditioning coaches. This conflict is detrimental to the teams and to the organization as a whole because it can interfere with each team's ability to

improve its performance level and thereby win more games for the university.

Functional conflict, on the other hand, is beneficial to the organization; in fact, organizations that do not have functional conflict often lack the energy and creativity necessary to generate new ideas (Nelson & Quick, 2013). For example, if two NHL team owners are engaged in conflict about how to support another team that is struggling financially, their conflict may push other owners and the league commissioner to consider multiple ways to support the league's teams. Perhaps one of the owners involved in the conflict will advocate for increased revenue sharing among teams, whereas the other will support generating more revenue for all teams by removing the hard cap on player salaries and imposing a luxury tax on teams that exceed a soft cap. This conflict, if properly managed, could lead to new and better ways to support all NHL teams, including those that are struggling financially.

Types of Conflict

Conflict in sport organizations can be categorized into four types: personal, intragroup, substantive, and procedural. As the label suggests, personal conflict results from differences between people; it may relate to values, personalities, or goals. Personal conflict can be damaging to the individuals involved, and participants in this type of conflict often report disliking the other person or making fun of or being angry with that person. This type of conflict can also be detrimental to the workplace because it sows distrust, bad feelings, and animosity among co-workers, which can inhibit people's ability to carry out their work tasks and meet the organization's goals (Jehn, 1997). For instance, imagine joining a minor league baseball team's front office staff, which includes only 10 full-time employees. In your first month on the job, you realize that the marketing director and the box office manager are in conflict because they are both highly competitive and jealous of one another's successes. As a result, it is difficult to coordinate marketing initiatives in order to sell more tickets, which of course negatively affects the organization's success.

Intragroup conflict is defined as conflict involving two or more members of an organization (Jehn, 1985). This type of conflict manifests in two forms—task conflict and relational conflict. Task conflict is based on the content of group decisions and includes perceptions of disagreement between group members as a result of differing viewpoints, opinions, or ideas. Thus task conflict is comparable to substantive conflict, which is based on work-related tasks, activities, or goals. In substantive conflict, individuals in the organization have differing ideas about how to accomplish work-related functions.

Returning to the example of the minor league front office, if the marketing director and the box office manager are in conflict about the most important fan group to target and the best promotions to use for Friday evening games, then they are engaged in both task and substantive conflict. The marketing manager may believe that family-friendly promotions would best increase attendance on Friday nights, whereas the box office manager may believe that after-work promotions directed toward the 25-and-over crowd would work best. Clearly, this conflict could become dysfunctional for the organization. When managed properly, however, substantive conflict can lead to positive outcomes for the organization. One way to properly manage this particular conflict would be to ask each person to compromise: For instance, the promotions could be offered on alternating weekends for the first half of the season, after which the more successful one would be used for the second half of the season.

The second form of intragroup conflict is relationship conflict, which, similar to personal conflict, is based on the "perception of interpersonal incompatibility"

(Medina, Munduate, Dorado, Martínez, & Guerra, 2005, p. 220). Relationship conflict can include conflict over personal values, beliefs, or norms (Medina et al., 2005). It can also develop among employees who hold different political views (e.g., progressive versus conservative), different valuations of time spent with family, or different expectations for prioritizing work over personal time.

Procedural conflict involves different ideas about how work should be carried out. In the example of the minor league team, even if the marketing director and box office manager agree to try the promotions on alternating Fridays, they could still have procedural conflict about *how* to carry them out. For instance, the marketing manager might want all full-time staff to participate in the promotional events, whereas the box office manager might believe that these tasks should be handled by summer interns and part-time employees. If this conflict is not resolved, it could negatively affect a promotion's success and reduce the sponsor's willingness to support it for the following season.

Levels of Conflict

Conflict in organizational behavior can occur on the individual level or the group level; within these categories, conflict on the individual level can be either interpersonal or intrapersonal. Interpersonal conflict involves two or more individuals—for example, the co-owners of a health club who disagree about how to support and compensate personal trainers on the staff. Intrapersonal conflict, on the other hand, is experienced within an individual; for instance, one of the health club owners might struggle to justify spending so much time at work and not enough time with his or her young children.

Similarly, conflict on the group level can be intergroup or intragroup. Intergroup conflict occurs between two or more work groups. For example, the research and development team for a sports apparel company might be in conflict with the marketing team regarding the best time to announce the release of a new basketball shoe that is still in development. Intragroup conflict, in contrast, involves members of a single work group. For instance, members of the marketing team at the sports apparel company might be in conflict about the most appropriate social media platform to use for announcing the release of the new shoe.

Conflict Management Strategies

Because conflict has the potential to be either positive (constructive) or negative (destructive), we must manage it properly in order to maximize positive outcomes and minimize negative ones. Conflict management strategies can focus on either behavioral change or attitudinal change. Managing conflict by focusing on behavioral change is a superficial and short-term solution, whereas focusing on attitudinal change addresses the root cause of the conflict (Slack & Parent, 2006). Therefore, we begin this discussion by describing strategies for behavioral change, then move on to strategies for attitudinal change that provide a longer-term solution. The strategies presented here can be classified as either lose-lose (wherein no one gains from the conflict resolution), win-lose (wherein one party sees the conflict resolved at the expense of another), or—the best option—win-win (wherein the parties resolve the conflict without either gaining or losing an advantage).

Avoidance

One way to manage conflict is through avoidance, which may not seem like managing at all since it does not address the underlying attitudinal challenge. This approach is considered a lose-lose strategy because one person either directs attention away from the conflict or ignores its existence altogether. For example, an athletic director might fail to respond to repeated meeting requests from a volleyball coach who is upset about budget decisions affecting her team. Similarly, a youth basketball coach might avoid having a conversation about playing time with a player's parent at a team dinner. In both cases, the conflict does not go away, and the underlying issues are not resolved.

Authority

One common way to manage conflict is to use one's positional or formal authority to reduce or eliminate the conflict. For instance, the athletic director might manage conflict with the volleyball coach by reminding the coach that final decisions regarding budgets are made at the sole discretion of the athletic director. A similar argument could be made by the youth basketball coach, who could remind the parent of the signed agreement which prohibits arguments over playing time as a condition for having one's child join the team. The use of authority is a win-lose strategy that fails to produce attitudinal changes; instead, it favors one group or individual at the expense of another. Thus, like avoidance, the use of authority is merely a short-term strategy for managing conflict.

Increase in Resources

When conflict results from lack or scarcity of needed resources, one solution (where possible) is to increase the resources. Though it may be difficult to increase financial resources, other types of resources may help reduce the conflict. For example, consider a director of event operations for a collegiate athletic department who is engaged in conflict with her staff regarding the number of events that each person must work in a given week. To resolve the conflict, the director might try to recruit unpaid, part-time interns from the college's sport management program to work at some events and thereby reduce the burden on her paid full-time staff. This action may offer only a partial solution, and the interns will require supervision and training, but it does offer something of an alternative if the director lacks the budget to hire another staff member. This approach is a win-win strategy because it addresses the needs of both parties; specifically, the director retains coverage for all sport events while relieving the workload stress on her staff.

Confrontation and Negotiation

Confrontation is a potentially risky strategy but one that may establish a basis for future collaboration (Slack & Parent, 2006). It requires both (or all) parties engaged in the conflict to come together and discuss the issues. This face-to-face interaction can be challenging, and it requires people to set aside their emotions and deal directly with the issues at hand. The confrontation process also involves negotiation as the sides try to reach an agreement in order to minimize the conflict. This process depends on all parties to work to find areas of agreement rather than focusing only on points of difference. Professional sport organizations often use negotiation when handling conflict between players and team owners, as is often the case during renewal talks for a league's contract with the players union. For example, one change made during negotiations over the NBA's collective bargaining agreement was an increase in the size of the standard team roster from a maximum of 13 players to a maximum of 14 (D. Feldman, 2017). This negotiation approach is another example of a win-win strategy, because both parties are able to resolve their conflict by raising all relevant issues during the confrontation and addressing them during the subsequent negotiation.

Job Rotation

Some conflicts result from failure to understand the challenges, demands, or constraints imposed on a person because of his or her job. This type of conflict can be minimized by giving members of the organization the chance to rotate among jobs, which allows them to learn about the issues and challenges involved in each other's work. Job rotation can be easier to accomplish in smaller organizations, where individuals work closely together and can be more easily trained to carry out different tasks. For instance, a minor league hockey team could use job rotation to help the public relations director understand the challenges faced by the community relations director, and vice versa. This strategy is not viable, however, for some conflict scenarios. For example, the public relations director could not change positions with the team's head coach, because the two jobs require very different and specific skill sets. When it is feasible, though, job rotation is a win-win strategy that addresses conflict by developing understanding of and appreciation for the needs of others.

NEGOTIATION

Suppose that you are responsible for coordinating athlete appearances for a professional soccer team and one of your star players has a conflict with a scheduled event at a local school. You must reach out to the school to discuss either changing the date or bringing another athlete to the appearance. Here's another scenario: You are offered your first full-time job, as assistant director of facility management for a community recreation center, and have heard from friends that you should not accept the job without asking for more salary or better benefits. Both of these situations call for you to engage in negotiation, which can be thought of as a "process of making joint decisions when the parties involved have different preferences" (Uhl-Bien et al., 2014, p. 224).

In sport organizations, negotiation can take any of four forms: two-party, group, intergroup, and constituency. In two-party negotiation, one person negotiates directly with another—for example, a new employee negotiating over salary with the hiring manager. In group negotiation, members of a group work toward a common decision. For instance, members of a college baseball team might negotiate team rules, such as game-night curfews and how many hours to spend in a group study session. Intergroup negotiations occur between two or more groups. For example, in determining the format of a promotional event to kick off the college basketball season, the marketing department might want the event to take place on a Friday night with a DJ and interactive games in order to maximize student attendance, whereas the head basketball coach might prefer an open practice on a Saturday afternoon followed by an autograph session for children. Finally, in constituency negotiation, each party involved in the negotiation process represents a broad constituency. This type includes negotiations between professional sport leagues and players unions to reach a collective bargaining agreement that addresses, among other things, maximum salaries, player benefits, revenue distribution, and roster sizes.

Negotiation Outcomes

The negotiation process is associated with two main types of goals: relationship goals and substance goals. Relationship goals address outcomes related to how well the parties involved in the negotiation (and any others they represent) are able to work together once the process has concluded. For example, in a constituency negotiation focused on a collective bargaining agreement, the relationship goals would focus on how well the players and team owners can work together once an agreement is reached. Substance goals, on the other hand, address outcomes related to the specific content under negotiation—for instance, the maximum salary for veteran players or the amount of league revenue to be distributed to players. The negotiation process is considered to be effective when both relationship and substance goals are met—that is, when the content outcomes are satisfactory for all involved

and positive interpersonal relationships are maintained (Uhl-Bien et al., 2014). In the collective bargaining example, an optimal negotiation will leave both sides pleased with the plan for revenue distribution and satisfied that the other side is committed to working together to support positive development of the players and the league.

Negotiation Strategies

Negotiation can take the form of two broad strategies: distributive negotiation and integrative negotiation. In distributive negotiation, which focuses on the positions of the involved parties, each side hopes to gain access to its fair share of the pie. In integrative negotiation, which focuses on the specific merits of the issues at hand, the parties work to make the pie larger and to share it in the best possible way. Thus distributive negotiation can take on a win-lose dynamic, whereas integrative negotiation takes a win-win approach. Consider the example of a collegiate athletic department that is deciding how to determine budgets for all teams. If the coaches engage in distributive negotiation, they will each lobby the athletic director for the largest possible budget. If, on the other hand, they engage in integrative negotiation, they will work together with the athletic department to determine how to increase revenues so that more financial resources are available for all teams to share. We will now discuss these two strategies in more detail.

Distributive Negotiation

In distributive negotiation, each party (e.g., individual, group) approaches the negotiation as a win-lose proposition. If one party seeks to get its own way and maximize self-interest, the result is a "hard" distributive negotiation, in which each side tries to dominate the other side in order to "win" the process. For example, if coaches in an athletic department take this approach in negotiating the budget with the athletic director, the coaches would each seek to gain every possible

IN THE BOARDROOM
Unfair Pay in the WNBA?

The collective bargaining agreement between the WNBA and the players association is a negotiated agreement that sets parameters for the working conditions, salaries, and benefits provided to players. When conducted optimally, such negotiations produce satisfactory results in terms of both substance goals and relationship goals. The most recent agreement in the WNBA was signed in 2014, and, given that both sides signed it, they both agreed to the conditions it laid out. However, analysis by Dave Berri (2015, 2017) calls into question the fairness of the agreement for players, because it appears that the WNBA engaged in more of a distributive negotiation than an integrative one. Citing data from the WNBA and the NBA, Berri notes that in 2015 NBA players received 50 percent of league revenue whereas WNBA players received only 33 percent (and that figure declined to less than 22 percent in 2017). Thus it appears that the negotiation process did not result in an optimal outcome for WNBA players. Given this disparity, if the WNBA wants to avoid conflict with its players down the line—which could result in a player lockout or strike—it should work on a more integrative negotiation that leads to more equitable revenue distribution for players, as well as ways to increase revenue generation for all parties.

dollar regardless of the effect on others. In contrast, in a "soft" distributive approach, one or more of the parties makes concessions in order to end the process. Thus the soft approach hinges on compromise as at least one party gives up something valued in order to reach an agreement and end the negotiation. For instance, in the case of the athletic department budget, if the women's basketball coach takes a soft distributive approach, she might give up a team trip during the holiday break if the athletic director agrees to purchase new travel gear for the team.

Integrative Negotiation

In integrative negotiation, the parties seek to work together to achieve a win-win result; therefore, this is a less confrontational approach than distributive negotiation. In this mode, it is critical that both parties be willing to negotiate based on the merits rather than trying to maximize self-interest. For integrative negotiation to succeed, the parties must

trust one another, which makes it essential that they maintain a positive relationship throughout the process. The parties must also be willing to share information with each other that can provide each side with an understanding of what is needed to reach an effective resolution; without having this information it will be difficult to reach an effective resolution that satisfies the needs of the parties involved. In addition, in order to facilitate information sharing, the parties must be willing to ask and answer specific, concrete questions (Uhl-Bien et al., 2014). Returning to the example of the athletic department budget, the athletic director could share with coaches all relevant information regarding expenses for all teams, and the women's basketball coach could share a list of areas where she sees the potential to cut costs for her team. Both parties could then work together to determine how to meet the team's needs while also looking for money-saving ideas that will benefit all teams in the department.

INDIVIDUAL TYPES OF POWER

Power is understood as the ability to exert influence on others (individuals or groups) in order to change their behaviors, actions, or attitudes (Raven, 2008). In sport organizations, power is most often associated with control over resources, such as money, information, decisions, and work assignments. In this section, we describe six kinds of power held by individuals in sport organizations: legitimate, reward, coercive, referent, expert, and informational. When reading about the types of individual power, keep in mind that they can be held simultaneously by a given individual. For example, the commissioner of a professional sport league has the power to negotiate player contracts on behalf of the league (legitimate power), can suspend or fine a player for violating league rules (coercive power), can provide incentives to high-performing teams (reward power), has expertise on media rights agreements (expert power), and may be charismatic (referent power).

Legitimate Power

Legitimate power is derived from an individual's position in the organization. Thus it does not result from any special qualities or attributes possessed by the person; rather, it exists because the organization's norms provide the occupant of a certain position with the right to influence others. For instance, the general manager of a baseball team holds legitimate power based on title, and all other individuals in the organization recognize that power.

Reward Power

Individuals hold reward power when they are able to provide rewards to others (e.g., employees, volunteers); thus they can influence others by promising to provide them with rewards they value. This type of power is often held in positions that can provide incentives or bonuses to others for performance. For example, a director of

ticket sales can offer cash bonuses or vacation days to employees who meet or exceed a sales quota for a season. Similarly, an athletic director can use reward power to incentivize coaches for successful seasons on the field (in terms of win-loss record) and in the classroom (in terms of team GPA). For instance, if a coach reaches the NCAA tournament or the team achieves a high GPA, the athletic director can reward the coach with a bonus over and above base salary.

Coercive Power

Coercive power is similar to reward power but involves the distribution of punishments rather than rewards in order to influence others. Individuals who hold coercive power are able to distribute negative consequences if expectations are not met. For instance, if a coach fails to meet expectations, the athletic director can wield coercive power by withholding the coach's bonus; moreover, if performance continues to fall short of expectations, the athletic director can fire the coach.

Referent Power

Referent power is held by individuals based on personal qualities or characteristics. Those who hold referent power command a sense of presence or charisma that compels others to follow. Referent power can develop "when members of the sport organization identify very strongly with values espoused by their leader" (Slack & Parent, 2006, p. 202). Indeed, many high-profile coaches in both professional and intercollegiate sport have wielded referent power based on a charismatic personality. For instance, Geno Auriemma, longtime and highly successful coach of the UConn women's basketball team, holds referent power as an influential voice in the college basketball community and beyond.

Expert Power

Expert power derives from the possession of expertise, knowledge, or skill in a par-

IN THE BOARDROOM
Changing the Face of NBA Coaching

Head coaching positions in the NBA have always been filled by men (Lapchick, 2017). However, current league commissioner Adam Silver has stated that the NBA "'definitely will' have a female head coach and that it will happen 'sooner, rather than later'" (Gaines, 2017, n.p.). That statement looks like more than mere PR spin when considered in light of actions taken by Gregg Popovich, head coach of the San Antonio Spurs. In 2014, Popovich used legitimate, expert, and referent power when he hired former WNBA star player Becky Hammon as an assistant coach for the Spurs. Popovich holds legitimate and referent power as a highly respected coach and possesses expert power as the winningest NBA coach for a single team. More specifically, his team has "won five NBA titles in six NBA Finals appearances since 1999 and also hold the NBA record for most consecutive seasons (17) with at least 50 wins" (Wells, 2017, n.p.). Popovich, who has spoken out on racial inequality as well (Gatto, 2017), has been vocal in his support of Hammon and her coaching skills, referring to her as "just a natural" (Gaines, 2017, n.p.) and indicating that she has what it takes to be an NBA head coach. His support for Hammon, coupled with his sources of power, can influence other coaches and professional sport owners to look for other talented women when filling vacant coaching positions.

ticular area; it does not have to be related to legitimate power in an organization. For example, in any sport organization, expert power is held by individuals who possesses technology-related skills, especially if the network crashes and employees cannot perform their work. Expert power is also held by a video technician who possesses the skills to edit video in order to help coaches review plays and prepare for upcoming games.

Informational Power

Informational power differs from expert power in that it is held by an individual in a particular situation. Thus, whereas expert power involves accumulated knowledge, skills, and expertise, informational power is wielded when one individual explains to another how to carry out a particular job or task. For example, an event operations employee for a minor league hockey team holds informational power when instructing new interns about how to write an

event script detailing the tasks required during a home hockey game.

SUMMARY

This chapter opened with a discussion of conflict, which permeates all levels of sport—from youth sport through the professional ranks. Conflict can be either positive (constructive) or destructive (negative); if not properly managed, it can lead to problems in an organization. Four types of conflict can occur in sport organizations: personal, substantive, procedural, and intragroup. Personal conflict results from differences between people in terms of values, personalities, or goals. Substantive conflict involves work-related tasks, activities, or goals and occurs when individuals have differing ideas about how to accomplish work-related functions. Procedural conflict involves differences in regard to the specifics of how work should be carried out or how tasks should be completed.

CASE STUDY

Balancing Power
in Intercollegiate Athletics

Intercollegiate sport played at the Division I Football Bowl Subdivision (FBS) level has become a significant source of revenue for universities competing in the Power Five conferences (i.e., the Big Ten, Big 12, SEC, ACC, and PAC-12). For instance, in the 2014-2015 season, Texas A&M University's athletics program brought in $192 million, and head football coach Kevin Sumlin earned more than $5 million in salary. Yet Sumlin was not the highest paid coach that year, as Jim Harbaugh earned more than $7 million from the University of Michigan. Football coaches command such high salaries because their programs usually bring in the most revenue for the athletic department. Schools that lack a revenue-producing football team may still generate significant revenue through a men's basketball team. In one such program, Rick Pitino, then head coach of the men's basketball team at the University of Louisville, earned more than $6 million in 2015. As a result of their generation of revenue, these coaches and others wield considerable power in their athletic departments, universities, and communities.

In fact, a high-profile coach is often the highest-paid employee on the university's—and perhaps the state's—payroll. Data gathered by the *Chronicle of Higher Education* revealed that only 10 percent of college presidents had a salary of more than $1 million and that of the 154 public-university employees who do make more than $1 million, 70 percent were coaches (Newman, 2014). Public sentiment is beginning to shift away from support of such high salaries as both the cost of college and the amount of student loan debt continue to rise. In a survey conducted in 2016, more than 60 percent of respondents agreed that college coaches should not be the highest-paid employees on college campuses (Camera, 2016).

The organizational structure in a typical athletic department designates the athletic director as the senior-most employee and indicates that all coaches report to the director. However, when a coach earns a higher salary than the athletic director and the university president, some aspects of power are shifted away from these designated authority figures and into the hands of the coach. Therefore, in light of the many sources of power available to individuals in a sport organization, athletic directors must work to support the demands of highly compensated coaches while also maintaining control of the athletic department and attending to other sport programs that do not generate significant revenue. Even as public sentiment shifts away from paying such high salaries, the job market for high-profile coaches has continued to support big contracts. The challenge going forward, then, is for university presidents and athletic directors to find a way to hire and retain the best coaches while also allaying public concern about coaches' high salaries.

Case Study Questions

1. What sources of power do athletic directors have that might help them rein in the salaries of high-profile coaches while still attracting the best candidates? Support your answer with details.

2. What sources of power do high-profile coaches have to enable the rise in their salaries? Support your answer with details.

3. What negotiation strategy would you recommend for an athletic director engaged in contract renewal talks with a men's basketball coach who wants a raise that will make him the highest-paid employee on campus?

4. What areas of conflict might develop if the coach does not secure the desired raise during this negotiation process?

5. What specific advice would you provide to the athletic director for managing this potential conflict?

Intragroup conflict involves two or more members of an organization and manifests in two forms—task conflict and relational conflict.

Because conflict can be both positive (constructive) and negative (destructive), we must manage it properly in order to maximize positive outcomes and minimize negative ones. Conflict management strategies can focus on eliciting either behavioral change or attitudinal change. These strategies can be further classified as lose-lose (in which no one gains from the conflict resolution), win-lose (in which one individual or group sees the conflict resolved at the expense of another), or, optimally, win-win (in which the parties come together to resolve the conflict without gaining or losing advantage).

Negotiation is the process of making joint decisions when the parties involved prefer different outcomes. It addresses two overall types of goals: substance goals and relationship goals. Substance goals relate to the specific content under negotiation, whereas relationship goals are concerned with how well the involved parties (and any others they represent) are able to work together once the negotiation has been concluded. Broad strategies to consider in negotiation include distributive negotiation, which focuses on the positions held by the involved parties, and integrative negotiation, which focuses on the specific merits of the issues at hand. Distributive negotiation can be marked by a win-lose dynamic, whereas integrative negotiation is more focused on a win-win approach.

Finally, power is understood as the ability to exert influence over individuals or groups in order to change their behaviors, actions, or attitudes. In sport organizations, power is most often associated with control over resources, including money, information, decisions, and work assignments. Types of individual power in sport organizations include legitimate, reward, coercive, referent, expert, and informational.

DISCUSSION QUESTIONS

1. How can conflict be both positive and negative in a sport organization?
2. Describe two types of conflict that can occur between individuals in a sport organization.
3. Describe two of the six forms of power that can be held by a person working in a sport organization.
4. Describe one way in which conflict between two individuals in a sport organization might be resolved.
5. What types of power do professional athletes hold?

PART IV
MANAGING THE ORGANIZATION

In parts I, II, and III of the book, we covered the fundamentals of organizational behavior and the management of individuals and groups. Now, in part IV, we tackle some of the ways in which sport managers can help bring clarity to people's work, build a culture that people wish to be part of, and deal with change, which is a reality in any organization. The three chapters in this part of the book highlight what we believe that leaders, managers, and employees need to appreciate as they go about their work in any sport organization.

Chapter 13 begins by introducing the interpersonal nature of communication, then details how communication flows in an organization, from both an internal view and an external view. The chapter addresses written, oral, and nonverbal communication with an eye toward reducing ambiguity and working effectively in a cross-cultural environment.

Chapter 14 details the various ways in which artifacts, values, and beliefs hold meaning for people at work. It also addresses ways in which they can be used by managers to convey important messages about how work should be done in the organization. In addition, the chapter addresses how the environment can shape what employees perceive to be most important.

Chapter 15 details some of the classical models for understanding change and addresses how people in an organization can either support or resist change. It also addresses various contemporary issues in sport relative to the change models.

Chapter 13

Communication in the Organization

Chapter Objectives

After studying this chapter, you will be able to

- describe the interpersonal communication process,

- detail ways in which personal communication can be more effective,

- elaborate on the pros and cons of social media as a communication tool,

- describe the importance of both verbal communication and nonverbal communication (e.g., body language), and

- appreciate communication differences in a cross-cultural environment.

Every day, we are bombarded with communication in many forms. Often, we find ourselves in situations that require multiple forms of communication—spoken, body, and written language—sometimes simultaneously. Thus clear communication is integral to functioning well in any relationship; moreover, communication influences a great proportion of our work, our preferences for work, and the tasks we are able to perform.

The topic of communication carries implications at the individual, group, and organizational levels. At the individual level, interpersonal communication hinges on the variety of ways in which people use language, tone of voice, body position, facial expressions, and even speaking speed—all of which can indicate personal preferences and attitudes that convey meanings between sender and receiver.

A person's choice of communication mode (e.g., email, face-to-face interaction, public or private message) can influence group performance. In sport settings, groups often form due to their particular role in the organization and may create their own ways of communicating in order to expedite messages exchanged between members. Thus, when we examine communication in a sport organization, we must recognize how a group's communication is affected by its role (e.g., marketing, finance, human resources). Moreover, though it is common to consider subcultural formations in terms of job task and function (e.g., marketing, finance), when we look at sport we must also consider other forms of segregation (e.g., offense, defense, rookie, veteran) based on specialized units and roles.

In any organization, various intra- and interorganizational communications occur, which can either aid or hinder the pursuit of organizational objectives. The leadership of the organization must communicate important messages—regarding, for example, policies, procedures, and expectations—to the employee base in an effort to ensure that people clearly understand what they are expected to do. However, such unidirectional messages do not necessarily produce the desired understanding, given that they are often codified, or written. Consequently, important messages also need to be discussed and reinforced.

In every sport organization, the leadership must be able to produce communication that helps employees develop a good understanding of corporate, group, and person-task or job objectives. When leaders clearly articulate corporate or organizational objectives that are both written and reinforced through various mechanisms (e.g., leadership behavior, dialogue, rewards), they can help build a shared understanding of important expectations for employee behavior. However, the leadership role in communication goes beyond the intraorganizational communication chain. Indeed, perhaps more today than ever before, sport organizations and their leaders also engage frequently in external communication with stakeholders (e.g., fans, sponsors, potential consumers), thus making it essential that they communicate consistently, clearly, and responsively.

INTERPERSONAL COMMUNICATION

According to one definition, "communication evokes a shared or common meaning" (Nelson, Quick, Armstrong, & Condie, 2015, p. 123). It is perhaps easiest to grasp how this process works if we approach it first in terms of basic interpersonal communication, which can include as few as (but at least) two people. At this basic level,

we can see clearly that the communication process involves a sender, a receiver, a message, a channel (e.g., face-to-face interaction, email, Skype, phone), various types of noise, and ideally, feedback, within a particular environment (Robbins & Judge, 2008).

Communication can be one-way or two-way. In one-way communication, a message is sent to a person without any opportunity for the recipient to ask questions, provide feedback, or interact in any way with the sender. Of course, we see both one-way and two-way communication employed in sport organizations. One-way communication offers the potential benefits of being fast, directive in nature, and (if simple to understand) useful when articulated clearly. Thus it can be helpful in emergency situations (e.g., military, firefighting) and in many coaching situations. For example, during a time-out in sport, the coach has limited time in which to communicate and therefore tends to be directive about expectations and which play to run. Two-way communication, on the other hand, allows for interaction and feedback.

Whether using a one-way or a two-way mode, effective interpersonal communication can help engender and foster good will among colleagues. The resulting rapport is critical to the process of creating a positive work environment in both administrative and athletic-based settings in sport.

The Basic Interpersonal Communication Process

In interpersonal communication (figure 13.1), a message originates at the source and is transferred to the recipient. Although this process may seem simple, it is complicated by a number of factors, such as the environment in which the message is delivered, which can influence how the message is understood. The message's delivery may be adequate if the environment is free of noise and distraction; however, many aspects of the environment can hinder the communication process, including, for example, distractions from other people in the office, loud or noisy equipment, and technological breakdowns. Noise in this context can consist of any factor that distorts the message during any part of the process (Robbins & Judge, 2008); thus it may involve, for instance, physical distractions, differences in status (e.g., an organizational leader communicating with an employee of lower rank), cultural differences, or poor or absent feedback.

In addition, the sender and receiver each have what is called a "perceptual screen" that influences the quality, clarity, and accuracy of communication (Nelson et al., 2015; Robbins & Judge, 2008). A person's perceptual screen can be influenced by personal values and beliefs, cultural influences, and even demographic factors such as gender and age. Perceptual screens underlie many of the challenges involved in communicating accurately. For instance, the sender is responsible for initiating and encoding a clear message but may do so in a way that indicates a bias or preference that the receiver may not understand. In other words, the message may be sent or received, or both, with some form of distortion because of a person's

perceptual screen. For example, a person's perceptual screen may be influenced by a power relationship between the sender and receiver; consider, for instance, the differences involved in communicating with a colleague, a supervisor, and an employee. A perceptual screen may also relate to a person's individual biases, preferences about the subject matter at hand, or judgment of how the message is delivered and conveyed by the sender. To put it another way, sometimes we simply "hear what we want to hear."

In delivering the message, the sender makes various key decisions, such as what channel to use (e.g., written, oral, nonverbal), which give the message certain characteristics that are then decoded by the receiver and thus influence his or her perception of the message's meaning (Robbins, & Judge, 2008). Nonverbal communication, in particular, plays an important role in the receiver's interpretation of the message; therefore, it is extremely important for the sender to ensure that any nonverbal elements are consistent with the intended meaning of the message. Moreover, because written communication is devoid of the nonverbal component, the sender must take care to

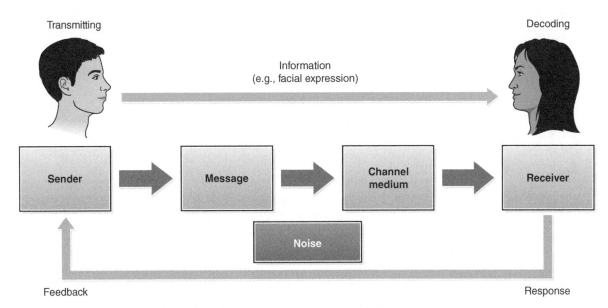

Figure 13.1   Interpersonal communication process model.

make it clear, succinct, and free of overly technical terminology.

Another key aspect of basic interpersonal communication is the process of encoding. In this part of the process, the communicator (the sender) decides how to express and deliver the message. The receiver then decodes the message and decides how to interpret it. Again, depending on the environment and the channel selected, the communication may be affected by issues such as noise and perceptual screens. The final stage of the communication process involves feedback, which provides an evaluation of how successfully the message has been transferred. Therefore, giving and receiving feedback is crucial to becoming a more effective communicator because it can increase understanding. When it occurs through oral communication, the feedback process requires skillful and attentive listening.

The basic interpersonal communication process of encoding and then sending a message to be received and decoded by the recipient is simple in sequence but entirely complex and varied in reality. Even if the sender has clearly articulated the message—that is, said what was intended in a way that can presumably be easily interpreted and understood—the receiver may decode it in a way that distorts the sender's intended meaning and favors an interpretation preferred by the receiver. In any case, the receiver can then encode a message based on his or her own thoughts and ideas and, if given the opportunity, create and deliver a feedback message.

For example, at the start of a new recreational baseball season, a volunteer coordinator may use oral communication to articulate a message about rule changes to the captains of the various teams. The coordinator may provide examples of new rules and then refer the captains to the league's website for the rest of the relevant information. However, depending on the noise in the room—or the perceptual screens of the captains—one or more receivers may fail to attach significance to the coordinator's message or may question the rationale for the changes without having the opportunity to engage in dialogue in front of the group. Noise in the environment (whether consisting of audio or visual distractions) could also introduce distortions into the message. For instance, if the meeting takes place in a public setting where other people are mingling or TVs are playing, participants may get distracted. Thus, the clarity of the message can be affected (enhanced or hindered) by factors such as the choice of venue, seating arrangements, and the use of technology within the environment that may interrupt or distort the message being delivered.

Distortion can also occur due to attribution error, in which we try to establish whether a person's behavior is caused by internal factors or external forces, thus

IN THE BOARDROOM
Asking Questions

It is sometimes difficult for a novice to ask for clarification of an organizational policy or procedure due to fear of being judged as incompetent by someone who holds higher status. Most managers, however, would tell you that it is much better to ask a question than to remain unsure and therefore possibly contribute to discordance in the organization's operations. Indeed, a good manager or leader allows employees to freely ask questions in order to perform their work effectively; in this way, feedback can function as a critical part of the process of interpersonal communication.

perhaps judging the behavior without having sufficient information to do so (Kelley, 1971). Kelley (1971) proposed that we make attributions based on three types of information cues: consensus (others behave the same way), distinctiveness (the person behaves the same way in other situations), and consistency (frequency in person's behavior is consistent over time). The premise is simply that people assign reasons to a person's behavior based on these cues and that the various bases of information can lead us to make internal (personal) attributions or external (situational) attributions. Internal attributions relate to the form of a person's effort, commitment, or ability, whereas external attributions relate to factors outside of the person's control (e.g., luck). For instance, when someone is promoted from assistant coach to head coach, we might reason either that the person was in the right place at the right time or that the person works hard, possesses relevant skills, and deserves the opportunity. Either way, we may be engaging unknowingly in an attribution error.

In another example, a manager might assume that an employee's poor performance results from lack of effort rather than attributing it to an external reason such as lack of support or issues with equipment (Matthewman, Rose, & Hetherington, 2009). Thus attribution error can damage an employee who is not at fault but in fact needs more support, more direction, or better equipment in order to do the job. For instance, if personnel at a fitness facility do not have functioning equipment to accurately assess a person's body composition, strength, and flexibility, then the patron may be upset and complain to management that his or her needs are going unmet. A manager who hears only this side of the story may believe that the person performing the assessment is not skilled enough to perform the job adequately, thus erroneously making an internal attribution for the problem.

As these examples illustrate, when we assign reasoning of any sort to a person's behavior without knowing the person's story, we run the risk of wrongful accusations. We may even be discriminatory if we assign such reasoning based on factors such as gender, age, or disability. Consequently, we should take care to avoid attribution error; instead, we should attempt various forms of communication to overcome any attribution not formed on the basis of reasoning and fact.

Effective Communication

According to Schermerhorn, Hunt, and Osborn (2004), "effective communication occurs when the intended meaning of the source and the perceived meaning of the receiver are virtually the same" (p. 279). Consequently, both the sender and the receiver influence the communication process. This influence may be moderated by a person's mood, experiences they bring to the communication, and general attitude and perception of the discussion taking place (e.g., favorable, negative). For effective communication to take place, the key is to remain sensitive, aware, and patient so that one does not leap to conclusions or fall into knee-jerk reactions. In addition, the receiver should ask for clarification if needed and confirm the message's meaning by asking if his or her interpretation matches the sender's intention.

In one-on-one communication, we tend to engage in more thorough dialogue when communicating in person and face to face than when communicating in written form (e.g., email) because we can do so more quickly. In-person dialogue also allows us to use nonverbal cues that are absent from written communication, and these cues provide information for both the sender and the receiver that can aid understanding. In addition, in-person communication—particularly with a friend or close colleague—typically provides a conducive environment in which to ask for clarification in a nonjudgmental way. For example, in professional sport, a rookie often needs mentoring and counsel from a veteran player, and it is helpful if the veteran can set aside time for one-on-one, in-person discussions with the rookie.

Time, in fact, is a key consideration for effective communication. Having sufficient time to engage in feedback helps ensure that messages are delivered and interpreted accurately. For instance, if time is short, the sender may feel rushed and therefore fail to use body language that correctly emphasizes particular words; consequently, he or she may have meant to say one thing verbally but confused or skewed that message through inconsistent body language. In addition, the rushed situation may prevent the receiver from seeking clarification or checking facts. Thus, when oral communication is hurried, it is good practice for the receiver to ask for a written follow-up message; this request allows the sender to clearly articulate the message in written form, which may correct any mistakes or gaps in the oral communication.

As you can see, then, effective communication requires more than simply listening. It also requires being adept at observing, questioning, giving and receiving feedback, and appreciating the power of nonverbal cues (both from oneself and from the other party). These factors "support such second-order interpersonal skills as assertiveness, influencing, persuading, negotiating, leading, managing conflict, and team-working" (Matthewman et al., 2009, p. 133).

Given the importance of effective interpersonal communication, it is critical to understand where breakdowns may occur. Communication problems can derive from a variety of reasons. For instance, the sender of the message may speak too quickly, use unclear or overly technical language, provide irrelevant information, or use confusing nonverbal cues. Problems can also result from the communication channel chosen by the sender—for instance, a distracting, noisy, public space where other people may be listening. In turn, these various factors may be decoded and interpreted by the receiver on the basis of personal differences, perceptual screen, poor or inattentive listening, or various attributions and biases that can increase ambiguity or distortion and cause further breakdown in communication between sender and receiver.

Flow of Communication

As we have seen, the interpersonal communication process is complex, and it can be complicated further by the dynamics of communication flow in organizational life. Communication flow consists of the exchanging of messages among individuals and groups within the organization, as well as with external stakeholders. Thus it carries consequences for how people interpret and perform their work. Here we consider four types of communication flow: downward, upward, lateral, and external.

In downward communication, the message originates from someone higher in the group or organization and is delivered to someone in a lower position; for example, a coach informs players of their upcoming training schedule. Downward communication is used in order to be directive, clarify objectives, address problems that need to be fixed, delegate tasks, announce policies and regulations, and facilitate various kinds of organizational control efforts. Many times, downward communication is unidirectional, or one-way, meaning that there is no opportunity for a feedback loop from the point of view of the recipient (Robbins & Judge, 2008).

In upward communication, on the other hand, the message originates from lower in the hierarchy of the group or organization and is delivered to someone at a higher level. This type of communication can help leaders make more informed decisions; for instance, a member of the service staff might inform someone in upper management about customer issues that need to be dealt with. Upward communication is helpful because leadership needs feedback from the various employee levels in order to understand problems and be aware of progress on the front lines. Because members of the service staff regularly encounter customers, they may know of equipment failures, merchandising issues, and other problems that need attention from the leadership.

In lateral communication, the messages flow from one party to another at the same level. This type of communication is very prominent in team-based sports, university departments, and other groups that have a relatively informal hierarchy made up of individuals who hold a similar stake in the organization's success. For example, the promotions team for a collegiate sport event might communicate laterally with the marketing department about how to reach a particular segment of the desired demographic (Robbins & Judge, 2008).

In external communication, a message flows from the organization to the external environment with the purpose of providing information to interested stakeholders. Sport organizations commonly conduct external communication through various tools, such as newspapers, magazines, television, radio, Internet, and social media. In the traditional model, sport organizations delivered much of their external communication through print media, TV, and radio. Today, of course, the web, and in particular the various forms of social media, give sport organizations instantaneous reach and allow for both one-way and two-way information flow. More specifically, various online resources—including blogs, message boards, and content communities—allow people to share photos, text, and audio and video files and to exchange thoughts and opinions with individual athletes and sport organizations. This array of communication options presents management with strategic challenges in terms of how much communication to engage in, which platforms to use for which target demographics, and what messages to convey in support of the desired corporate image. In additional, the rise of handheld devices has created a world marked by a constant flow of and demand for communication.

COMMUNICATING THROUGH SOCIAL MEDIA

In the current information age, it is critical for sport organizations to reach sport consumers with important pieces of information, such as team schedules, results, records, tickets, promotions, and parking, to name only a few. Faced with this demand, sport organizations can use a variety of mass media forms to reach specific market segments, all of which can play a role in the organization's success. Sport managers must use these forms of mass media to communicate effectively by getting their message across and responding when needed. Although traditional channels are still used—and sometimes even preferred—sport organizations increasingly integrate the web (and, in particular, social media) into their strategies for communicating with stakeholders through both one-way messages and two-way formats that enable dialogue. As a result, recent years have seen the emergence of research examining the use of social media tools by sport organizations (MacIntosh, Abeza, & Lee; 2017; O'Shea & Alonso, 2011).

In this high-tech environment, Twitter has emerged as a preferred platform in sport because it provides a powerful way to reach fans (Williams & Chinn, 2010). Its benefits include speed and the possibility for exchanges of information between a sport organization and external constituents. For sport organizations, the most important aspect of the dialogue that occurs on Twitter and other social media platforms involves communication between fans themselves (MacIntosh, Abeza, & Lee, 2017). The sport organization can act as a catalyst by starting the conversation on a topic of interest to fans and, from time to time, furthering the fan dialogue by adding interesting internal commentary to the discussion.

Of course, the use of social media is not without its pitfalls for organizations, including fan speculation and fact checking regarding the accuracy of organizational statements, as well as the potential for the organization to lose control of its messages. Indeed, the very nature of social media creates an empowered audience whose members can communicate in any way they want. This freedom strips away the traditional top-down and unidirectional flow of information. For more on key considerations related to social media, see this chapter's case study (Creating a Social Media Policy). Furthermore, social media platforms have the capability to easily distort facts, which can require an organization and its leadership to deal with situations that might not otherwise arise. Challenging situations can result, for instance, from the use or abuse of social media by employees (whether administrative staff, coaches, or players) and from questions raised by fans and consumers about organizational operations or initiatives.

COMMON COMMUNICATION FORMS

Each day, we communicate with others by means of various forms, whether written (e.g., email), oral (e.g., face-to-face, Skype), or nonverbal (e.g., body language). In sport, it is also common to engage in cross-cultural communication, particularly at the high-performance level. We discuss each of these forms in more detail in the following sections.

Written Communication

Mastering written communication is not a simple task. Students begin learning to write very early in the educational process—from forming letters to learning parts of speech to constructing sentences, paragraphs, and essays. When one's career begins, writing takes on a whole new dimension in the form of agendas, executive summaries, organizational documentation (e.g., policies, regulations), and other types of business and organizational communication. Although some academic programs help students learn this type of writing, many do not.

Written communication has the advantage of being tangible; that is, you can save or store the message for reference or use at a later date. In addition, it typically serves a clear purpose. In an organization, written communication helps employees make sense of their work. For instance, relatively permanent documents—such as organizational statements of vision, mission, philosophy, and values—can help employees understand the organization's direction and their specific jobs. However, written communication can also become burdensome.

Consider a typical day in the life of a sport camp manager, who may receive any number of emails from parents, memos from the head office, advertisements for camp-related products and services, questions from interested parties, and, of course, many other items. In addition to the exchanges that these emails may initiate, the camp manager must also produce written documents to track camp activities for record-keeping purposes—for example, daily written reports charting the number of participants. Such documents are often mundane, simple, and repetitive. As discussed in chapter 6, these aspects of the job may be unmotivating to the person responsible for them. However, monitoring and reporting are important parts of many jobs, particularly if an incident occurs (e.g., a camper is hurt). Therefore, both the sport camp and its stakeholders rely on this manager's leadership in receiving, encoding, decoding, and transmitting appropriate messages—whether internally to staff or externally to stakeholders. In both internal and external communication, the message should be kept as simple as possible. This is particularly true when managing emails or any form of online communication, which can sometimes be overly (and unnecessarily) verbose. Good communication is succinct and avoids jargon and overly technical language.

Oral Communication

Oral communication offers the benefits of speed and feedback (Robbins & Judge, 2008). Spoken language allows people to exchange ideas more easily than is possible through the written word. Oral communication can also be filled with jargon and inside jokes that help people create bonds and group understanding, particularly through the use of acronyms or technological language. At the same time, this type of insider communication can alienate people who do not know what is going on in the conversation.

When people communicate by speaking face to face, they can use nonverbal communication to aid in the delivery of the message. In one study (Mehrabian, 1970), body language accounted for 55 percent of the message, voice tone accounted for 38 percent, and only 7 percent was derived from verbal content. More generally, experts agree that anywhere from 65 percent to 90 percent of a typical conversation is interpreted on the basis of nonverbal cues (Kinicki & Kreitner, 2008). For example, the sender may use hand signals, facial expressions, arm movements, or direct eye contact. Today, of course, the oral form of communication can also be used through advanced technology that allows face-to-face communication when people are not in the same physical space. For instance, video conferencing (teleconferencing) is increasingly used when people cannot meet in person or when business expenses need to be minimized. In sport-related workplaces, communication platforms such as Skype and FaceTime are becoming increasingly common.

Despite the benefits of this technology, body language can be difficult to fully interpret when a communication platform shows only a portion of a person's body (e.g., head and shoulders). However, in such situations, oral communication can still be aided by some forms of body language, such as eye contact and facial expressions.

One note of caution regarding oral communication involves the workplace "grapevine," which is notorious for passing along rumors and misinterpretations—that is, for losing the sender's intended message. When details are passed along from one person to another, each iteration is subject to decoding and then reencoding when the receiver creates a new message for the next recipient. This process can produce messages that differ greatly from the original intended message and therefore can spread misinformation. At times, the grapevine can produce gossip that rises to the level of organizational misbehavior, particularly when it is negative or malicious (Wilson, 2010). This issue can be compounded if the language used is overly technical or subject to cultural barriers.

Nonverbal Communication

As we have noted, body language is an important form of communication, particularly with in-person and other face-to-face encounters. Body language can be telling in both the sender and the receiver and can occur in the form of eye contact, facial expressions, arm positions, overall posture, and other displays. This form of communication provides the sender and the recipient with crucial information to decode.

In both oral and written communication, people sometimes suppress their true sentiments or employ filters when encoding feedback. Even so, body language may allow the sender to discern the receiver's mood based on factors such as eye contact (or lack thereof), posture, and body positioning. However, nonverbal behavior can also be influenced by what is considered acceptable practice in various cultures; that is, it can vary widely from one country or region to another. For example, cultures vary greatly in the level of comfort assigned to certain physical distances between one person and another. Greetings can also differ greatly—for instance, in terms of nonverbal practices such as acceptable norms related to handshakes, bowing, hugging, or kissing. In addition, friendly hand gestures in one culture (e.g., a thumbs-up in North America) may be seen as vulgar in another. Thus what one person experiences as the norm in communication may be associated with controversy or distaste in another person's culture.

The study of individual space (proxemics) can help us understand people's comfort zones. For example, in intimate relationships (e.g., marriage), personal space decreases, whereas other personal relationships (e.g., close acquaintanceship) often require more space. Physical space increases further in social spheres (e.g., among business associates) and further again in the public sphere (e.g., among strangers). In this way, nonverbal cues related to physical space during conversations reflect what we find acceptable—that is, our boundaries in private and public life.

Thus, during our various communication encounters, it is crucial that we consider physical space, as well as other nonverbal factors such as dress codes. We must also consider our posture and body position when meeting new people, working in intercultural settings, and delivering important and potentially sensitive messages. Other key factors include seating arrangements around a meeting table, the amount of hand gesturing we use, and the costs of speaking out of turn. Such formalities convey signs of respect or disrespect and are seen as key parts of being professional in many cultures. However, as noted earlier, they can vary greatly across cultures. In some cultures, for instance, it is considered inappropriate for men to look at women. In others, it is considered appropriate to slightly bow the head in the company of a superior in order to avoid making direct eye contact, whereas in North America direct eye contact is viewed as appropriately honest and forthright. Consequently, we must be aware both of our own communication strengths and weakness and of the diverse practices that characterize communication in intercultural settings.

Cross-Cultural Communication

In professional sport, and increasingly in high-level amateur sport as well, people come together from different cultural backgrounds to work toward achieving shared goals. As a result, sport organizations are faced with the reality that their people come with differences in how they work, how they expect work to be performed, and how they function in groups with their colleagues. Of course, this diversity includes

IN THE BOARDROOM
Communicating Confidence and Competence in Interviews

As a prospective employee, you need to make your first impression a good one. There are several ways to do so beyond the basic ability to clearly articulate answers to the questions you are asked. To really impress, you must be aware of your nonverbal communication, starting with the professional attire you select for the interview. It is also important to remember your posture, maintain good eye contact, and avoid fidgeting with your hands. It sounds simple, and it is: Your nonverbal cues can convey a strong and confident person, and these characteristics can help you secure the position you seek.

differences in communication styles and preferences. For instance, a simple laugh or smile, which conveys happiness or friendship in North America, may be interpreted differently by a person from Russia who considers it simplistic or even naive. Similarly, a handshake is a customary greeting in many parts of the world—but not all. In other examples, being punctual means something entirely different to a person in the Caribbean than it does to someone in Switzerland, and attending social activities outside of official work hours is a common way to bond in many parts of Asia but is seen as exclusionary in some other places. As these examples illustrate, appropriate and preferred methods of communication vary around the world; therefore, sport managers need to be aware and appreciative of cultural differences.

When working in an intercultural environment, keep an open mind and avoid ethnocentrism—the tendency to see things only from your own cultural perspective. A person who is ethnocentric evaluates individuals of a different race or culture according to criteria that are specific to his or her own understanding of how things

should be done (MacIntosh, Bravo, & Li, 2011). This type of behavior can result in several negative consequences, including misunderstandings, conflict, and poor performance. To communicate effectively in such settings, engage fully in listening, invite elaboration about topics with which you are not entirely familiar, and engage in reflective discussion (by summarizing the points as you understand them and asking if that is what the speaker meant).

SUMMARY

Effective communication requires a certain skill set, and exchanges between senders and receivers are subject to a variety of factors that can impede accurate understanding of the intended messages. Becoming an effective communicator does not happen overnight; it is a seemingly simple but actually complex process that requires trial and error. Communicating effectively in oral, written, and nonverbal forms is a challenging task, and most people need development in one or more of these areas in order to become a good manager.

IN THE BOARDROOM
Public Speaking: Keeping It Simple

Communicating in front of a crowd requires a certain skill set, and this is particularly true if you are addressing an audience with a different first language than yours. When you are tasked with presenting your work for any audience, it is important to clearly enunciate your words. This need is amplified in international settings, where it is also critical that you speak slowly and use fewer technical words, which can cause confusion. It is better to play it safe, use simpler words, speak slowly, and fully articulate each word. You should also attend to nonverbal forms of communication, including your attire (formal or informal), the amount of hand and head gesturing you use, and the importance of eye contact with the audience. It is always good practice to get to know the audience's behavioral norms before you take the stage. Generally, when presenting to an international audience, it is good practice to keep hand gestures to a minimum in order to avoid making the message any more complicated than it may already be due to the language barrier. Of course, there will be times when you should use your hand to signal or emphasize a key point, but it is not advisable to be particularly demonstrative in your body language.

CASE STUDY
Creating a Social Media Policy

The use of social media continues to increase on the personal, professional, and organizational levels as various social media tools make their way into households and corporate settings. It is now common for staff members to use Facebook and other platforms to set up groups for both personal and business use. This blurring of the line between the personal and the professional has created a need for managers to establish guidelines for the use of social media. These platforms can also be problematic for organizations when they give the public a window into the private lives of organizational representatives.

As a result, in recent years, many sport organizations have developed social media policies to protect themselves and their various stakeholders (e.g., athletes, sponsors). For example, the International Olympic Committee (IOC) has, on one hand, stated its support for athletes who want to post videos and pictures of their experience at the Games on their social media accounts. On the other hand, the IOC has also provided guidelines for safe posting and established repercussions for abuse of social media, including commercial uses during the Games that conflict with Olympic sponsors.

In order to communicate such policies to those who are most affected by them, sport organizations would benefit from including representatives from those stakeholder groups in the process of creating the policy. This approach can help the organization create a viable policy and communicate it effectively to key audiences. In this way, the communication becomes less unidirectional and more inclusionary, as the stakeholder representatives help ensure that the policy and its rationale are communicated to their constituents—which, in the case of the IOC, includes all athletes participating in the Games.

The IOC policy indicates that social media activity should not imply any unauthorized association of a third party with the IOC, the Olympics Games, or the Olympic movement (International Olympic Committee, 2011). For example, the policy document indicates that blogs and tweets should conform to the spirit of Olympism as laid out in the Olympic Charter and that postings should be in good taste and respectful of others; of course, many social media platforms (e.g., Snapchat) are difficult to police for such matters. The policy also asserts the sanctity of the Olympic Village and indicates that this area should be characterized by respect for the rights of each person in it. The policy allows for athletes to post photos of themselves but requires prior written consent before posting photos of others.

Case Study Questions

1. What are the benefits of creating a social media policy for a sport organization such as the IOC?
2. What role does an athlete representative play in communicating IOC policy regarding social media?
3. In your view, why does IOC policy restrict athletes' use of social media?
4. Why is the Olympic Village in particular viewed as a place of sanctity in the IOC social media policy?

A review of the process of interpersonal communication reminds us that when we deliver messages, we need to ensure that the receiver has the space and time to respond in a way that secures the intended meaning of that message. With that goal in mind, the receiver needs to be assured that asking questions and seeking clarification are critical parts of the feedback loop in an effective communication process.

Research shows that messages are constantly at risk of being misinterpreted because of the environment in which they are delivered, the potential for noise in the selected communication channel, and our own personal biases and perceptions. These types of distortion can hinder the communication process and lead to interpersonal conflict. Minimizing the causes of distortion in an organization enables more effective interpersonal and group communication. This is particularly true in today's information age, where readily available technology has revolutionized the ways in which we communicate on a daily basis. Therefore, it is vitally important for sport managers to find the most appropriate channels for communication, both internally (inward to the organization) and externally (outward to stakeholders).

DISCUSSION QUESTIONS

1. Identify five ways in which a person can demonstrate effective communication.
2. Identify some aspects of nonverbal communication that might hinder a receiver's understanding and interpretation of a message.
3. If you were to design a sport organization's media policy, what would you include in the policy to ensure professional communication, and why?
4. What are some factors that might interfere with understanding and interpretation of a message in a cross-cultural setting?

Chapter 14

Organizational Culture

Chapter Objectives

After studying this chapter, you will be able to

- identify levels of awareness of organizational culture;
- describe how culture is both tangible and intangible;
- explain the various ways in which leaders can shape, manage, and reinforce a desired culture;
- describe how management can use the concept of organizational culture as a strategic toolkit;
- discuss how organizational culture faces both inward and outward; and
- describe the difference between espoused and perceived values.

If there is one topic synonymous with organizational behavior, it is the phenomenon known as organizational culture (OC), which in turn is linked to other important topics such as leadership, diversity, and change. OC affects both individual and group work and, ultimately, influences the organization's performance. Whether you are a new entrant or have been with an organization for some time, OC influences your role, the people around you, and the attitudes and behaviors that are common in the company.

One basic way to understand organizational culture is to consider "how things are done" and what is expected of a person in the organization. Prominent scholar Edgar Schein (e.g., 1985, 1991) conceived of OC as including the artifacts, core values, beliefs, and basic assumptions in an organization that help to guide and coordinate member behavior. Schein's extensive work on OC has helped to shape management research and understanding of the concept's many influences in organizational life. His work has pointed out that OC helps people in an organization learn to solve work challenges and complex problems by adopting expected ways of behavior.

Although the concept may appear simple enough, it is layered with complexity due in part to how OC forms, how it is continuously shaped, and the dynamic forces in an organization's internal and external environments. In sport, it is common to hear about the need to change an organizational culture, but it is very difficult to do so. When people talk about OC, the term *values* (or *core values* or *key values*) is often used in describing an organization and how it functions, which may at times indicate a need for change. Indeed, values do lie at the heart of OC, and they relate closely to attitude formation and behavior. In Rokeach's (1973) seminal work on this topic, he suggested that people's attitudes and behaviors are influenced by a set of instrumental and terminal values. In this context, an individual's values are considered to constitute an enduring belief that a certain mode of conduct or end state of existence is personally or socially preferable to an opposite or converse mode of conduct or end state of existence (Rokeach, 1973). More specifically, instrumental values (e.g., intellect, ambition) were considered by Rokeach to be preferable modes of behavior that help achieve an end or terminal value (e.g., happiness, comfortable life). As you can see, then, the term *values* holds both organizational and personal meaning.

Given that organizations are run by people—and that people do not arrive at work as blank slates but already have their own values, which influence their behavior—it is important to consider how personal values can influence people's work lives. At the same time, many researchers have questioned the validity of Rokeach's (1973) work by raising concerns about how he reduced the rich range that occurs in people's values into a relatively parsimonious set. Others, such as Schwartz (1994), have produced thoughtful research on the structure of value relations and how values interact with each other and can be complementary. In any case, research consistently notes that once a value is held, whether by a person or by an organization, it is difficult to change.

Before we can discuss any type of fundamental value change in an organization's culture, we must first understand what comprises OC. In essence, a value in organizational life can help guide decision making in terms of what is the right or wrong way to go about solving a problem. A more colloquial way to think of it is provided by the expression "how things are done around here," which indicates what people expect in terms of behavior at work. We will touch more on organizational values shortly.

Another way to think about OC is by examining it in terms of what is both tangible and intangible, or observable and unobserved. OC originates in the organizational founder's thoughts and intentions (Schein, 1985), which are often conveyed in written forms—such as statements of philosophy, mission, vision, and objectives—that are easily observed. Observable cues about what is important in an organization are also provided by the ways in which leaders act (and react) on a daily basis. These observable behaviors, such as showing up to meetings on time and having an open- or closed-door policy, highlight features of the organization's culture that can help explain and predict others behaviors. Other aspects of work are less easily observed, such as stories shared, insiders' common (and colloquial) language, and the ways in which people converse or mingle in the lunchroom—all of which contribute to office lore or jokes that are understood only by members. Even the arrangement of physical space can indicate what is important in work life. Thus we see once again that while OC may appear simple on the surface, it is actually complex.

To further understand the concept of OC, it is helpful to know how it emerged in academia, the levels of awareness through which we can conceptualize the phenomenon, and the types of OC research that have been conducted in sport management and beyond.

WHERE OC RESEARCH BEGAN AND WHERE IT IS TODAY

Emerging from concepts in psychology and anthropology (c.f., Pettigrew, 1979), the concept of OC has been linked to why people behave as they do in an organizational context. Although the study of culture has strong roots in anthropology, our understanding of culture in an organizational setting has been consolidated by the merging of several bodies of literature, including that of social psychology. These literatures have also helped management science understand additional related concepts, such as person–job fit, group behaviour, person–organization fit, and various performance-related outcomes and measures.

In North America, the focus on organizational culture began in the mid-1980s, when burgeoning global competition created pressure for a more internationalized business model. In a review of OC research periods, Weber and Dacin (2011) noted two prominent waves of research that have helped develop the field.

- The first wave, which occurred in the 1980s (Weber & Dacin, 2011), focused on collective meanings; for instance, it examined and theorized processes and structures at the collective level of analysis (such as the organization). It also addressed the basic characteristics of an organizational culture and conceptualized the concept itself as being stable in organizational values and beliefs. Generally, then, this wave focused on control and structure.

- The second wave, which occurred in the late 1980s and the 1990s, discussed culture not as a regulatory force but as a phenomenon composed of various social processes. Essentially, this period of research posited increased agency in both individuals and organizations that exercised the idea of organizational culture as a pragmatic resource. For instance, management can use OC either privately (internally) or publically (externally, to inform stakeholders outside of the organization). Ultimately, this wave focused on cultural agency as a resource (i.e., toolkit, skill set, array of strategies) with an external cultural context that the leadership of the organization could exploit to create a favorable image (front-stage, public, audiences). Indeed, one way in which leaders can create a positive public image for an organization is by viewing OC as a strategic investment, particularly from an external (marketing-oriented) point of view where they can market what their company stands for or intends to represent.

Over the past 40 years, research has illuminated several key aspects of OC—for instance, values and their effects on people and on corporate image. Today, the concept of OC is particularly linked to the formation of organizational strategy through the paradigm of leadership. For example, research by Rindova, Dalpiaz, and Ravasi (2011) noted that when OC is viewed as a toolkit for management, it enables leadership to take action toward instituting change initiatives (e.g., desired identity). For example, management may seek to initiate a change in response to an identity issue, and therefore, when OC is viewed as a toolkit, a strategy of internal integration and external marketing may help the organization create a more favorable identity. This way of thinking removed the notion that OC was only an internal phenomenon and made clear that stakeholders outside of the imaginary organizational boundary can also be influenced by "how things are done" in the organization. (See work of Hatch and Schultz, 1997, for more details on how OC can affect corporate image.)

LEVELS OF AWARENESS

In the case of staging sport events, temporary organizations can ingrain important values and ways to behave in new recruits (employees and volunteers) by using the concept of OC as a means of cultural resource incorporation and identity formation (Parent & MacIntosh, 2013). More specifically, the leadership of a temporary organization can embed aspects of the desired culture by incorporating statements of vision, mission, and core values into the training documents provided to new recruits, by establishing company dress codes, and even through the use of key artifacts (e.g., pictures) that convey important messages. Thus the organization's leaders play a fundamental role in forming, reinforcing, and shaping for the new recruits the culture that they wish to create.

For instance, as described by Wry, Lounsbury, and Glynn (2011), the production of important stories of and from an organization's leadership can shape the attention and perception of various audiences and help legitimize direction at the group and organizational levels. Wry et al. note that "the meaning and labels associated with a collective identity are narrative constructions that are bound to the stories communicated by members" (p. 450). Thus stories, as well as organizational documents and formative training mechanisms, can help new entrants and groups establish identity in the organization; they can also help new recruits (and even those outside of the traditional organizational boundaries) come to know about the organization's culture.

While there are many ways to come to know an OC generally, three levels of awareness are considered important in uncovering aspects of the concept: artifacts, values and beliefs, and basic assumptions.

Artifacts

Artifacts are visible, tangible items that are readily available in any organization and signal what is considered important there (Rafaeli & Pratt, 2006); in other words, artifacts are cultural symbols in the work environment. For instance, sport organizations often display trophies, pictures of important moments, statues, numbers that have been retired, relics from the past, and other easily observable items that convey messages about what is important in the organization. Most of these symbols highlight a basic assumption in sport: Winning is important.

Since sport occurs in the public domain, especially in the professional and high-level amateur ranks, it is common to see greatness personified or recognized in the

form of retired numbers and other special tributes to important players (e.g., David Ortiz, Derek Jeter). These sport heroes and icons are associated with the concept of leadership (described in chapter 9) and hold a special place in their organization's history and in the hearts and minds of their fans. When they retire, they themselves become artifacts that indicate what is important in the organization, such as hard work, dedication, and heroism.

Artifacts also play a meaningful role in other ways. For instance, sport teams typically name captains, flag bearers, and even ambassadors. Designating a person for such a role sends a signal, both inwardly to the group and outwardly to the public, about the characteristics and qualities deemed admirable in the organization. The decision-making process behind selecting these individuals considers many factors that relate to performance on the field of play and to qualities exhibited in the locker room and in public. These designations and displays convey what management wants to propagate in terms of team values, attitudes, and behavior; ultimately, then, they help build the organizational culture and reinforce expected ways of doing things.

In enduring sport organizations, evidence of history's great leaders can be seen around the arena or field of play, sometimes in the form of statues and often in the form of celebrated moments captured in pictures and memorabilia. These artifacts tell compelling stories and illuminate important values, including, for example, teamwork, persistence, passion, and competitive spirit. In addition, other artifacts of organizational life that are easily identifiable include how people dress for work and how physical space is arranged (e.g., desks, open or closed doors). Both dress code and physical arrangement of office space can be indicative of the levels of formality expected at work and can help to reinforce what is considered to be expected ways of behavior. Another way of reinforcing what is considered important in an organization is through the use of rituals. For instance, pride in team and country are reinforced in professional sport by the singing of a national anthem prior to the game and in high-level amateur sport by the raising of a national flag to recognize the winner. When these rituals are violated in any way—for example, by taking a knee during the national anthem or keeping a hat on during the flag raising—some people feel upset and attention is drawn to the involved individuals and their motives. Due to the public nature of high-performance sport, such actions have been used to send political messages.

As you can see, the use of artifacts, the purposeful creation of space, and the uses of that space are key considerations for sport managers (Parent & MacIntosh, 2013). Indeed, the strategic and purposeful use of physical space, along with the various artifacts easily seen within the work environment, provide management with ways to help people in the organization understand how work is expected to be performed.

Values and Beliefs

It is not until a person becomes more embedded in an organization—or pays particular attention to the vision, mission, objectives, and other forms of organizational articulation—that the deeper levels of organizational culture become known. Such organizational documents commonly denote key expectations for behavior (as in an ethics code), formalized modes of communication, and other means of behavioral coordination. Thus, at this level of awareness, a person gets a better sense of the inner workings and expectations of an organization. This level focuses on values and beliefs expressed in ways that are less readily identifiable than artifacts. Schein (1985) argued that this level helps form a person's expectations of how to behave, thus allowing the person to navigate desirable versus undesirable modes.

Indeed, at the level of values, the person develops a greater awareness of what is most important in terms of behavior in the organization.

Values and beliefs, and changes in them, are also shaped by institutional pressures that emanate from the organization's external environment (Danisman, Hinings, & Slack, 2006). Consequently, we can deduce that regulatory bodies, governments, and successful competitors play an important role in understanding how organizational values evolve. For example, in the NFL and NHL in particular, recent rule changes regarding concussion protocols and contact to the player's head have stemmed in part from external concern over the value of an athlete's health and well-being. Specifically, the leaders of these leagues (Roger Goodell in the NFL and Gary Bettman in the NHL) have faced pressure from external parties, including former and current players, to make rule changes aimed at better protecting players from the physical trauma inherent in their sports. Lawsuits are still pending, but these league leaders have had to respond to the pressure to embrace player safety and health as core values of their organizations, even if their responses have arguably been made partly with an eye toward monetary and branding implications.

Research has shown that people are guided by the values and beliefs known to be reinforced by an organization's leaders (for more on this topic, see chapter 9). More specifically, the ways in which leaders go about their work, react to critical incidents, and reinforce and reward behavior send important messages about the values they hold to be important. In this sense, values are relatively stable and help people distinguish appropriate from inappropriate ways of doing things. Research has generated important findings regarding the importance of values and their influence on people's behavior (e.g., Carmeli & Tishler, 2004; Kolodinsky, Giacalone, & Jurkiewicz, 2008; Suddaby, Elsbach, Greenwood, Meyer, & Zilber, 2010). Consequently, future scholarship on the subject would be well-served to examine the influence of leadership on organizational values and the subsequent effect on members of the organization (MacIntosh & Doherty, 2005).

Basic Assumptions

The last level of organizational culture is that of basic assumptions—the unconscious and taken-for-granted beliefs (e.g., winning is important, effort is valued, teamwork is needed), habitual perceptions (e.g., the importance of practice and healthy habits), and thoughts and feelings about working in the organization (e.g., pride, historical legacy). This level sheds light on the deep, underlying reasons that people do what they do in organizational life. For the most part, these assumptions operate unconsciously and are perceived consciously only when they are violated. At this level, for instance, notions of time and space help construct the reality of work life—for instance, through the assumption that punctuality shows professionalism and care. Is it acceptable to show up late for a meeting? Can you knock on the CEO's door without a scheduled meeting? Are you allowed to take an hour-long lunch break?

Basic assumptions are informed in part by the leadership's expectations that have helped rationalize the company's existence, but they are also composed of basic modes of behavior that have developed over time and become entrenched as "how things are done" and how they are expected to be done. These values may form due to cultural norms (Hofstede, 1980), or attitudes and behaviors that have become normalized in society and in the organization; they are not openly discussed—they are just accepted. Thus people go about their activity in ways that are expected of them without questioning the behavior. As a result, change at this level is difficult to implement and slow to develop; in fact, it takes a profound, often revolutionary shift in philosophy and a fundamentally new

expectation for how to behave (for more on organizational change, see chapter 15).

Overall, these levels of OC awareness can help people come to know the organization better and go about their work with a strong understanding of desirable attitudes and behaviours. Thus, coming to know OC helps people explain their work lives, informs their decision making, guides their communication, and generally helps them fit well with the intended direction of the organization. Whether you are a sport manager, athlete, coach, trainer, or other organizational stakeholder, your performance depends in large part on understanding the organization's preferred ways of doing things—both stated and unstated.

ESPOUSED VERSUS EXPERIENCED OC

Although it is good practice to get to know the OC through the various levels of awareness, many differences can exist between what is said to be important and what is lived by people in the organization (e.g., MacIntosh & Doherty, 2005; MacIntosh & Spence, 2012). The mere fact of stating that something is important and valued in the organization does not mean that it is experienced as important by employees and volunteers (though one would certainly hope it is). For example, even though most organizations develop vision, mission, and values statements, the majority of people who work for an organization may not perceive, adopt, or agree with the sentiments advanced in these artifacts; nor may their behavior align with them. This, then, is one of the key challenges of management—to create an espoused culture (what is said to be valued) and then realize that culture's values through people's behavior (what is enacted).

In recent years, considerable scholarship has argued that leaders of organizations should engage in what is known as management by values (MBV; c.f., Dolan

& Garcia, 2002) as a way to both espouse and create authentically lived cultures. In this view, establishing a value system that is both espoused and lived (or, put another way, is *congruent*) helps an organization develop more effective and more successful operations (Hamm, MacLean, Kikulis, & Thibault, 2008). The theory holds that dissonance between what is said or espoused and what is lived or perceived makes failure more likely (Hamm et al., 2008). With this risk in mind, several authors have expressed the need to understand where gaps exist in an organizational value system (e.g., Adkins, Ravlin, & Meglino, 1996; Bell-Laroche, MacLean, Thibault, & Wolfe, 2014; Detert, Schroeder, & Mauriel, 2000: MacIntosh & Spence, 2012). For instance, Bell-Laroche at al. (2014) argued that sport managers need to begin incorporating values into the organization's strategic planning. The idea is that MBV can help leaders produce more positive organizational outcomes when values are aligned with human resource practices and adopted as part of a strategic plan (Kerwin, MacLean, & Bell-Laroche, 2014). Ultimately, the goal of MBV is to under-stand the gaps (or incongruences) in the value system, create ways to address that dissonance, and thus not only enforce but also live the important principles of the organization (MacIntosh & Spence, 2012).

INTEGRATING THE EMPLOYEE INTO THE CULTURE

When bringing on a new employee, management must focus on teaching that new person important aspects of how things are done in the organization. Doing so requires an authentic approach that reflects the organization's culture.

One of the defining features of the sport world is the high turnover of personnel (e.g., athletes, coaches, frontline staff, service staff), and each new hire brings new experiences, skill sets, and ideas about their role and about the organization itself. As a result, it can be difficult to establish a solid foundation of core values with every new entrant. Over time, however, a person's ongoing interaction and negotiation with members of the organization (e.g., veterans, coaches) through socialization

IN THE BOARDROOM
Value Checking

Do you know your organization's values? Do you think they accurately reflect what goes on in the organization? One example in professional sport can be found in the Philadelphia Eagles value of being green—not merely in the team's primary uniform color but in the practice of being energy efficient and environmentally friendly. The Eagles organization espouses the value of being green through a "Go Green" marketing campaign and has incorporated several environmental features into its daily business operations in order to ensure that the value is not merely stated to be important but is observable in and around game-day activities. For instance, the organization has established recycling initiatives, composting time of products sold (how long it takes for the product to decompose), green energy production through solar power systems and wind turbines, carbon footprint reduction, and the use of green cleaning products. These and other initiatives have been strategically employed in the management of the team and in the branding of the organization.

tactics (see chapter 8) can engender a stronger (or weaker) value system and more (or less) congruence. With these challenges in mind, the integration process should focus on teaching the new entrant long-established core values and inculcating the organization's vision and mission.

Due to the large and international talent pool in professional sport (and, to some degree, in North American college sport), talent acquisition requires leaders to appreciate background differences and understand new entrants' transition needs. Therefore, the integration process may need to include language instruction as well as training in other aspects of work life. For example, a new employee in a college athletic department may not be aware of the many terms used to ensure that the department is in compliance with NCAA regulations; this is especially true if the person has not previously worked in intercollegiate athletics. Similarly, if a minor league baseball team hires a new employee who has no previous work experience in sport but is experienced in a corporate setting (e.g., retail customer service), that employee may need to be integrated into the expectation of working long days and late nights during the season. Thus, helping a new entrant transition from prior experience to new realities is one of the key challenges faced by managers in fostering a strong understanding of cultural expectations and practices.

Another important consideration is the presence of subcultures in an organization. Subcultures develop when a subset of employees, such as the marketing department, develops its own set of values or way of doing things that differs from the dominant or desired culture of other departments or of the organization as a whole. Subcultures can develop on the basis of job functions, geographical separation of organizational units, or other characteristics such as age and gender (MacIntosh & Doherty, 2005; Martin, 1992, 2002). When a group differs in its work-related beliefs, particularly from the other groups in the

company, these differences can produce incongruences (or gaps) that may account for some sources of conflict (Martin, 1992). At the same time, some organizational theorists have argued that the notion of a shared or homogeneous organizational culture is idealistic and rarely occurs and that it is more common to find shared values and beliefs within organizational subcultures than throughout an entire organization (Martin, 2002). In such cases, group members' values and beliefs may help them develop close ties due to factors that differ from the dominant cultural values espoused at the organizational level (Martin, 2002). Although this dynamic may foster strong team or group work, it can be confusing and anxiety producing for the new entrant. Thus, during the integration process, it is important for the new entrant to meet as many people as possible across the organization so that they can understand both the general work environment as well as the specific environment for their particular unit (e.g., human resource department) and observe some of the key nuances between the organizational units.

OC SCHOLARSHIP IN SPORT

The phenomenon of organizational culture has received strong attention in sport management scholarship. In 2010, for instance, *European Sport Management Quarterly* published a special issue on sport management cultures, in which Girginov (2010) noted that the key role played by people in constantly shaping and changing organizational values requires sport managers to pay attention to the various aspects of work life that employees and the organization's leaders jointly influence. Several other papers in the special issue also stress that it is important for management to consider how organizational culture influences people and their performance. Four years later, the same journal published a special issue on value co-creation in sport management. In that issue, Woratschek, Horbel, and Popp (2014) argued that a variety of

IN THE BOARDROOM
Subcultures in Sport Events

It has been suggested that multi- and single-sport events (e.g., Pan American Games, FIFA World Cup) can produce subcultures based on job functions within the vertical and horizontal management structure of an organization staging an event (MacIntosh & Walker, 2012). In these temporary organizations, jobs are often highly specialized (e.g., promotions, finance, volunteer recruitment), thus increasing the potential for development of subcultures, which, if not managed properly, can create incongruence, conflict, and organizational inefficiency. For management, then, it is critical to establish the organization's values, vision, and mission statements sooner rather than later and to embed them in the recruitment and hiring processes for all job functions. Reinforcing these important statements early on and throughout the life cycle of the event can help managers, employees, and volunteers understand what is expected of them, which is a crucial factor in staging an effective event given that these groups must rely on each other in order to perform their work.

people play a role in producing value in the organization, including those traditionally considered outside of (or external to) it. Drawing these studies together, we can see that in the world of sport, values are propagated, reinforced, and reshaped through constant communication efforts among leaders, employees, and clients in what can be a rather complex stakeholder network influencing organizational culture.

In particular, the influence of leadership—both in helping to strengthen organizational culture and in using various methods to build values—has been a strength of OC scholarship in sport to date (e.g., Kent & Weese, 2000; MacIntosh & Doherty, 2005, 2010; Wallace & Weese, 1995; Weese, 1995). Without question, leaders play a critical role in both shaping and reinforcing organizational culture. For instance, their responses to crises or critical incidents, both internal and external, say a great deal about what is most important in the organization; these responses indicate whether leaders "walk the talk" and demonstrate commitment to upholding the organization's core values. The same is true on a more daily basis as

well; that is, organizational culture is also shaped and reinforced by what leaders pay attention to, how they behave, and what they reward or punish in day-to-day work life. For instance, do leaders reinforce the organization's values by demonstrating commitment to hiring policies, helping develop talent, and living out their stated philosophy regarding work–life balance? Do they train employees and give them opportunities to grow? The answers can tell us a great deal about what is truly valued in organizational life. Research has also found that leadership's ability to manage cultural diversity can provide OC benefits such as an increased ability to gather important information regarding resource acquisition and innovative thinking perhaps not as easily obtained in a homogeneous work setting (Doherty & Chelladurai, 1999; MacIntosh & Spence, 2012; MacIntosh, Li, & Bravo, 2011).

We know less, however, about the ways in which organizational culture is shaped, reinforced, and propagated by employees and external clients. Moreover, despite the many aspects of organizational culture that have been

CASE STUDY
The Way Things Are Done Here

One intriguing example of cultural differences in sport is provided by the soccer teams FC Barcelona (Barça) and Real Madrid. Historically, Real Madrid has recruited and retained many international players and coaches with very different backgrounds and languages. Real Madrid, despite having its fair share of Spanish nationals on the roster, has been more prone to the *galácticos* policy of recruiting superstars from around the world. Although Barça also has international stars (e.g., Lionel Messi, Luis Suárez), Real Madrid has tended to be more internationally diverse in its athletic and coaching talent, including current coach Zinedine Zidane.

In contrast, FC Barcelona has maintained a strong focus on its local community. In fact, at the core of its operations, the club has been a guardian of the Catalonian identity, even going so far as to strategically develop local talent from a young age. The club has also been vocal in expressing belief in the importance of maintaining Catalonian heritage and democratic law (e.g., the 2017 independence referendum), supporting local citizens in their political endeavors in part by playing a game with an empty stadium due to their displeasure with league organizers (La Liga) whom did not agree that a game should be canceled. Indeed, FC Barcelona has taken pride in creating an organization that is purposefully focused on the importance of local culture through education programs and celebrating the Catalonian heritage.

What is most interesting about the FC Barcelona strategy is that the organization's values have been taught to young and older players alike through instruction and practice going back to the early days of La Masia (the club's training facility). As part of this effort, the club focuses on the intellectual, personal, and social development of its younger sportspeople. As noted in chapter 8, instilling specific behavioral expectations, particularly during the encounter phase, is a method by which organizational leaders can ensure clarity and help new entrants come to know the environment in which they are operating.

Teams such as Barça and Madrid are giant global brands. As a result, their particular ways of doing things resonate outwardly into the global marketplace, thus reflecting their core values around the world.

Case Study Questions

1. In terms of organizational culture, what aspects are important for sport managers to consider teaching a new internationally acquired talent (player or coach)?
2. Identify some management tactics for building an organizational value system that is both strongly espoused and authentically experienced.
3. In what ways might an organization's culture (e.g., values, beliefs) resonate outwardly into the global marketplace?

investigated—including how it forms, who is responsible for shaping it and by what methods, how it influences people and performance, and where gaps exist in cultural values—the research has not yet delved deeply into how to change the culture for the greater good of the organization and its people.

SUMMARY

Organizational culture is one of the more important and more complex of the various phenomena that influence an organization and its management. The concept has strong links to other important topics, including leadership, which is integral to the functioning of every organization. Given that the world of sport management is so diverse, organizational management in both enduring and temporary organizations can benefit from understanding the levels of awareness of OC and learning how to reinforce (and even reimagine) the values and beliefs that they wish to instill in employees and volunteers.

Sport is a highly consumed product and a popular arena of business that engages many stakeholders (e.g., media, fans, other businesses). As we seek to understand these aspects of sport, OC not only helps explain and predict how work is performed internally but sheds light on how organizations develop their external images. More specifically, research has demonstrated that OC is not simply an internal phenomenon that influences employee attitudes and behaviors; to the contrary, its messaging extends beyond the imaginary boundary of the organization and into the marketplace.

In the coming years, OC research may be influenced by the emergence of value co-creation as an important area of management consideration. For example, OC can be used as a strategic tool to help explain an organization's work and form its image. Hence, it is possible that involving consumers in propagating what is most important to the organization may reinforce—or change—certain deeply held values and beliefs. Can external stakeholders influence an organization's core values, and if so how? Thus the coming research on OC and value co-creation may produce new strategies for sport managers to consider. In any case, one thing is certain: The phenomenon of OC and its importance to the people of sport organizations are not going away.

DISCUSSION QUESTIONS

1. Identify the three layers of organizational culture.
2. What is the difference between espoused and experienced organizational culture?
3. In what ways can leadership demonstrate the values that are important to an organizational culture?
4. If you consider organizational culture as a toolkit, what strategies might management use to ensure that the organization's values and beliefs are well understood?
5. How might a person go about changing the culture of an organization?

Chapter 15

Organizational Change

Chapter Objectives

After studying this chapter, you will be able to

- define organizational change and explain why it happens in sport organizations,
- describe types of change that are common in sport organizations,
- provide reasons that people commonly resist change,
- explain Lewin's and Greiner's change models,
- identify areas in current sport practices where change is needed, and
- discuss methods and best practices that management can use to help people deal with organizational change.

As in life, the one constant in sport organizations is change. It comes in many forms, from the daily unexpected and small changes to the large and perhaps unanticipated changes that can send shock waves through an organization. Small or large, these changes mean that people who work in organizational settings are continuously influenced by a shifting environment.

As a topic of investigation, organizational change is typically associated not with day-to-day variations in business operations but with planned strategic changes that organizations implement in order to gain or retain a competitive advantage (Slack & Parent, 2006). Even so, employees and other stakeholders can also be affected by rumors of change; actual changes in work expectations; and new or altered roles or rules. Depending on how a change is communicated and managed, people may embrace it, develop with it, or resist it. Therefore, communicating the

change, and the reasoning for it, is one of the most important aspects of effectively managing it.

As noted by Slack and Parent (2006), various perspectives are available for thinking about the topic of organizational change. One of the more dominant approaches in the realm of sport management is institutional theory, which posits that organizations tend to acquire and adopt similar characteristics in order to obtain legitimacy and become accepted in the industry of which the organization is part (DiMaggio & Powell, 1983; W.R. Scott, 2001). This theory holds that organizations adopt resilient aspects of the social structure—such as rules, regulations, and norms—that have become the established way in which things get done.

In a review of institutional theory and sport management research, Washington and Patterson (2011) highlighted the need to further examine the concept of institutional change in sport. They noted the shift in dominant view from organizations as stable to organizations of change in which people possess power and influence with which to enable change. Research has also discussed the notion of institutional entrepreneurship, which may help explain how individuals act agentically to shape their environments (e.g., Dowling & Smith, 2016; Edwards, Mason & Washington, 2009). For instance, Lawrence and Suddaby (2006) noted that stakeholders can bring about various types of change in an organization that create new opportunities or disrupt the status quo. These lines of research share a common notion that people possess various types of power in their organizations or institutional fields, which (along with external forces in the environment) can galvanize efforts to make change a reality.

Even a cursory review of the academic literature points up the importance of change in both general management and sport management. Anecdotally, it is evident that change is a regular occurrence in sport generally and in sport organizations, and the topic of organizational change has been linked to both planned strategy and unplanned or uncontrollable events. Regardless of whether change is planned or unplanned, it is critical for management scholars to understand how people react to and are influenced by the reality of change.

Instilling substantial change in an organization can be a long and challenging process. Furthermore, although certain types of change can be simple (e.g., altering a physical layout or instituting a new dress code), even these changes can influence an organization's culture (see chapter 14). Revolutionary change can be particularly hard to come by, especially for older, well-established organizations in which the shared values and belief system are already instilled and perceived.

Sport organizations typically look at player and coach personnel as movable and changeable parts in a larger system for producing wins on the field as well as business success. This is particularly true in the realm of professional sport but also occurs in high-level amateur sport (Amis, Slack, & Hinings, 2004). For example, when the board of directors of a national sporting body decides that it is time for a change in the position of president, that change in leadership can produce anxiety among employees, who may fear for the well-being of the organization or for their own continued employment. Typically, an extended search would be conducted for

IN THE BOARDROOM
Personnel Changes and Team-Building Strategies

One of the realities for athletes in professional sport is that team owners view them as commodities; thus players are often traded, placed on waivers, or cut. When new players become part of the team environment, it is good management practice for coaches to engage in team-building activities, both yearly and in-season. During these exercises, coaches should encourage feedback, discuss strategies, and provide opportunities for players to reflect and tell stories in order to bond new players into the team and clearly articulate the team's values and expectations. Many teams—for example, the Toronto Maple Leafs—conduct preseason and training camp activities for athletes and coaches that involve some form of physical activity and social exchange (e.g., paintball, ropes course).

the new person, but, depending on the urgency of the need, the board may act quickly. In the case of a professional sport team, we often see changes in the role of general manager, and, here again, the length of time required to find a good fit for the organization may vary.

The effects on the employee base depend largely on how the need for the change is communicated by top leadership and on the time frame in which the change must take place. It behooves the leadership to provide a clearly articulated rationale for the change and, if possible, to talk about the influence of the time frame. The need to fill a position in a "timely fashion" (whether that means in days, weeks, or even months) is a critical consideration when undertaking planned and even unplanned change initiatives involving personnel. Sometimes, a short-term replacement is immediately necessary (as in the case of finding service staff to care for customers); in other cases, personnel changes are less urgent and management has more time to recruit and hire the appropriate person for the job.

ORGANIZATIONAL CHANGE IN SPORT

In today's sporting environment, change may occur at any time (e.g., pre-, mid-, or postseason) and for any of a myriad of reasons. For instance, it may occur because of a person's needs and wants, political or economic structures that elicit (or force) organizational change and adaptation, or the ongoing need to keep up with the competition and ensure that the organization's products or services are the best they can be. There are also many ways in which organizational change can occur in sport, as well as many possible consequences of both the change itself and the process by which it occurs.

Especially among professional sport teams, it is very common from year to year, and even during a season, to see many human changes in the form of new personnel, either to replace a person who has been fired (e.g., a coach) or a player who has been injured, demoted, or traded. These types of personnel changes alter the composition of the team and create new task roles for administrators, teammates, and coaching staff as they help the new personnel adapt. Thus, perhaps unlike any other industry, sport sees change as a common factor in the typical yearly and seasonal planning cycle. Consider, for example, the amount of turnover in fitness industry personnel (MacIntosh & Doherty, 2010). The service sector of the sport industry tends to suffer from high rates of turnover because of seasonal issues, and much of the work that is required is done by part-time employees. Often, this type of work is poorly compensated and offers little challenge to workers in terms of using their full skills and aptitudes; it is also characterized by relatively low autonomy and is often formalized (e.g., written rules) in regard to the expectations of the work itself.

Moreover, change in the ranks of customer service staff, personal trainers, or sales staff in a fitness industry setting requires management to rethink its business cycles. For example, many of the jobs are part-time, non-career-based positions that are typically filled by students. Thus management must plan its business cycle to recruit, hire, and train staff based on seasonal predictions of turnover; this is planned organizational change. In addition, due to the high turnover, human resource management is faced with the difficult and important task of ensuring that the practices of recruiting, hiring, and training are continuously monitored and upgraded. Management must articulate to employees the need for this ongoing change and the means by which the organization goes about filling spots (based on, for example, educational background); of course, it must also assist in the transition of job-related tasks for those who are directly influenced.

Cruickshank, Collins, and Minten (2015) posited that in order for planned change to be successful in sport, management must align the perceptions of internal and external stakeholders. In many ways, this idea is similar to that of decreasing levels of incongruence between leadership and the employee base in an organization's value system (see chapter 14). In both professional sport and high-level amateur sport—where performance and outcomes are measured primarily in terms of wins and podium appearances—planned organizational change often comes in the form of hiring a new coach, which in turn may entail a central change in strategy that influences, players, employees, and other organizational stakeholders.

Organizations in the sport industry continuously deal with change due to factors such as technological innovations (e.g., in-game hotspots within venues, increased presence on social media, online streaming), government funding and regulations (e.g., support for hosting sport events, athlete assistance funding), and competition in the marketplace. Because a sport organization's external environment is constantly changing, the organization must recognize and adapt to these shifts in order to remain effective and thrive. Consider for a moment the various forces of change that can occur in business—for instance, new labor laws, continued downsizing or rightsizing trends, and the globalization of sport brands. In order to succeed in the midst of such changes, organizations must take steps to address the new conditions and embrace the changes.

For management, this ongoing need to adapt requires an appreciation of local, regional, national, and even international changes. Hence, it is good practice for management to monitor the external environment and report on relevant changes (whether occurring or impending) that could alter the organization's situation and therefore the strategies needed. For instance, Canada is the site of social pressures to find ways to increase people's physical activity levels across the age spectrum, including ways to help people maintain sport participation in the long term (e.g., from youth soccer programs into adult soccer) (J. Legg, Snelgrove, & Wood, 2016). As noted by J. Legg et al. (2016), such situations sometimes call for a radical change in how sport is organized in order to address larger social goals. Implications for organizations may include deciding how to communicate the change to stakeholders—for instance, determining the role of the board of directors in describing the need for it—and ensuring the needed capacity within the organization to implement it.

Internal Change

Internal changes are common in sport and involve actions such as succession planning, promoting from within, and bringing in an assistant coach who is already familiar with the team's system of play. The person who comes into a role through such a change is familiar with the inner working environment, rules, regulations, and culture and therefore needs less time to adapt. This type of change is more common during the season and in high-business times. Internal changes can also result from a shift in corporate objectives or from a person resigning, getting sick, or taking a leave.

These influencers on work life can produce change in organizational structural pieces, such as the composition of work groups, which can alter the nature of work for people in those groups, particularly if the change is unexpected. For example, Golden State Warriors head coach Steve Kerr unexpectedly missed several months during the 2015-2016 season due to complications from back surgery. At the same time, such changes can create opportunities for others to fill the resulting void. As for the organization as a whole, it is typically left to fill the void quickly. As a result, the decision is often made to fill it with an internal resource; the Warriors, for instance, turned to assistant coach Luke Walton. In other cases, however, the change brings in someone entirely new, from outside of the organization. The rationale here is that the organization wants to find a person who possesses not only a strong skill set and relevant knowledge of the sport but also a new vision. When making an external hire, most sport organizations wait until the playing season is over. Whatever approach is preferred, the competitive, high-performance nature of sport means that personnel changes are likely whenever an organization's performance expectations go unmet.

Pressure to win is not, however, the only factor that prompts change in sport organizations; in fact, many other types of external pressures can prompt a change. For instance, when Ottawa Senators owner Eugene Melnyk wanted a new venue closer to the downtown core of the city, he appointed Tom Anselmi as president and CEO because of Anselmi's experience in negotiating and building sport venues (e.g., the Air Canada Centre in Toronto) in his work with Maple Leaf Sports and Entertainment. Installing Anselmi in place of the previous president, Cyril Leeder, constituted a rather profound change in the organization's leadership core. Many employees and customers were upset by the change, but others came to understand the rationale despite not necessarily favoring the change when it was first announced.

Another example involves the concussion lawsuits filed against the NFL and NHL due to brain trauma experienced by players. These collective actions from former and current players have helped create a movement in which many stakeholders are galvanized by a heightened sense of the importance of player health and safety. These external pressures for change are forcing the leagues and their leaders (e.g., management, board of directors) to engage in dialogue about ways to address the problem for players and control the business implications

of the controversy. In response, some teams are creating positions to be filled by people who are knowledgeable about the prevention and treatment of head trauma. As these examples show, an organization's external environment can produce many kinds of calls to action for organizational change.

Why Change Is Common

Change can happen for many reasons, including expectations from oneself and others to meet a certain level of performance according to various measurable indicators. When goals and objectives are specific, measurable, and assigned to someone, it is easier to describe the needed changes when expectations go unmet. This approach is used often in the world of sport due to the focus on improvement standards, win-loss records, and the desire to perform at the top of one's class or level. When such expectations are not fulfilled, change is viewed as necessary. Whether that change is planned strategically by the organization's management or is unplanned (e.g., someone falls ill, dies, or quits), employees may be influenced both directly and indirectly through structural or job-related factors. For instance, change can result in a new reporting structure, new functions within a work unit, new responsibilities, new communication procedures, and new or revised policies.

Resistance to Change

External forces such as globalization, workplace diversity, and technological evolutions can produce both planned and unplanned changes. Either way, it is likely that people will not all conform entirely to the change. In fact, it is not uncommon for people to resist change, and this is especially true among employees who are deeply affected by a change but have little or no say regarding it.

Employees and other stakeholders may resist a change for many reasons, including lack of motivation regarding the change, inability to cope with it, and misunderstanding of the need for it. Stakeholders often worry that change will cost them time, money, and effort while providing little payoff or return for their investment (Slack & Parent, 2006). Employees may also resist change because of desire to save face, fear of the unknown, unhappiness with the breaking of routines, or changes to personnel (McShane & Steen, 2012).

The good news is that resistance to change can be effectively managed through stakeholder education, employee communication, and inclusion of stakeholders in the change process (Slack & Parent, 2006). When employees lack motivation regarding a change, the change process is hindered by difficulty in obtaining the employees' commitment to it (McShane & Steen, 2012). In such cases, leadership must determine whether employees' resistance derives from lack of skill or inability to adapt to the change. For instance, employees may feel ill equipped to take on more responsibility in the job or may feel that the change creates uncomfortable role ambiguity. In response, management must not only communicate the need for the change but also demonstrate consideration for the people who may be directly affected by taking into account their needs and wants related to the change. For example, if a supervisor decides to leave for a new opportunity, the assistant supervisor may be asked to step into the higher role, either temporarily or permanently. This person may require some form of training, certification, or mentorship from a senior staffer in order to work through the transition period.

As noted by Lawrence (2008), people also tend to resist discipline and domination. Moreover, in his work on power and the role of those affected by change, Lawrence considers enclosure and surveillance as inward-looking forces of discipline involving routine practices and structures that influence employees. He argues that resistance is a neglected area of research and that most studies focus on the homogeneity of organizational responses to institutional pressures. There is, however, a body of literature in sport management that addresses the various forces at work (e.g., government rules), as well as the people who are influenced when change is enacted (e.g., O'Brien & Slack, 2003; Gammelsæter, 2010; Skirstad & Chelladurai, 2011). These works consider a variety of stakeholders in the change process—those who can provide input, those who are affected in various ways, and those who

IN THE BOARDROOM
Managing Employee Resistance

Though it is not easy to deal with resistance to change, there are some methods that management can consider in order to prevent, minimize, or alleviate dissonance. For instance, while changes are still being planned, it is good practice to discuss them with the people who will be most affected—for example, in one-on-one or group meetings—and provide a clear rationale. In addition, if possible, including employees in the change process itself can empower them by giving them a sense of voice. Consider, for example, succession planning in the case of a retiring leader. Enabling employees to provide their viewpoints about desirable leadership characteristics for the new hire can engender good will and ease the transition. Providing employees with a rationale for change and a sense of voice can make it easier for them to understand the need for, and even embrace, the new direction.

resist (and why they do so). These concerns need to be considered by management.

Other reasons for which people may resist change include poor communication from management and unilateral decision making that does not involve the people who will be affected by the change. This latter reason may not apply to organizations that are open to training employees and providing opportunities to enhance a person's abilities and skills.

LEWIN'S MODELS: CHANGE MANAGEMENT AND FORCE FIELD ANALYSIS

According to many models, organizational change usually occurs in distinct stages (Slack & Parent, 2006). Kurt Lewin, a German American psychologist, was a pioneer in the field of organizational change models and one of the first to consider the idea of enacting planned change. Lewin's change management model (1958; see figure 15.1), which dates back to the 1950s, is still applicable to modern organizations undergoing change and remains a commonly referenced source.

Lewin's (1958) model consists of three stages: unfreezing, moving, and refreezing. An organization can unfreeze by determining what needs to change; for example, a sport organization might decide that it can be more fiscally responsible by moving toward a virtual-office model, thereby reducing its office rental costs.

Typically, the catalyst for change derives from feelings of dissatisfaction or frustration with the current state of things. The unfreezing stage requires that people discard old ideas and behaviors in favor of the proposed changes; thus it shakes up the status quo. During this stage, upper management should provide guidance and support for the change and establish the underlying reasons for which the change is needed; in the previous example, if the sport organization reduces its rental cost, it can use the savings to better serve its membership base.

An organization enters the moving (or changing) stage when it is ready to take specific actions to change organizational structures. In this stage, attitudes, values, and behaviors are subject to change. Ideally, people who are influenced by the change understand the need for it and accept its effect on their role in the organization. For instance, in the example of the sport organization moving toward a virtual-office model, the change means that some work tasks will have to be completed outside of the traditional office environment. They key here is to mobilize employees to embrace the change through effective communication.

Once the change has occurred, the organization refreezes in order to sustain the change. In this stage, new attitudes, values, and behaviors are integrated, and the new way of doing things is stabilized; thus a new status quo is established. As we discussed in chapter 14, it is very

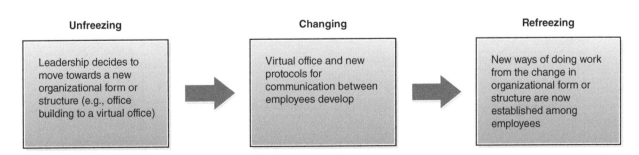

Figure 15.1   Lewin's change management model.

difficult to achieve a fundamental change in deeply held values and beliefs. Though it may be simple (though not always cheap) to change artifacts, the essence or deeper levels of the organization and its culture present a bigger challenge, and efforts to enact change at these levels are more difficult (MacIntosh & Doherty, 2005). Thus changes of this magnitude require much planning and a strategy that is both well thought out and well communicated.

In order to understand the nature of resistance and conformity to change, it is helpful to consider Lewin's (1958) force field analysis model (see figure 15.2). This model posits two sets of forces that work, respectively, for and against change. One set, made up of driving forces, pushes the organization to make changes (e.g., new rules regarding player contact, new protocols for player safety), whereas the other set, made up of restraining forces, resists change and tends to block its progression (e.g., by invoking the centrality of tackling, aggression, and toughness in football).

In recent years, for example, player safety has been at the forefront of league and player relations, particularly in the NFL and the NHL. In these cases, the driving forces of change have included the prevalence of concussion and head trauma, bouts of drug addiction for pain management, and severe depression suffered by players in both leagues. Perhaps

the strongest driving force, however, has come from player suicides, including those of former NHL enforcers Derek Boogaard and Wade Belak and former hard-hitting NFL stars Junior Seau and Andre Waters.

For the leagues and their players, maintaining the status quo and going about business as usual was no longer an option in the face of deaths attributed to the violence inherent in these sports. Therefore, the leagues had to unfreeze; it was time for them to break through the restraining forces of the status quo. Specifically, the leagues had to move, in terms of their values related to violence and injury, and adapt to the reality of the external demands coming from fans, players, and the media. They needed to act in the interest of players' health, safety, and well-being, which meant that rules and norms of the game had to change—for instance, through the "instigator penalty" (aimed at reducing fights), rules against "head shots," and the institution of concussion protocols. At the same time, however, restraining forces continue to support the status quo, including people who advocate for retaining the old rules and the deeply ingrained notion that overcoming supposedly short-term pain and injury outweighs long-term health consequences. These restraining forces generate resistance to implementing the new rules and protocols when, for

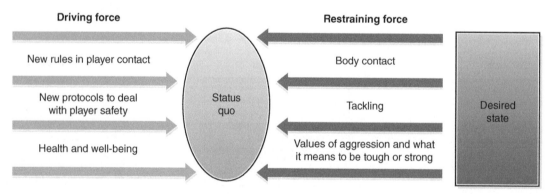

Figure 15.2 Lewin's force field analysis model.

example, players violate body-contact rules by delivering head shots.

As of now, we are seeing a reduction in fighting across the NHL, but the shift in values, attitudes, and behaviors related to violence has not eradicated fighting from the sport. The same is true for head shots in both the NHL and the NFL, where some players in each league continue to violate the rules. Consequently, the need remains for both leagues, as well as the players, coaches, and officials, to continue acting as driving forces for desired changes. To put it in terms of Lewin's (1958) change management model (figure 15.1), the new leaguewide rules and behavioral changes are unfinished because the organizations have yet to refreeze in support of the new way of doing things. Although evidence does show new attitudes and behaviors forming, a great deal of work remains to be done in order to ensure that these sports become and stay as safe as possible for the players.

GREINER'S PATTERNS OF ORGANIZATIONAL CHANGE

Similar to Lewin's (1958) change management model, Greiner's (1967) patterns of organizational change model posits that change occurs in stages. However, unlike the relatively simplistic notions of unfreezing, moving, and refreezing, Greiner's conception suggests a six-stage pattern of organizational change.

1. Pressure and arousal
2. Intervention and reorientation
3. Diagnosis and recognition
4. Invention and commitment
5. Experimentation and search
6. Reinforcement and acceptance

Greiner's model fills some gaps in Lewin's (1958) approach. For instance, the diagnosis and recognition stage (which involves diagnosis of problem areas and the recognition of a problem by the leaders and managers that follows) demonstrates that despite a person's willingness to change, problem areas may arise that can hinder and even stop change from occurring. For example, poor delegation or communication regarding a new assignment from the leadership can hinder an employee from doing work that would support the desired change. In another example, unforeseen consequences of power redistribution when a new entrant joins the organization can cause job conflict (see chapter 12). Greiner's model also accounts for the presence of various pressures from different stakeholders (internal and external), which may alter the rate of change taking place and possibly even the change itself from happening. In addition, the model acknowledges that solutions may not be known at the start of the change process and may require creativity and innovation along the way. Ultimately, Greiner's work portrays a more complex and dynamic change process than that of Lewin's.

At the same time, as with most models of organizational behavior, Greiner's work has its own shortcomings. For instance, it does not adequately address the periodic shifts and stages when change does (or does not) take place. In reality, organizational change initiatives are not neat and tidy, moving directly from one phase to the next; instead, they are often characterized by starts, pauses, restarts, deviations, and the like. In addition, Greiner's model fails to consider the different types of attitudes and behaviors that change agents may exhibit throughout the change process, as well as their influence on whether change happens at all. Still, the Greiner model, like Lewin's model, provides management with an account of moving through a planned change while noting that turbulence will occur on the way to the desired end state— that is, the establishment of effective and accepted new practices.

Another approach to organizational change, known as the contextualist approach (Pettigrew, 1987), argues that implementing change is a long-term endeavor primarily because of three factors:

1. Context—both outer (involving elements external to the organization) and inner (involving organizational elements such as structure and culture)
2. Content (e.g., technology, human resources)
3. Process (e.g., actions, reactions, and interactions)

The premise here is that the context, content, and process of change operate dynamically and that any substantial organizational change will take time to initiate and complete. In fact, as noted by Pettigrew, transformational (substantive) change may even challenge an organization's dominant ideology and culture. If so, it can upset interpersonal relationships among the people who make up the workforce and lead to conflict and dissent; the challenges of undertaking change at the deeper levels of organizational meaning are addressed further in chapter 14.

SPORT MANAGEMENT RESEARCH ON ORGANIZATIONAL CHANGE

The sport industry is rife with research opportunities to examine concepts and theories of organizational change. In fact, there is already a solid body of research on organizational change in sport management, including Slack and Hinings' (1992) work addressing the importance of understanding the overall change process for management; Greenwood and Hinings' (1988, 1993) discussion of archetypes, tracks, and strategic choice; and Kikulis, Slack, and Hinings' (1995) research regarding change in decision making in National Sport Organizations (NSOs). Taken as a whole, research in the early 1990s focused on understanding the various influencers of change and the responses of organizations in dealing with change as a reality of being competitive in the sport industry

(e.g., Horch, 1994; Kikulis, 2000; Theodoraki & Henry, 1994; Thibault, Slack, & Hinings, 1991, 1993).

With regard to personnel, we know that organizational change in sport often involves coaches and players (Frontiera, 2010). In fact, personnel changes occur on a fairly consistent basis on professional and amateur sport teams and in administrative teams in the sport industry. In the realm of professional sport, for instance, team owners hold the power to enact changes not only in player and coach personnel but also in the administrative leadership (e.g., president, general manager) depending on where they want to go as an organization, either philosophically or financially.

In regard to coaching changes in professional sport, Soebbing, Wicker, and Weimar (2015) noted that it can take upwards of two months to identify any positive effects from a change in leadership. Moreover, they argued that a new leader needs time in which to handle change-related consequences before any performance improvements can be demonstrated. Therefore, given that most coaching changes result from unmet performance expectations, a new coach must be given time to instill needed changes and manage expectations realistically. For instance, in professional sport, if a coach is fired midseason, top leadership often hires an "interim coach," who, depending on the team's success during the rest of the year, may (or may not) become the new coach.

Given that most change initiatives involve undertaking a process to become different or better at something, sport organizations act as a microcosm for some of the larger and more prominent issues in society. Consider for a moment the composition (or makeup) of the employee base—in particular, top leadership—in sport organizations. Sport management research has highlighted inequality in regard to diversity (e.g., gender; see Cunningham, 2015) and one notable example of an organization that is actively trying to lead a change toward more equality is the

International Paralympic Committee (IPC). The IPC has created a special commission to reduce gender inequality and developed a summit to promote women's leadership and ensure that people do not merely acknowledge but truly understand the importance of diversity in the workplace for a sport organization (Le Clair, 2011; D. Legg, Fay, Hums, & Wolfe, 2009; Misener & Darcy, 2014). These IPC works shine a light on changes that need to be made not only in the Paralympic movement but also in sport organizations overall.

Although we can look back on periods in sport where revolutionary change has been made in regard to inequality—for instance, Jackie Robinson's breaking the color barrier in Major League Baseball—it is also important to recognize the gradual changes, such as the ongoing development of parasport, that help shift the ground in both professional and amateur sport toward eliminating barriers and stereotypes. Despite these advancements, however, there remains much room for improvement in providing equal opportunity for all. Indeed, many players in MLB and other sports at all levels still experience racism (e.g., racial slurs) originating from both fans and other players. The reality is that sport organizations and leagues are far from perfect, and change is both wanted and needed for many reasons. Depending on the content and context of change, various parts of an organization can undertake initiatives that may include reorganization of leadership and management roles as well as communication campaigns to highlight new policies.

As the research in sport management has shown, sport organizations have been and remain in a constant state of flux. Therefore, the leadership of a sport organization must remain attentive to the external environment in order to stay relevant and effective (Wagstaff, Gilmore, & Thelwell, 2016) while also attending to the internal organizational environment and, in particular, ensuring that staff understand the need for change and are ready to act as driving forces for it. To embrace change, management must first identify the organization's current state—what it is lacking—and what approaches are needed for improvement. Significant changes are accepted only if it is proven to those who are affected that the present way of doing things is more painful than the pain that accompanies transition. Thus the pain of the present is the prime impetus for movement into the future.

SUMMARY

Change is a common phenomenon in any sport organization, and—whether minor or major, evolutionary or revolutionary—it affects people in the organization and beyond. Regardless of the magnitude of the change and whether it is planned or unexpected, people respond in accordance with their beliefs and abilities by either resisting the change or helping to promote it. Lewin's idea that an organization "unfreezes" in order to change the status quo is appealing in its simplicity, but we know from research that change is not linear, that it can take time, and that many people can be affected by it (Pettigrew, 1987).

Sport organizations constantly undergo changes due to demands emanating both internally (from within the organization) and externally (from the environment in which organization operates). There is no shortage of reasons for change in sport organizations; examples range from athlete drug dependency to illness to social inequality and beyond. For management, then, the change process hinges on understanding the need for change and determining how best to communicate that rationale to organizational stakeholders.

Even in the best change process, employee resistance is simply a fact that management has to deal with. This reality requires management to have both a plan A and a plan B. The process of change itself can in fact be of benefit to the person who

Changes in Top Leadership

Planned organizational change can take many forms. For instance, an organization's board of directors may decide to hire a new top-level leader, and this type of decision can be stressful for the organization's personnel. Such high-level changes have occurred in the national governing body of university sport in Canada, which is known as U Sports (formerly CIS). In recent years, the organization has not only rebranded itself with its new name—which in itself constitutes a major shift in marketing strategy—but also experienced a major change in top leadership. For employees, a change in top management can be especially challenging, because it requires them to learn about the new individual, his or her leadership style, and the new vision that will direct the organization. In addition, it often requires employees to learn new patterns of behavior, such as the new leader's preferences for communication, and perhaps new work roles as well.

In many cases, leadership changes of this magnitude are implemented because the board of directors wants the organization to shift its operations or vision, produce new or better outcomes, or perhaps alter the very structure of the organization or the composition of the employee base. Such changes ultimately challenge the organization's work dynamics as people learn new ways of doing their jobs, take on new roles and responsibilities, and form new groups to get work done. Some people will embrace the changes and become motivated and excited, whereas others may see the changes as unnecessary or upsetting and choose to act as a restraining force resisting the change.

For U Sports in Canada, finding a new leader and settling that person into the top leadership role was a crucial step toward instilling desired and strategic change for the intercollegiate sport system. Even though the impetus for the change was a desire for a new vision and direction, the organization gains a measure of stability if the new leader is able to remain in the job and lead the intended change.

Case Study Questions

1. What role can the board of directors play in helping people understand the leadership change?
2. What reasons might there be for an employee to resist a change in leadership?
3. Given the recent leadership and branding changes at U Sports, where does the organization now stand in terms of Greiner's patterns of organizational change model?

may be resisting at first, particularly if the change is well thought out and not overly rigid in its implementation strategy. Will the employee end up being a comrade or a combatant in the change process? It is the responsibility of the organization's leaders to understand and appreciate the various forces of change and the influence that their decision making and communication can exert on the people in the organization. At the same time, it is the responsibility of employees to raise any questions or concerns about the change through dialogue with management. After all, employees will play a major role in the success of the coming change for the organization.

DISCUSSION QUESTIONS

1. Identify a current or recent example of change in a sport organization with which you are familiar. Is it an internal or external change? According to Lewin's model, at what stage does it stand now?

2. Give an example of an external force that pressures sport organizations to undertake change initiatives.

3. Why do people resist change, and how can management help them overcome their resistance?

4. If you were a manager, in what general ways would you go about communicating intended changes with your employee base, and why?

REFERENCES

Chapter 1

Barney, J.B. (1991). Firm resources and sustained competitive advantage. *Journal of Management, 17*, 99-120.

Chappelet, J., & Bayle, E. (2005). *Strategic and performance management of Olympic sport organisations.* Champaign, IL: Human Kinetics.

Chelladurai, P. (2014). *Managing organizations for sport and physical activity: A systems perspective* (4th ed.). Scottsdale, AZ: Holcomb Hathaway.

Halbwirth, S., & Toohey, K. (2001). The Olympic Games and knowledge management: A case study of the Sydney Organising Committee of the Olympic Games. *European Sport Management Quarterly, 1*(2), 91-111.

Heisig, P. (2009). Harmonisation of knowledge management: Comparing 160 KM frameworks around the globe. *Journal of Knowledge Management, 13*(4), 4-31.

MacIntosh, E., & Parent, M. (2017). Athlete satisfaction with a major multi-sport event: The importance of social and cultural aspects. *International Journal of Event and Festival Management, 8*(2), 136-150.

Mintzberg, H. (1994). *The rise and fall of strategic planning.* New York, NY: Prentice Hall.

Mullin, B.J., Hardy, S., & Sutton, W. (2014). *Sport marketing* (4th ed.). Champaign, IL: Human Kinetics.

Nelson, D.L., Quick, J.C., Armstrong, A., & Condie, J. (2015). *ORGB* (2nd Canadian ed.). Toronto, Canada: Nelson Education.

Nonaka, I., & Takeuchi, H. (1995). *The knowledge-creating company.* New York, NY: Oxford. University Press.

North American Society for Sport Management. (n.d.). Purpose & history. www.nassm.org/NASSM/Purpose

O'Boyle, I. (2017). Strategic management in non-profit sport. In T. Bradbury & I. O'Boyle (Eds.), *Understanding sport management: International perspectives* (pp.116-129). London, UK: Routledge.

O'Reilly, N., & Knight, P. (2007). Knowledge management best practices in national sport organisations. *International Journal of Sport Management and Marketing, 2*(3), 264-280.

Parent, M.M., MacDonald, D., & Goulet, G. (2013). The theory and practice of knowledge management and transfer: The case of the Olympic Games. *Sport Management Review, 17*, 205-218.

Szymanski, M., & Wolfe, R.A. (2017). Strategic management. In R. Hoye & M.M. Parent (Eds.), *The Sage handbook of sport management* (pp.24-38). Thousand Oaks, CA: SAGE.

Thibault, L., Kihl, L., & Babiak, K. (2010). Democratization and governance in international sport: Addressing issues with athlete involvement in organizational policy. *International Journal of Sport Policy, 2*(3), 275-302.

Chapter 2

Ackers, Silfer, Cafone, and Hemeon et al. v. University of Iowa. (2015). [Civil rights complaint filed with the U.S. Department of Education, Office for Civil Rights]. www.espn.com/pdf/2015/0204/espnw_complaintofstudentathletes.pdf

Acosta, V., & Carpenter, R. (2014). *A longitudinal, national study: Thirty-seven year update.* www.acostacarpenter.org

Banaji, M.R., & Greenwald, A.G. (1994). Implicit stereotyping and prejudice. In M.P. Zanna & J.M. Olson (Eds.), *The psychology of prejudice: The Ontario symposium* (Vol. 7, pp. 55-76). Hillsdale, NJ: Erlbaum.

Bohnet, I. (2016). *What works: Gender equality by design.* Cambridge, MA: Harvard University Press.

Bohnet, I., & Morse, G. (2016, July-August). Designing a bias-free organizations. *Harvard Business Review,* 3-7.

Brinson, W. (2014, September 15). NFL hiring female advisers to shape domestic violence policies. CBS Sports. www.cbssports.com/nfl/news/nfl-hiring-female-advisers-to-shape-domestic-violence-policies

Burton, L.J. (2015). Underrepresentation of women in sport leadership: A review of research. *Sport Management Review, 18*(2), 155-165.

Burton, L.J., Borland, J., & Mazerolle, S.M. (2012). "They cannot seem to get past the gender issue": Experiences of young female athletic trainers in NCAA Division I intercollegiate athletics. *Sport Management Review, 15*(3), 304-317.

Burton, L.J., Grappendorf, H., & Henderson, A. (2011). Perceptions of gender in athletic administration: Utilizing role congruity to examine (potential) prejudice against women. *Journal of Sport Management, 25*(1), 36-45.

Canadian Human Rights Act, R.S.C., 1985, c. H-6. http://laws-lois.justice.gc.ca/eng/acts/h-6/FullText.html

Chalabaev, A., Sarrazin, P., Fontayne, P., Boiché, J., & Clément-Guillotin, C. (2013). The influence of sex stereotypes and gender roles on participation and performance in sport and exercise: Review and future directions. *Psychology of Sport and Exercise, 14*(2), 136-144.

Colquitt, J. A., Conlon, D. E., Wesson, M. J., Porter, C. O., & Ng, K. Y. (2001). Justice at the millennium: a meta-analytic review of 25 years of organizational justice research. 425-445.

Cox, T. (1994). *Cultural diversity in organizations: Theory, research, and practice.* San Francisco, CA: Berrett-Koehler.

Cunningham, G.B. (2006). The influence of demographic similarity on affective reactions to physical activity classes. *Journal of Sport and Exercise Psychology, 28,* 127-142.

Cunningham, G. B. (2009). Understanding the diversity-related change process: A field study. *Journal of Sport Management, 23*(4), 407-428.

Cunningham, G. B. (2011). Creative work environments in sport organizations: The influence of sexual orientation diversity and commitment to diversity. *Journal of Homosexuality, 58*(8), 1041-1057.

Cunningham, G.B. (2015). *Diversity and inclusion in sport organizations* (3rd ed.). New York, NY: Routledge.

Cunningham, G.B., Ferreira, M., & Fink, J.S. (2009). Reactions to prejudicial statements: The influence of statement content and characteristics of the commenter. *Group Dynamics: Theory, Research, and Practice, 13*(1), 59.

Cunningham, G.B., & Sagas, M. (2005). Access discrimination in intercollegiate athletics. *Journal of Sport and Social Issues, 29*(2), 148-163.

ESPN. (n.d.). About: Mission. www.facebook.com/pg/ESPN/about

ESPN. (n.d.). Diversity, inclusion, & wellness. https://espncareers.com/working-here/diversity-inclusion-wellness

Fink, J.S. (2016). Hiding in plain sight: The embedded nature of sexism in sport. *Journal of Sport Management, 30*(1), 1-7.

Fink, J.S., & Pastore, D.L. (1999). Diversity in sport? Utilizing the business literature to devise a comprehensive framework of diversity initiatives. *Quest, 51*(4), 310-327.

Goldin, C., and C. Rouse (2000), "Orchestrating Impartiality: The Impact of "Blind" Auditions on Female Musicians." *The American Economic Review* 90(4), 715-741.

Hawkins, B.J., Carter-Francique, A.R., & Cooper, J.N. (Eds.). (2016). *Critical race theory: Black athletic sporting experiences in the United States.* New York, NY: Springer.

Hitt, M.A., Miller, C.C., & Colella, A. (2015). *Organizational behavior* (4th ed.). Hoboken, NJ: Wiley.

Joseph, B. (2016, November 7). Explaining the lack of black head coaches in college football. *The Journal of Blacks in Higher Education.* www.jbhe.com/2016/11/explaining-the-lack-of-black-head-coaches-in-college-football

Kahane, L., Longley, N., & Simmons, R. (2013). The effects of coworker heterogeneity on firm-level output: Assessing the impacts of cultural and language diversity in the National Hockey League. *Review of Economics and Statistics, 95*(1), 302-314.

Lapchick, R. (2016). *The racial and gender report card.* www.tidesport.org/reports.html

LaVoi, N. M. (2017, February). Head coaches of women's collegiate teams: A report on select NCAA Division-I institutions, 2016-17. Minneapolis: Tucker Center for Research on Girls & Women in Sport. Retrieved from http://www.cehd.umn.edu/tuckercenter/library/docs/research/WCR_2016-17_Head_Coaches_FBS_DI.pdf

LaVoi, N.M. (Ed.). (2016). *Women in sports coaching*. Oxford, UK: Routledge.

Lee, W., & Cunningham, G.B. (2015). A picture is worth a thousand words: The influence of signaling, organizational reputation, and applicant race on attraction to sport organizations. *International Journal of Sport Management, 16*, 492-506.

Nishii, L.H. (2013). The benefits of climate for inclusion for gender-diverse groups. *Academy of Management Journal, 56*(6), 1754-1774.

Pellegrino, G., D'Amato, S., & Weisberg, A. (2011). The gender dividend: Making the business case for investing in women. Deloitte. www2.deloitte.com/content/dam/Deloitte/global/Documents/Public-Sector/dttl-ps-thegenderdividend-08082013.pdf

Powell, M. (2016, April 1). Men of soccer don't get it, as usual. Retrieved from https://www.nytimes.com/2016/04/02/sports/soccer/womens-soccer-pay-powell.html

Roberson, L., Kulik, C. T., & Pepper, M. B. (2003). Using needs assessment to resolve controversies in diversity training design. *Group & Organization Management, 28*(1), 148-174.

SGB Media. (2017, January 16). Nike expands support for diversity with two new partnerships. https://sgbonline.com/nike-expands-support-for-diversity-with-two-new-partnerships

Steele, C. M., & Aronson, J. (1995). Stereotype threat and the intellectual test performance of African Americans. *Journal of personality and social psychology, 69*(5), 797.

The Guardian (2017, April 5). U.S. women's national soccer team resolves pay dispute with federation. Retrieved from https://www.theguardian.com/football/2017/apr/05/us-womens-national-soccer-team-federation-dispute

Title VII of the Civil Rights Act of 1964 (Pub.L. 88–352, 78 Stat. 241). www.eeoc.gov/laws/statutes/titlevii.cfm

Title IX of the Education Amendments of 1972, 20 U.S.C. §§ 1681-1688.

U.S. Department of Education. (2017). Equity in athletics data analysis. https://ope.ed.gov/athletics/#

U.S. Equal Employment Opportunity Commission. (2009, November 21). Federal laws prohibiting job discrimination: Questions and answers. www.eeoc.gov/facts/qanda.html

U.S. Lacrosse. (n.d.). *Diversity and inclusion assessment toolkit for leaders*. www.uslacrosse.org/sites/default/files/public/documents/programs/diversity-inclusion-assesment-toolkit-for-leaders.pdf

Walker, N.A., & Melton, E.N. (2015). The tipping point: The intersection of race, gender, and sexual orientation in intercollegiate sports. *Journal of Sport Management, 29*(3), 257-271.

Chapter 3

Babiak, K., & Wolfe, R. (2009). Determinants of corporate social responsibility in professional sport: Internal and external factors. *Journal of Sport Management, 23*(6), 717-742.

Branch, J. (2016). N.H.L. commissioner Gary Bettman continues to deny C.T.E. Link. *The New York Times*. www.nytimes.com/2016/07/27/sports/nhl-commissioner-gary-bettman-denies-cte-link.html?_r=0

Brown, M.E., & Mitchell, M.S. (2010). Ethical and unethical leadership: Exploring new avenues for future research. *Business Ethics Quarterly, 20*(4), 583-616.

Brown, M.E., & Treviño, L.K. (2006). Ethical leadership: A review and future directions. *The Leadership Quarterly, 17*(6), 595-616.

Coaches Code of Ethics (2017). National Federation of State High School Associations. Retrieved from https://www.nfhs.org/nfhs-for-you/coaches/coaches-code-of-ethics/

Cunningham, G.B. (2015). *Diversity & inclusion in sport organizations* (3rd ed.). New York, NY: Routledge.

DeSensi, J., & Rosenberg, D. (2010). *Ethics and morality in sport management* (2nd ed.). Morgantown, WV: FiT.

Goodwyn, W. (2017, February 8). Baylor sanctioned by Big 12 after new revelations about sexual assault controversy. NPR Sports. www.npr.org/2017/02/08/514172776/baylor-sanctioned-by-big-12-after-new-revelations-about-football-team-controvers

Hancock, M., & Hums, M. (2015). Applying a principled and ethical approach to sport leadership. In G. Kane, J. Borland, & L. Burton (Eds.), *Sport leadership in the 21st century*, pp. 105-126. Burlington, MA: Jones & Bartlett.

Hobson, W., & Boren, C. (2016). New court documents suggest others at Penn State knew of Jerry Sandusky abuse. *The Washington Post*. www.washingtonpost.com/sports/colleges/new-court-documents-suggest-others-at-penn-state-knew-of-jerry-sandusky-abuse/2016/07/12/9752f5a6-4853-11e6-90a8-fb84201e0645_story.html?utm_term=.ced680d0afd1

Knight Commission on Intercollegiate Athletics (2017). Retrieved from https://www.knightcommission.org/

Lupica, M. (2016, March 25). NFL's brain trust drops the ball. Sports on Earth. www.sportsonearth.com/article/169056550/nfl-concussions-bruce-arians-jerry-jones

Martin, K.D., & Cullen, J.B. (2006). Continuities and extensions of ethical climate theory: A meta-analytic review. *Journal of Business Ethics, 69*(2), 175-194.

Mulki, J.P., Jaramillo, J.F., & Locander, W.B. (2008). Effect of ethical climate on turnover intention: Linking attitudinal and stress theory. *Journal of Business Ethics, 78*(4), 559-574.

Nahavandi, A., Denhardt, R.B., Denhardt, J.V., & Aristigueta, M.P. (2013). *Organizational behavior*. London, UK: SAGE.

National Basketball Association. (n.d.). NBA FIT. http://fit.nba.com

Nike. (n.d.). About Nike. http://about.nike.com/pages/our-ambition

Pfleegor, A., & Seifried, C. (2016). Ethical decisions in sport: Etho-conventional decision-making model for sport managers. *International Journal of Sport Management, 17*, 383-407.

Red Sox Foundation. (n.d.). Our mission. www.redsoxfoundation.org/about/our-mission

Schwarz, A., Bogdanich, W., & Williams, J. (2016, March 24). N.F.L.'s flawed concussion research and ties to tobacco industry. *The New York Times*. www.nytimes.com/2016/03/25/sports/football/nfl-concussion-research-to-bacco.html?_r=0

Segran, E. (2017, July 28). Escalating Sweatshop Protests Keep Nike Sweating. Retrieved from https://www.fastcompany.com/40444836/escalating-sweatshop-protests-keep-nike-sweating

Treviño, L.K., Brown, M., & Pincus-Hartman, L. (2003). A qualitative investigation of perceived executive ethical leadership: Perceptions from inside and outside the executive suite. *Human Relations, 56*, 5-37.

USA Hockey. (n.d.). Coaching ethics. www.usahockey.com/page/show/893032-coaching-ethics

Van Marrewijk, M. (2003). Concepts and definitions of CSR and corporate sustainability: Between agency and communion. *Journal of Business Ethics, 44*(2), 95-105.

Chapter 4

Chelladurai, P., & Ogasawara, E. (2003). Satisfaction and commitment of American and Japanese collegiate coaches. *Journal of Sport Management, 17*(1), 62–73.

Collins, C.J., Hanges, P.J., & Locke, E.A. (2004). The relationship of achievement motivation to entrepreneurial behavior: A meta-analysis. *Human Performance, 17*(1), 95-117.

Costa, C.A., Chalip, L., Green, B.C., & Simes, C. (2006). Reconsidering the role of training in event volunteers' satisfaction. *Sport Management Review, 9*, 165-182.

Day, D.V., & Schleicher, D.J. (2006). Self-Monitoring at Work: A Motive-Based Perspective. *Journal of Personality, 74*(3), 685-714.

De Raad, B. (2000). *The Big Five Personality Factors: The psycholexical approach to personality*. Hogrefe & Huber Publishers.

Dixon, M.A., Cunningham, G.B., Sagas, M., Turner, B.A. & Kent, A. (2005). Challenge is key: An investigation of affective organizational commitment in undergraduate interns. *Journal of Education for Business, 80*, 3.

Duda, J.L., & Hall, H.K. (2001). Achievement goal theory in sport: Recent extensions and future directions. In R.N. Singer, H.A. Hausenblas, & C.M. Janelle (Eds.), *Handbook of research in sport psychology* (2nd ed., pp. 417–434). New York, NY: Wiley.

Gajendran, R.S., & Joshi, A. (2012). Innovation in globally distributed teams. *Journal of Applied Psychology, 97*, 1252–1261.

Goleman, D. (1985). *Emotional intelligence*. New York, NY: Bantam Books.

Joseph, D.L., Jin, J., Newman, D.A., O'Boyle, E.H. (2015). Why does self-reported emotional intelligence predict job performance? A meta-analytic investigation of mixed EI. *Journal of Applied Psychology, 100*(2), 298-342.

Joseph, D.L., & Newman, D.A. (2010). Emotional intelligence: An integrative meta-analysis and cascading model. *Journal of Applied Psychology, 95*(1), 54-78.

Judge, T., Thoresen, C., Bono, J., & Patton, G. (2001). The job satisfaction–job performance relationship: A qualitative and quantitative review. *Psychological Bulletin, 127*, 376–407.

Judge, T.A., Heller, D., & Mount, M.K. (2002). Five-factor model of personality and job satisfaction: A meta-analysis. *Journal of Applied Psychology, 87*(3), 530–541.

Jung, H.S., & Yoon, H.H. (2012). The effects of emotional intelligence on counterproductive work behaviors and organizational citizen behaviors among food and beverage employees in a deluxe hotel. *International Journal of Hospitality Management, 31*, 369-378.

Keskin, H., Akgün, A.E., Ayar, H., & Kayman, ⊠.S. (2016). Cyberbullying victimization, counterproductive work behaviours, and emotional intelligence at workplace. *Procedia—Social and Behavioral Sciences, 235*, 281-287.

Kim, M., & Chelladurai, P. (2008). Volunteer preferences for training influences of individual difference factors. *International Journal of Sport Management, 9*(3), 233-249.

Kinicki, A.J., McKee–Ryan, F.M., Schriesheim, C.A., & Carson, K.P. (2002). Assessing the construct validity of the job descriptive index: A review and meta-analysis. *Journal of Applied Psychology, 87*, 14–32.

Krupat, E. (2017, March 2). Why the Wonderlic test is an outdated method of thinking about NFL intelligence. *Sports Illustrated.* www.si.com/nfl/2017/03/02/nfl-combine-wonderlic-test-draft-prospects

Lee, Y.H., & Chelladurai, P. (2016). Affectivity, emotional labor, emotional exhaustion, and emotional intelligence in coaching. *Journal of Applied Sport Psychology, 28*(2), 170-184.

Lyons, B.D., Hoffman, B.J., & Michel, J.W. (2009). Not much more than g? An examination of the impact of intelligence on NFL performance. *Human Performance, 22*(3), 225-245.

Mayer, J.D., Roberts, R.D., & Barsade, S.G. (2008). Human abilities: Emotional intelligence. *Annual Review of Psychology, 59*, 507-536.

McCrae, R.R., & John, O.P. (1992). An introduction to the five-factor model and its applications. *Journal of personality, 60*(2), 175-215.

Meyer, J. P., & Allen, N. J. (1991). A three-component conceptualization of organizational commitment. *Human resource management review, 1*(1), 61-89.

Mezulis, A.H., Abramson, L.Y., Hyde, J.S., & Hankin, B.L. (2004). Is there a universal positivity bias in attributions? A meta-analytic review of individual, developmental, and cultural differences in the self-serving attributional bias. *Psychological Bulletin, 130*(5), 711-747.

Nelson, D.L., & Quick, J.C. (2013). *Organizational behavior: Science, the real world, and you.* Mason, OH: Cengage Learning.

Ng, T.W., Sorensen, K.L., & Eby, L.T. (2006). Locus of control at work: A meta-analysis. *Journal of Organizational Behavior, 27*(8), 1057-1087.

Nieves, A. (2016, February 15). What is the Wonderlic test and why does the NFL use it? *Sports Illustrated.* www.si.com/nfl/nfl-combine-wonderlic-test-explained

Oh, I.-S., Charlier, S.D., Mount, M.K. and Berry, C.M. (2014). The two faces of high self-monitors: Chameleonic moderating effects of self-monitoring on the relationships between personality traits and counterproductive work behaviors. *Journal of Organizational Behavior, 35*, 92–111. doi:10.1002/job.1856

Park, S.H. (2010). The influence of respect from the organization and affective organizational commitment among volunteers for leisure service. *Journal of Leisure and Recreation Studies, 34*(3), 141-148.

Schmidt, F.L., & Hunter, J. (2004). General mental ability in the world of work: Occupational attainment and job performance. *Journal of Personality and Social Psychology, 86*(1), 162-173.

Son Hing, L.S., Bobocel, D.R., Zanna, M.P., & McBride, M.V. (2007). Authoritarian dynamics and unethical decision making: High social dominance orientation leaders and high right–wing authoritarian followers. *Journal of Personality and Social Psychology, 92*, 67–81.

Stephens, R.D., Dawley, D.D., & Stephens, D.B. (2004). Commitment on the board: A model of volunteer directors' levels of organizational commitment and self-reported performance. *Journal of Managerial Issues, 16*, 483-504.

Terborg, J.R. (1981). Interactional psychology and research on human behavior in organizations. *Academy of Management Review, 6*(4), 569-576.

Turner, B.A., & Chelladurai, P. (2005). Organizational and occupational commitment, intention to leave, and perceived performance of intercollegiate coaches. *Journal of Sport Management, 19*(2), 193-211.

Vandenberghe, C., Bentein, K., & Stinglhamber, F. (2004). Affective commitment to the organization, supervisor, and work group: Antecedents and outcomes. *Journal of vocational behavior, 64*(1), 47-71.

Wan, H.C., Downey, L.A., & Stough, C. (2014). Understanding non-work presenteeism: Relationships between emotional intelligence, boredom, procrastination, and job stress. *Personality and Individual Differences, 65*, 86-90.

Chapter 5

Bandura, A. (1986). The explanatory and predictive scope of self-efficacy theory. *Journal of social and clinical psychology, 4*(3), 359-373.

Bandura, A. (1989). Regulation of cognitive processes through perceived self-efficacy. *Developmental Psychology, 25*(5), 729-735.

Doherty, A., Misener, K., & Cuskelly, G. (2014). Toward a multidimensional framework of capacity in community sport clubs. *Nonprofit and Voluntary Sector Quarterly, 43*(2 suppl), 124S-142S.

ESPN. (n.d.). Learning & development. https://espncareers.com/working-here/learning-development

Fedor, D.B., Davis, W.D., Maslyn, J.M., & Mathieson, K. (2001). Performance improvement efforts in response to negative feedback: The roles of source power and recipient self-esteem. *Journal of Management, 27*(1), 79-97.

Gray, J.L. (1979). The myths of the myths about behavior mod in organizations: A reply to Locke's criticisms of behavior modification. *Academy of Management Review, 4*, 121–129.

Hamer, B. (2017, February 15). 4 tips on how to sell more season tickets (memberships). Sports Business Solutions. www.sportsbusiness.solutions/4-tips-on-how-to-sell-more-season-tickets-memberships

Hitt, M.A., Miller, C.C., & Colella, A. (2015). *Organizational behavior* (4th ed.). Hoboken, NJ: Wiley.

Judge, T.A., & Bono, J.E. (2001). Relationship of core self-evaluations traits—self-esteem, generalized self-efficacy, locus of control, and emotional stability—with job satisfaction and job performance: A meta-analysis. *Journal of Applied Psychology, 86*(1), 80-92.

Judge, T.A., Jackson, C.L., Shaw, J.C., Scott, B.A., & Rich, B.L. (2007). Self-efficacy and work-related performance: The integral role of individual differences. *Journal of Applied Psychology, 92*(1), 107-127.

Kreitner, R. (1982). Controversy in OBM: History, misconceptions, and ethics. In L. Frederiksen (Ed.), *Handbook of organizational behavior management* (pp. 71-91). New York, NY: Wiley.

Locke, E.A., Shaw, K.N., Saari, L.M., & Latham, G.P. (1981). Goal setting and task performance: 1969-1980. *Psychological Bulletin, 90*(1), 125-152.

Luthans, F., & Kreitner, R. (1985). *Organizational behavior modification and beyond.* Glenview, IL: Scott Foresman.

Mitchell, T.R., & Daniels, D. (2003). Observations and commentary on recent research in work motivation. *Motivation and work behavior, 7*, 225-254.

Nelson, D.L., & Quick, J.C. (2013). *Organizational behavior: Science, the real world, and you.* Mason, OH: Cengage Learning.

Peter, J. (2014, December 29). Behind Oregon's (Phil) Knight in shining armor. *USA Today.* www.usatoday.com/story/sports/ncaaf/pac12/2014/12/29/oregon-nike-phil-knight-college-football-playoff/21013009

Popp, N., Simmons, J., & McEvoy, C.D. (2017). Sport ticket sales training: Perceived effectiveness and impact on ticket sales results. *Sport Marketing Quarterly, 26*(2), 99-109.

Taylor, T., Doherty, A., & McGraw, P. (2015). *Managing people in sport organizations.* London, UK. Routledge.

Uhl-Bien, M., Schermerhorn, J., & Osborn, R. (2014). *Organizational behavior.* Hoboken, NJ. Wiley.

Warner, S., Tingle, J.K., & Kellett, P. (2013). Officiating attrition: The experiences of former referees via a sport development lens. *Journal of Sport Management, 27*(4), 316-328.

Wolverton, B., & Kambhampati, S. (2016, January 27). Colleges raised $1.2 billion in donations for sports in 2015. *The Chronicle of Higher Education.* www.chronicle.com/article/Colleges-Raised-12-Billion/235058

Chapter 6

Aisbett, L., & Hoye, R. (2015). Human resource management practices to support sport event volunteers. *Asia Pacific Journal of Human Resources, 53,* 351-369.

Allen, D.G. (2006). Do organizational socialization tactics influence newcomer embeddedness and turnover? *Journal of Management, 32,* 237–256.

Bang, H. (2015). Volunteer age, job satisfaction, and intention to stay. *Leadership & Organizational Development Journal, 36*(2), 161-176.

Bang, H., Ross, S., & Reio, T.G. (2012). From motivation to organizational commitment of volunteers in non-profit sport organizations: The role of job satisfaction. *Journal of Management Development, 32*(1), 96-112.

Chelladurai, P. (2014). *Managing organizations for sport and physical activity: A systems perspective* (4th ed.). Scottsdale, AZ: Holcomb Hathaway.

Chelladurai, P., & Ogasawara, E. (2003). Satisfaction and commitment of American and Japanese collegiate coaches. *Journal of Sport Management, 17*(1), 62-73.

Davar, S.C., & Bala, R. (2012). Relationship between job satisfaction and job performance: A meta-analysis. *Indian Journal of Industrial Relations, 48*(2), 290–305.

Deci, E.L., Koestner, R., & Ryan, R.M. (1999). A meta-analytic review of experiments examining the effects of extrinsic rewards on intrinsic motivation. *Psychological Bulletin, 125*(6), 627-668.

Deci, E.L., Ryan, M.R., Gagne, M., Leone, D.R., Usunov, J., & Kornazheva, B.P. (2001). Need satisfaction, motivation, and well-being in the work organizations of a former Eastern Bloc country: A cross-cultural study of self-determination. *Personality and Social Psychology Bulletin, 27*(8), 930-942.

Dixon, M.A., & Warner, S. (2010). Employee satisfaction in sport: Development of a multi-dimensional model in coaching. *Journal of Sport Management, 24*(2), 139-168.

Doherty, A. (2009). The volunteer legacy of a major sport event. *Journal of Policy Research in Tourism, Leisure, and Events, 1,* 185-207.

Dormann, C., & Zapf, D. (2001). Job satisfaction: A meta-analysis of stabilities. *Journal of Organizational Behavior, 22,* 483-504.

Elstad, B. (1996). Volunteer perceptions of learning and satisfaction in a mega-event: The case study of the XVII Olympic Winter Games in Lillehammer. *Festival Management & Event Tourism, 4,* 75-83.

Hackman, J.R., & Oldham, G. (1980). *Work redesign.* Reading, MA: Addison-Wesley.

Herzberg. F. (1966). *Work and the nature of man.* Cleveland, OH: World.

Herzberg, F. (1967). The motivation to work. In E.A. Fleishman (Ed.), *Studies in personnel and industrial psychology* (pp. 282-287). Homewood, IL: Dorsey Press.

Herzberg, F., Mausner, B., & Snyderman, B.B. (1959). *The motivation to work.* New York, NY: Wiley.

Hoeber, L., Doherty, A., Hoeber, O., & Wolfe, R. (2015). The nature of innovation in community sport organizations. *European Sport Management Quarterly, 15*(5), 518-534.

Hom, P.W., & Kinicki, A.J. (2001).Toward a greater understanding of how dissatisfaction drives employee turnover. Academy of Management Journal, 44, 975–987.

Kim, M., Kim, M.K., & Odio, M.A. (2010). Are you proud? The influence of sport and community identity and job satisfaction on pride of mega-event volunteers. *Event Management, 14,* 127-136.

Locke, E.A. (1976). The nature and causes of job satisfaction. In M.D. Dumnette (Ed.), *Handbook of industrial and organizational psychology* (pp. 1297-1349). Chicago, IL: Rand McNally.

MacIntosh, E., & Parent, M. (2017). Athlete satisfaction with a major multi-sport event: The importance of social and cultural aspects. *International Journal of Event and Festival Management, 8*(2), 136-150.

MacIntosh, E., & Walker, M. (2012). Chronicling the transient nature of fitness employees: An organizational culture perspective. *Journal of Sport Management, 26,* 113-126.

Maier, C., Woratschek, H., Strobel, T., & Popp, B. (2016). Is it really about money? A study on incentives in elite team sports. *European Sport Management Quarterly, 16*(5), 592-612.

Martensen, A., & Gronholdt, L. (2001). Using employee satisfaction measurement to improve people management: An adaptation of Kano's quality types. *Total Quality Management, 12*(7), 949-957.

Matzler, K., Fuchs, M., & Schubert, A. (2004). Employee satisfaction: Does Kano's model apply? *Total Quality Management & Business Excellence, 15*(9/10), 1179-1198.

McShane, S.L., & Steen, S. (2012). *Canadian organizational behaviour* (8th ed.). Toronto, Canada: McGraw-Hill Ryerson.

Morrison, E.W. (1996). Organizational citizenship behavior as a critical link between HRM practices and service quality. *Human Resource Management, 35*, 493-512.

Namasivayam, K. (2005). Connecting organizational human resource practices to consumer satisfaction. *International Journal of Service Industry Management, 16*(3), 253-270.

Robbins, S.P., & Judge, T.A. (2008). *Essentials of organizational behaviour* (9th ed.). Upper Saddle River, NJ: Pearson Prentice Hall.

Rogalsky, K., Doherty, A., & Paradis, K.F. (2016). Understanding the sport event volunteer experience: An investigation of role ambiguity and its correlates. *Journal of Sport Management, 30*, 453-469.

Sagas, M., & Cunningham, G. (2005).Work–family conflict among college assistant coaches. *International Journal of Sport Management, 6*, 183–197.

Silverberg, K.E., Marshall, E.K., & Ellis, G.D. (2001). Measuring job satisfaction of volunteers in public parks and recreation. *Journal of Park and Recreation Administration, 19*, 79-92.

Taylor, T., & Morgan, A. (2017). Managing volunteers in grassroots sport. In T. Bradbury & I. O'Boyle (Eds.), *Understanding sport management: International perspectives* (pp. 130-144). New York, NY: Routledge.

Tett, R.P., & Meyer, J.P. (1993). Job satisfaction, organizational commitment, turnover intention, and turnover: Path analyses based on meta-analytic findings. *Personnel Psychology, 46*(2), 259-293.

Townsend, K. (2004). Management culture and employee resistance: Investigating the management of leisure service employees. *Managing Leisure, 9*, 47-58.

Wilson, F. (2010). *Organizational behaviour and work: A critical introduction* (3rd ed.). New York, NY: Oxford University Press.

Withey, M.J., & Cooper, W.H. (1989). Predicting exit, voice, loyalty, and neglect. *Administrative Science Quarterly, 34*, 521-539.

Chapter 7

Arnold, R., & Fletcher, D. (2012). A research synthesis and taxonomic classification of the organizational stressors encountered by sport performers *Journal of Sport & Exercise Psychology, 34*, 397-429.

Bakker, A.B., Demerouti, E., & Verbeke, W. (2004). Using the job demands–resources model to predict burnout and performance. *Human Resource Management, 43*(1), 83-104.

Caddick, N., & Smith, B. (2014). The impact of sport and physical activity on the well-being of combat veterans: A systematic review. *Psychology of Sport & Exercise, 15*(1), 9-18.

Fletcher, D., & Hanton, S. (2003). Sources of organizational stress in elite sports performers. *The Sport Psychologist, 17*(2), 175-195.

Fletcher, D., Rumbold, J.L., Tester, R., & Coombes, M.S. (2011). Sport psychologists' experiences of organizational stressors. *The Sport Psychologist, 25*, 363-381.

Godbey, K.L., & Courage, M.M. (1999). Stress-management program: Intervention in nursing student performance anxiety. *Archives of Applied Nursing, 8*(3), 190-199.

Gustafsson, H., Kentta, G., & Hassmen, P. (2011). Athlete burnout: An interated model and future research directions. *International Review of Sport and Exercise Psychology, 4*(1), 3-24.

Gustafsson, H., Skoog, T., Davis, P., Kentta, G., & Haberl, P. (2015). Mindfulness and its relationship with perceived stress, affect, and burnout in elite junior athletes. *Journal of Clinical Sport Psychology, 9*, 263-281.

Hanton, S., Fletcher, D., & Coughlan, G. (2005). Stress in elite sport performers: A comparative study of competitive and organizational stressors. *Journal of Sports Sciences, 23*, 1129–1141.

Kristiansen, E., & Parent, M.M. (2014). Athletes, their families, and team officials: Sources of support and stressors. In D.V. Hanstad, M.M. Parent, & B. Houlihan (Eds.), *The Youth Olympic Games* (pp. 106–121). Oxon, UK: Routledge.

Kristiansen, E., & Roberts, G.C. (2011). Media exposure and adaptive coping in elite football. *International Journal of Sport Psychology, 42,* 339–367.

MacIntosh, E., & Nicol, L. (2012*)*. The athlete's sport event experience of the XIX Commonwealth Games in Delhi, India. *International Journal of Event and Festival Management, 3*(1), 12-29.

MacIntosh, E., & Parent, M. (2017). Athlete satisfaction with a major multi-sport event: The importance of social and cultural aspects. *International Journal of Event and Festival Management. 8*(2*), 136-150.*

Maslach, C., & Leiter, M.P. (1997). *The truth about burnout: How organizations cause personal stress and what to do about it.* San Francisco, CA: Jossey-Bass.

Maslach, C., & Leiter, M.P. (2008). Early predictors of job burnout and engagement. *Journal of Applied Psychology, 93*(3), 498-512.

McShane, S.L., & Steen, S. (2012*). Canadian organizational behaviour* (8th ed.). Toronto, Canada: McGraw-Hill Ryerson.

Mellalieu, S.D., Neil, R., Hanton, S., & Fletcher, D. (2009). Competition stress in sport performers: Stressors experienced in the competition environment. *Journal of Sport Sciences, 27*(7), 729-744.

Nelson, D.L., Quick, J.C., Armstrong, A., & Condie, J. (2015). ORGB (2nd Canadian ed.). Toronto, Canada: Nelson Education.

Parent, M., Kristiansen, E., & MacIntosh, E. (2014). Athletes' experiences at the Youth Olympic Games: Perceptions, stressors, and discourse paradox. *Event Management, 18,* 303-324.

Parent, M., & MacIntosh, E. (2013). Organizational culture evolution in temporary organizations: The case of the 2010 Olympic Winter Games. *Canadian Journal of Administrative Sciences, 30*(4), 223-237.

Raedeke, T.D. (1997). Is athlete burnout more than just stress? A sport commitment perspective. *Journal of Sport and Exercise Psychology, 19*(4), 396-417.

Selye, H. (1946). The general adaptation syndrome and the diseases of adaptation. *Journal of Endocrinology, 6,* 117.

Selye, H. (1956). *The stress of life.* New York, NY: McGraw-Hill.

Selye, H. (1974). *Stress without distress.* Philadelphia, PA: Lippincott.

Sharif, B.A. (2000). Understanding and managing job stress: A vital dimension of workplace violence prevention. *The International Journal of Health Education, 3*(2), 107-116.

Sonnentag, S., & Jelden, S. (2009). Job stressors and the pursuit of sport activities: A day-level perspective. *Journal of Occupational Health Psychology, 14*(2), 165-181.

Woodman, T., & Hardy, L. (2001). A case study of organizational stress in elite sport. *Journal of Applied Sport Psychology, 13,* 207-238.

Chapter 8

Adkins, C.L. (1995). Previous work experience and organizational socialization: A longitudinal examination. *Academy of Management Journal, 38,* 839–862.

Allen, D. (2006). Do organizational socialization tactics influence newcomer embeddedness and turnover? *Journal of Management, 32*(2), 237-256.

Ashforth, B.E., Saks, A.M., & Lee, R.T. (1998). Socialization and newcomer adjustment: The role of organizational context. *Human Relations, 51,* 897–926.

Bravo, G., Shonk, D., & Won, D. (2012). Psychological contract in the context of sport organizations. In L. Robinson, P. Chelladurai, G. Bodet, & P. Downward (Eds.), *Routledge handbook of sport management* (pp. 193-213). New York, NY: Routledge.

Cable, D.M., & Parsons, C.K. (2001). Socialization tactics and person–organization fit. *Personnel Psychology, 54,* 1-23.

Feldman, D.C. (1976). A contingency theory of socialization. *Administrative Science Quarterly, 21,* 433-452.

Fogarty, T.J., & Dirsmith, M.W. (2001). Organizational socialization instrument and symbol: An extended institutional theory perspective. *Human Resource Development Quarterly, 12*(3), 247-266.

Grøgaard, B., & Colman, H.L. (2016). Interpretive frames as the organization's "mirror": From espoused values to social integration in MNEs. *Management International Review, 56,* 171-194.

Hofstede, G., Neuijen, B., Ohayv, D.D., & Sanders, G. (1990). Measuring organizational cultures: A qualitative and quantitative study across twenty cases. *Administrative Science Quarterly, 35,* 286-316.

Jones, G.R. (1986). Socialization tactics, self-efficacy, and newcomers' adjustments to organizations. *Academy of Management Journal, 29,* 262–279.

Kennedy, A. (2016, August 8). NBA's rookie transition program schedule. *Basketball Insiders.* www.basketballinsiders.com/nbas-rookie-transition-program-schedule

Kinicki, A., & Kreitner, R. (2008). *Organizational behaviour: Key concepts, skills, and best practices* (3rd ed.). New York, NY: McGraw-Hill/Irwin.

Klein, H.J., & Weaver, N.A. (2000). The effectiveness of an organizational-level orientation training program in the socialization of new hires. *Personnel Psychology, 53,* 47–66.

MacIntosh, E., & Harris, J. (2017). The global sport environment. In T. Bradbury & I. O'Boyle, *Understanding sport management: International perspectives* (pp. 58-72). New York, NY: Routledge.

MacIntosh, E., Bravo, G., & Li, M. (2012). Intercultural management in sport organizations. In M. Li, E. MacIntosh, & G. Bravo (Eds.), *International sport management* (pp. 53-69). Champaign, IL: Human Kinetics.

McShane, S.L., & Steen, S. (2012). *Canadian organizational behaviour* (8th ed.). Toronto, Canada: McGraw-Hill Ryerson.

Morrison, E.W. (2002). Newcomers' relationships: The role of social network ties during socialization. *Academy of Management Journal, 45*(6), 1149-1160.

Ostroff, C., & Kozlowski, S.W.J. (1992). Organizational socialization as a learning process: The role of information acquisition. *Personnel Psychology, 45*(4), 849-874.

Parent, M., & MacIntosh, E. (2013). Organizational culture evolution in temporary organizations: The case of the 2010 Olympic Winter Games. *Canadian Journal of Administrative Sciences, 30*(4), 223-237.

Remme, M. (n.d.). Rookie transition program helps players adjust to NBA Life. [Official Site of the Minnesota Timberwolves]. www.nba.com/timberwolves/news/rookie-transition-program-helps-players-adjust-nba-life

Rousseau, D.M. (1989). Psychological and implied contract in organizations. *Employee Responsibilities and Rights Journal, 2,* 121-139.

Taormina, R.J. (2009). Organizational socialization: The missing link between employee needs and organizational culture. *Journal of Managerial Psychology, 24,* 660-676.

Taylor, T., Doherty, A., & McGraw, P. (2008). *Managing people in sport organizations: A strategic human resource management perspective.* New York, NY: Routledge.

Van Maanen, J., & Schein, E.H. 1979. Toward a theory of organizational socialization. *Research in Organizational Behavior, 1,* 209–264.

Wang, M., Kammeyer-Mueller, J., Liu, Y., & Li, Y. (2015). Context, socialization, and newcomer learning. *Organizational Psychology Review, 5*(1), 3-25.

Chapter 9

Avolio, B.J. & Gardner, W. (2005). Authentic leadership development: Getting to the root of positive forms of leadership. *The Leadership Quarterly,16,* 315-338.

Bass, B. (1985). *Leadership and performance beyond expectations.* New York, NY: Free Press

Bass, B., & Stogdill, R.M. (1990). *Bass and Stogdill's handbook of leadership: Theory, research, and managerial applications* (3rd ed.). New York, NY: Free Press.

Bennis, W., & Nanus, B. (1985). *Leaders: The strategies for taking charge.* New York, NY: Harper & Row.

Blake, R.R., & Mouton, J.S. (1964). *The managerial grid: The key to leadership excellence.* Houston: Gulf Publishing Co.

Bourner, F., & Weese, W.J. (1995). Executive leadership and organizational effectiveness in the Canadian Hockey League. *European Journal of Sport Management, 2,* 88-100.

Burnes, B., & O'Donnell, H. (2011). What can business leaders learn from sport? *Sport, Business and Management: An International Journal, 1*(1), 12-27.

Burns, J.M. (1978). *Leadership.* New York, NY: Harper & Row: Harper & Row.

Burton, L.J., Barr, C., Fink, J.S., & Bruening, J.E. (2009) "Think athletic director, think masculine?": Examination of the gender typing of managerial subroles within athletic administration positions. *Sex Roles, 61*, 416-426.

Burton, L.J., Grappendorf, H., & Henderson, A. (2011). Perceptions of gender in athletic administration: Utilizing role congruity to examine (potential) prejudice against women. *Journal of Sport Management, 25*(1), 36-45.

Burton, L.J., & Welty Peachey, J. (2013). The call for servant leadership in intercollegiate athletics. *Quest, 65*(3), 354-371.

Burton, L.J., & Welty Peachey, J. (2009). Transactional or transformational? Leadership preferences of Division III athletic administrators. *Journal of Intercollegiate Sport, 2*, 245-259.

Chelladurai, P. (1978). *A contingency model of leadership in athletics* (Unpublished doctoral dissertation). University of Waterloo, Canada.

Chelladurai, P., & Riemer, H. (1998). Measurement of leadership in sport. In J.L. Duda (Ed.), *Advances in sport and exercise psychology* (pp. 227-253). Morgantown, WV: Fitness Information Technology.

Chelladurai, P., & Saleh, S.D. (1980). Dimensions of leader behavior in sports: Development of a leadership scale. *Journal of Sport Psychology, 2*, 34-45.

Collins, J.C. (2001). *Good to great: Why some companies make the leap . . . and others don't.* New York, NY: Harper Collins.

Conger, J.A. (1998). *Charismatic leadership: The elusive factor in organizational effectiveness.* San Francisco, CA: Jossey-Bass.

Conger, J.A., & Kanungo, R.N. (1998). *Charismatic leadership in organizations.* Thousand Oaks, CA: Sage.

Dalakoura, A. (2010). Differentiating leader and leadership development: A collective framework for leadership development. *Journal of Management Development, 29*(5), 432-441. doi: 10.1108/02621711011039204

Danylchuk, K., & Chelladurai, P. (1999). The nature of managerial work in Canadian intercollegiate athletics. *Journal of Sport Management, 13*, 148-166.

DeFrantz, A.L. (1988). Women and leadership in sport. *Journal of Physical Education, Recreation & Dance, 59*, 46-48.

DeSensi, J. (2014). Sport: An ethos based on values and servant leadership. *Journal of Intercollegiate Sport, 7*, 58-63.

Doherty, A. (1997). The effect of leader characteristics on the perceived transformational/transactional leadership and impact of interuniversity athletic administrators. *Journal of Sport Management, 11*, 275-285.

Doherty, A.J., & Danylchuk, K. (1996). Transformational and transactional leadership in interuniversity athletics management. *Journal of Sport Management, 10*, 292-309.

Edginton, C.R., Hudson, S.D., & Ford, P.M. (1999). *Leadership in recreation and leisure service organizations* (2nd ed.). Champaign, IL: Sagamore.

Fiedler, F. E. (1967) *A Theory of Leadership Effectiveness*, New York: McGraw-Hill.

Fleishman, E. A. (1953). The description of supervisory behavior. *Journal of Applied Psychology, 37*(1), 1-6. http://dx.doi.org/10.1037/h0056314

Gardner, W.L., Avolio, B.J., Luthans, F., May, D.R., & Walumbwa, F. (2005). "Can you see the real me?" A self-based model of authentic leader and follower development. *The Leadership Quarterly, 16*, 343-372. doi: 10.1016/j.leaqua. 2005.03.003

Goleman, D. (1998) *Working with emotional intelligence*. New York, NY: Bantam Books.

Goleman, D. (2004). Never stop learning. *Harvard Business Review, 82*, 82-91.

Greenleaf, R. (2002). *Servant leadership: A journey into the nature of legitimate power and greatness*. Paulist Press, New Jersey.

Hemphill, J.K. (1950). Relations between the size of the group and the behavior of superior leaders. The Journal of Social Psychology, 32(1), 11-22. https://doi.org/10.1080/00224545.1950.9919026

Hersey, P. & Blanchard, K. H. (1969). Life cycle theory of leadership. *Training and Development Journal. 23(5),* 26–34.

Hersey, P., & Blanchard, K. H. (1977). *Management of Organizational Behavior 3rd Edition–Utilizing Human Resources*. New Jersey/Prentice Hall.

House, R.J. (1971). A path-goal theory of leader effectiveness. *Administrative Science Quarterly, 16*(3), 321-339.

Hutchinson, M., & Bouchet, A. (2014). Organizational redirection in highly bureaucratic environments: De-escalation of commitment among Division I athletic departments. *Journal of Sport Management, 28*(2), 143-161.

Kent, A., & Weese, W.J. (2000). Do effective organizations have better executive leaders and/or organizational cultures? A study of selected sports organizations in Canada. *European Journal for Sports Management, 7*(2), 4-21.

Kihl, L.A., Leberman, S., & Schull, V. (2010). Stakeholder constructions of leadership in intercollegiate athletics. *European Sport Management Quarterly, 10*(2), 241-275.

Kotter, J. (1999). On what leaders really do. *Harvard Business Review*.

Kouzes, J., & Posner, B. (2002). *The leadership challenge* (3rd ed.). San Francisco, CA: Jossey-Bass.

Ladkin, D., & Taylor, S.S. (2010). Enacting the "true self": Towards a theory of embodied authentic leadership. *The Leadership Quarterly, 21*, 64-74.

Likert, R. (1961). *New patterns of management*. New York, NY: McGraw-Hill.

MacIntosh, E., & Doherty, A. (2005). Leader intentions and employee perceptions of organizational culture in a private fitness corporation. *European Sport Management Quarterly, 5*(1), 1-22.

McShane, S.L., & Steen, S.L. (2012). *Canadian organizational behavior* (8th ed.). New York, NY: McGraw-Hill.

Sagas, M., & Wigley, B.J. (2014). Gray area ethical leadership in the NCAA: The ethics of doing the wrong things right. *Journal of Intercollegiate Sport, 7*, 40-57.

Schein, E.H. (1990). *Organizational culture and leadership*. San Francisco, CA: Jossey-Bass.

Scott, D.K. (1999). A multiframe perspective of leadership and organizational climate in intercollegiate athletics. *Journal of Sport Management, 13*, 298-316.

Sosik, J.J., & Megerian, L.E. (1999). Understanding leader emotional intelligence and performance: The role of self–other agreement on transformational leadership perceptions. *Group & Organization Management, 24*, 367–390.

Stogdill, R.M. (1948). Personal factors associated with leadership: A survey of the literature. *Journal of Psychology, 25*, 35-71.

Stogdill, R.M. (1963). *Manual for the leadership behavior description questionnaire*. Fisher College of Business. Ohio State University.

Wallace, M., & Weese, J. (1995). Leadership, organizational culture, and job satisfaction in Canadian YMCA organizations. *Journal of Sport Management, 9*, 182-193.

Walumbwa, F.O., Avolio, B.J., Gardner, W.L., Wernsing, T.S., & Peterson, S.J. (2008). Authentic leadership: Development and validation of a theory-based measure. *Journal of Management, 34*(1), 89-126. doi: 10.1177/0149206307308913

Weese, J. (1994). A leadership discussion with Dr. Bernard Bass. *Journal of Sport Management, 8*, 179-189.

Weese, J. (1995). Leadership and organizational culture: An investigation of Big Ten and Mid-American Conference campus recreation administrations. *Journal of Sport Management, 9*, 119-134.

Weese, J., & Beard, S. (2012). Rethinking the teaching of leadership in sport management. *Sport Management Education Journal, 6*, 1-7.

Welty Peachey, J., & Burton, L.J. (2011) Male or female? Exploring leader effectiveness and female leadership advantage with athletic directors. *Sex Roles, 64*, 416-425.

Welty Peachy, J., Zhou, Y., Damon, Z.J., & Burton, L.J. (2015). Forty years of leadership research in sport management: A review, synthesis, and conceptual framework. *Journal of Sport Management, 29*, 570-587.

Yukl, G. (2008). *Leadership in organizations* (7th ed.). Upper Saddle River, NJ: Prentice Hall.

Chapter 10

Bishop, G. (2015, December 22). Behind the Superdome blackout. *Sports Illustrated*. www.si.com/nfl/2015/12/22/super-bowl-xlvii-blackout-superdome

Cohen, L.J., & DeBenedet, A.T. (2012, July 17). Penn State cover-up: Groupthink in action. *Time*. http://ideas.time.com/2012/07/17/penn-state-cover-up-group-think-in-action.

Heitner, D. (2013, June 22). Are executive search firms worth the cost to college athletic departments? *Forbes*. www.forbes.com/sites/darrenheitner/2013/06/22/are-executive-search-firms-worth-the-cost-to-college-athletic-departments/#6749b9042075

Hitt, M.A., Miller, C.C., & Colella, A. (2015). *Organizational behavior* (4th ed.). Hoboken, NJ: Wiley.

Hutchinson, M., & Bouchet, A. (2014). Organizational redirection in highly bureaucratic environments: De-escalation of commitment among Division I athletic departments. *Journal of Sport Management, 28*(2), 143-161.

Hutchinson, M., Nite, C., & Bouchet, A. (2015). Escalation of commitment in United States collegiate athletic departments: An investigation of social and structural determinants of commitment. *Journal of Sport Management, 29*(1), 57-75.

Isenberg, D.J. (1986). Group polarization: A critical review and meta-analysis. *Journal of Personality and Social Psychology, 50*(6), 1141-1151.

Janis, I.L. (1982). *Groupthink* (2nd ed.). Boston, MA: Houghton Mifflin.

Lapchick, R. (2016). *The racial and gender report card*. Retrieved from www.tidesport.org/reports.html

LaVoi, N. M. (2017, February). Head coaches of women's collegiate teams: A report on select NCAA Division-I institutions, 2016-17. Minneapolis: Tucker Center for Research on Girls & Women in Sport. Retrieved from http://www.cehd.umn.edu/tuckercenter/library/docs/research/WCR_2016-17_Head_Coaches_FBS_DI.pdf

Lunenburg, F. (2012). Devil's advocacy and dialectical inquiry: Antidotes to groupthink. *International Journal of Scholarly Academic Intellectual Diversity, 14*, 1-9.

Nelson, D.L., & Quick, J.C. (2013). *Organizational behavior: Science, the real world, and you*. Mason, OH: Cengage Learning.

Nickerson, R.S. (1998). Confirmation bias: A ubiquitous phenomenon in many guises. *Review of General Psychology, 2*(2), 175-220.

Schrotenboer, B., & Axon, R. (2013, June 6). Search firms come under scrutiny after Rutgers flap. *USA Today*. www.usatoday.com/story/sports/ncaaf/2013/06/06/parker-executive-search-ncaa-rutgers/2398487

Simon, H.A. (1956). Rational choice and the structure of the environment. *Psychological Review. 63*(2): 129–138.

Simon, H.A. (1987). Bounded rationality. In J. Eatwell, M. Milgate, & P. Newman (Eds.), *Utility and probability* (pp. 15-18). New York, NY: Macmillan.

Slack, T., & Parent, M.M. (2006). *Understanding sport organizations: The application of organization theory* (2nd ed.). Champaign, IL: Human Kinetics.

Solomon, J. (2016b, April 12). College football coach search firms: Are they worth the money? CBS Sports. www.cbssports.com/college-football/news/college-football-coach-search-firms-are-they-worth-the-money

Uhl-Bien, M., Schermerhorn, J., & Osborn, R. (2014). *Organizational behavior*. Hoboken, NJ: Wiley.

Washington, M., & Zajac, E.J. (2005). Status evolution and com- petition: Theory and evidence. *Academy of Management Journal, 48*, 282–296.

Chapter 11

Beal, D.J., Cohen, R.R., Burke, M.J., & McLendon, C.L. (2003). Cohesion and performance in groups: A meta-analytic clarification of construct relations. *Journal of Applied Psychology, 88*, 989-1004.

Gore & Associates. (n.d.). Our beliefs and principles. www.gore.com/about/our-beliefs-and-principles

Gratton, L., & Erickson, T.J. (2007, November). 8 ways to build collaborative teams. *Harvard Business Review*, 101-109.

Jackson, C.L., & LePine, J.A. (2003). Peer responses to a team's weakest link: A test and extension of LePine and Van Dyne's model. *Journal of Applied Psychology, 88*, 459-475.

Karau, S.J., & Williams, K.D. (1993). Social loafing: A meta-analytic review and theoretical integration. *Journal of Personality and Social Psychology, 65*, 681-706.

Liden, R.C., Wayne, S.J., Jaworski, R.A., & Bennett, N. (2004). Social loafing: A field investigation. *Journal of Management, 30*(2), 285-304.

Mumford, T.V., Van Iddekinge, C., Morgeson, F.P., & Campion, M.A. (2008). The team role test: Development and validation of a team role knowledge situational judgment test. *Journal of Applied Psychology, 93*, 250–267

National Collegiate Athletic Association. (n.d.). Women's Basketball Oversight Committee Ad Hoc Working Group on Recruiting. www.ncaa.org/governance/committees/womens-basketball-oversight-committee-ad-hoc-working-group-recruiting

Paradis, K.F., & Martin, L.J. (2012). Team building in sport: Linking theory and research to practical application. *Journal of Sport Psychology in Action, 3*, 159-170.

Rock, D., & Grant, H. (2016, November 4). Why diverse teams are smarter. *Harvard Business Review.* https://hbr.org/2016/11/why-diverse-teams-are-smarter

Rock, D., Grant, H., & Grey, J. (2016, September 22). Diverse teams feel less comfortable—And that's why they perform better. *Harvard Business Review.* https://hbr.org/2016/09/diverse-teams-feel-less-comfortable-and-thats-why-they-perform-better

Taylor, T., Doherty, A., & McGraw, P. (2015). *Managing people in sport organizations.* London, UK: Routledge.

Tuckman, B.W., & Jensen, M.A.C. (1977). Stages of small-group development revisited. *Group & Organization Studies, 2*(4), 419-427.

Uhl-Bien, M., Schermerhorn, J., & Osborn, R. (2014). *Organizational behavior.* Hoboken, NJ: Wiley.

Chapter 12

Berri, D. (2015, August 12). Basketball's gender wage gap is even worse than you think. Vice Sports. https://sports.vice.com/en_us/article/basketballs-gender-wage-gap-is-even-worse-than-you-think

Berri, D. (2017, September 20). Basketball's growing gender wage gap: The evidence the WNBA is underpaying players. Forbes. www.forbes.com/sites/davidberri/2017/09/20/there-is-a-growing-gender-wage-gap-in-professional-basketball/#636a4cc536e0

Camera, L. (2016, March 16). Coaches' salaries shouldn't best presidents'. *U.S. News & World Report.* www.usnews.com/news/articles/2016-03-15/new-survey-college-coaches-shouldnt-make-more-than-college-presidents

Feldman, D. (2017, January 20). Detailed summary of changes under the NBA's new collective bargaining agreement. NBC Sports. http://nba.nbcsports.com/2017/01/20/detailed-summary-of-changes-under-the-nbas-new-collective-bargaining-agreement

Gaines, C. (2017, March 29). Gregg Popovich compared Becky Hammon to Steve Kerr and says she has what it takes to be an NBA coach. *Business Insider.* www.businessinsider.com/gregg-popovich-becky-hammon-nba-coach-2017-3

Gatto, T. (2017, February 3). Gregg Popovich's words on racial inequality, white privilege will fire up all sides. *Sporting News.* www.sportingnews.com/nba/news/gregg-popovich-white-privilege-black-history-month-san-antonio-spurs-coach-donald-trump/a4naeipiyrzyznmpe85j07pb

Jehn, K.A. (1995). A multimethod examination of the benefits and detriments of intragroup conflict. *Administrative Science Quarterly, 40*, 256-282.

Jehn, K.A. (1997). A qualitative analysis of conflict types and dimensions in organizational groups. *Administrative science quarterly*, 530-557.

Lapchick, R. (2017). The 2017 racial and gender report card: National Basketball Association. Retrieved from http://nebula.wsimg.com/74491b38503915f2f148062ff076e698?AccessKeyId=DAC3A56D8FB782449D2A&disposition=0&alloworigin=1

Medina, F.J., Munduate, L., Dorado, M.A., Martínez, I., & Guerra, J.M. (2005). Types of intragroup conflict and affective reactions. *Journal of Managerial Psychology, 20*(3/4), 219-230.

Newman, J. (2014, May 16). Coaches, not presidents, top public-college pay list. *The Chronicle of Higher Education.* www.chronicle.com/blogs/data/2014/05/16/coaches-not-presidents-top-public-college-pay-list

Raven, B.H. (2008). The bases of power and the power/interaction model of interpersonal influence. *Analyses of Social Issues and Public Policy, 8*(1), 1-22.

Slack, T., & Parent, M.M. (2006). *Understanding sport organizations: The application of organization theory* (2nd ed.). Champaign, IL: Human Kinetics.

Uhl-Bien, M., Schermerhorn, J., & Osborn, R. (2014). *Organizational behavior.* Hoboken, NJ: Wiley.

Wall, J.A., Jr., & Callister, R.R. (1995). Conflict and its management. *Journal of Management, 21*, 515–558.

Wells, A. (2017, February 14). Gregg Popovich breaks NBA record for most wins with single franchise. Bleacher Report. http://bleacher-report.com/articles/2691087-gregg-popovich-breaks-nba-record-for-most-wins-with-single-franchise

Chapter 13

International Olympic Committee. (2011). Social media policy: Blogging and Internet guidelines for participants and other accredited persons at the London Olympic Games (Version 31). https://stillmed.olympic.org/Documents/Games_London_2012/IOC_Social_Media_Blogging_and_Internet_Guidelines-London.pdf

Kelley, H.H. (1971). *Attribution in social interaction.* New York, NY: General Learning Press.

Kinicki, A., & Kreitner, R. (2008). *Organizational behavior: Key concepts, skills, and best practices* (3rd ed.). New York, NY: McGraw-Hill/Irwin.

MacIntosh, E., Abeza, L., & Lee, J. (2017). Enriching identity in the fan nation: The role of social media in the case of a professional sport team. *Sport, Business and Management: An International Journal, 7*(3), 315-331.

MacIntosh, E., Bravo, G., & Li, M. (2011). Intercultural management in sport organizations. In Li, M., MacIntosh, E., & Bravo (Eds.), *International sport management* (pp. 53-69). Champaign, IL: Human Kinetics.

Matthewman, L., Rose, A., & Hetherington, A. (2009). *Work psychology: An introduction to human behavior in the workplace.* New York, NY: Oxford University Press.

Mehrabian, A. (1970). *Tactics of social influence.* Princeton, NJ: Prentice Hall.

Nelson, D.L., Quick, J.C., Armstrong, A., and Condie, J. (2015). *ORGB* (2nd Canadian ed.). Toronto, Canada: Nelson Education.

O'Shea, M., & Alonso, A.D. (2011). Opportunity or obstacle? A preliminary study of professional sport organizations in the age of social media. *International Journal of Sport Management and Marketing, 10*(3/4), 196-212.

Robbins, S.P., & Judge, T.A. (2008). *Essentials of organizational behaviour* (9th ed.). Upper Saddle River, NJ: Pearson Prentice Hall.

Schermerhorn, J.R., Hunt J.G., & Osborn R.N. (2004). *Core concepts of organizational behavior.* Danvers, MA: Wiley.

Williams, J., & Chinn, S. (2010). Meeting relationship-marketing goals through social media: A conceptual model for sport marketers. *The International Journal of Sport Communication, 3*, 422-437.

Wilson, F. (2010). *Organizational behaviour and work: A critical introduction* (3rd ed.). New York, NY: Oxford University Press.

Chapter 14

Adkins, C.L., Ravlin, E.C., & Meglino, B.M. (1996). Value congruence between coworkers and its relationship to outcomes. *Group and Organization Management, 21*, 439-462.

Bell-Laroche, D., MacLean, J., Thibault, L., & Wolfe, R. (2014). Leader perceptions of management by values within Canadian National Sport Organizations. *Journal of Sport Management, 28*, 68-80.

Carmeli, A., & Tishler, A. (2004). The relationships between intangible organizational elements and performance. *Strategic Management Journal, 25*, 1257-1278.

Danisman, A., Hinings, C.R., & Slack, T. (2006). Integration and differentiation in institutional values: An empirical investigation in the field of Canadian national sport organizations. *Canadian Journal of Administrative Sciences, 23*, 301-317.

Detert, J.R., Schroeder, R.G., & Mauriel, J.J. (2000). A framework for linking culture and improvement initiatives in organizations. *Academy of Management Review, 25*(4), 850-863.

Doherty, A.J., & Chelladurai, P. (1999). Managing cultural diversity in sport organizations: A theoretical perspective. *Journal of Sport Management, 13*(4), 280-297.

Dolan, S.L., & Garcia, S. (2002). Managing by values: Cultural redesign for strategic organizational change at the dawn of the twenty-first century. *The Journal of Management Development, 21*(2), 101-117.

Girginov, V. (2010). Culture and the study of sport management. *European Sport Management Quarterly, 10*(4), 397-417.

Hamm, S., MacLean, J., Kikulis, L., & Thibault, T. (2008). Value congruence in a Canadian non-profit sport organisation: Case study. *Sport Management Review, 11,* 123-147.

Hatch, M.J., & Schultz, M. (1997). Relations between organizational culture, identity, and image. *European Journal of Marketing, 31*(5/6), 356-365.

Hofstede, G. (1980). *Culture's consequences: International differences in work-related values* (Cross-cultural research and methodology series, vol. 5). Beverly Hills, CA: Sage.

Kent, A., & Weese, W.J. (2000). Do effective organizations have better executive leadership and/or organizational cultures? A study of selected sport organizations in Canada. *European Journal for Sport Management, 7*(2), 4-21.

Kerwin, S., MacLean, J., & Bell-Laroche, D. (2014). The mediating influence of management by values in nonprofit sport organizations. *Journal of Sport Management, 28*(6), 646-656.

Kolodinsky, R.W., Giacalone, R.A., & Jurkiewicz, C.L. (2008). Workplace values and outcomes: Exploring personal, organizational, and interactive workplace spirituality. *Journal of Business Ethics, 81,* 465-480.

MacIntosh, E., & Doherty, A. (2005). Leader intentions and employee perceptions of organizational culture in a private fitness corporation. *European Sport Management Quarterly, 5*(1), 1-22.

MacIntosh, E., & Doherty, A. (2010). The influence of organizational culture on job satisfaction and intention to leave. *Sport Management Review, 13,* 106-117.

MacIntosh, E., Li, M., & Bravo, G. (2011). Intercultural management in sport organizations. In M. Li, E.W. MacIntosh, & G.A. Bravo (Eds.), *International sport management* (pp. 53-69). Champaign, IL: Human Kinetics.

MacIntosh, E., & Spence, K. (2012). An exploration of stakeholder values: In search of common ground within an international sport and development initiative. *Sport Management Review, 15,* 404-415.

MacIntosh, E., & Walker, M. (2012). Chronicling the transient nature of fitness employees:

An organizational culture perspective. *Journal of Sport Management, 26*(2), 113-126.

Martin, J. (1992). *Cultures in organizations: Three perspectives.* New York, NY: Oxford University Press.

Martin, J. (2002). *Organizational culture: Mapping the terrain.* Thousand Oaks, CA: Sage.

Parent, M., & MacIntosh, E. (2013). Organizational culture evolution in temporary organizations: The case of the 2010 Olympic Winter Games. *Canadian Journal of Administrative Sciences, 30*(4), 223-237.

Pettigrew, A.M. (1979). On studying organizational cultures. *Administrative Science Quarterly, 24*(4), 570-581.

Rafaeli, A., & Pratt, M.G. (2006). *Artifacts and organizations: Beyond mere symbolism.* Mahwah, NJ: Erlbaum.

Rindova, V., Dalpiaz, E., & Ravasi, D. (2011). A cultural quest: A study of organizational use of new cultural resources in strategy formation. *Organization Science, 22,* 413-431.

Rokeach, M. (1973). The nature of human values. New York, NY: Free Press.

Schein, E.H. (1985). *Organizational culture and leadership,* San Francisco, CA: Jossey-Bass.

Schein, E.H. (1991). The role of the founder in the creation of organizational culture. In P.J. Frost, L.F. Moore, M.R. Louis, C.C. Lundberg, & J. Martin (Eds.), *Reframing organizational culture* (pp. 14-25). Beverly Hills, CA: Sage.

Schwartz, S.H. (1994). Are there universal aspects in the structure and contents of human values? *Journal of Social Issues, 50*(4), 19-45.

Suddaby, R., Elsbach, K.D., Greenwood, R., Meyer, J.W., & Zilber, T.B. (2010). Organizations and their institutional environments—Bringing meaning, values, and culture back in: Introduction to the special research forum. *Academy of Management Journal, 53*(6), 1234-1240.

Wallace, M., & Weese, J.W. (1995). Leadership, organizational culture, and job satisfaction in Canadian YMCA organizations. *Journal of Sport Management, 9,* 182-193.

Weber, K., & Dacin, M.T. (2011). The cultural construction of organizational life: Introduction to the special issue. *Organization Science, 22,* 287-298.

Weese, J.W. (1995). Leadership and organizational culture: An investigation of Big Ten and

Mid-American Conference campus recreation administrations. *Journal of Sport Management, 9,* 110-134.

Woratschek, H., Horbel, C., & Popp, B. (2014). Value co-creation in sport management. *European Sport Management Quarterly, 14*(1), 1-5.

Wry, T., Lounsbury, M., & Glynn, M.A. (2011). Legitimating nascent collective identities: Coordinating cultural entrepreneurship. *Organization Science, 22,* 449-463.

Chapter 15

Amis, J., Slack, T., & Hinings, C.R. (2004). Strategic change and the role of interests, power, and organizational capacity. *Journal of Sport Management, 18,* 158-198.

Cruickshank, A., Collins, D., & Minten, S. (2015). Driving and sustaining culture change in professional sport performance teams: A ground theory. *Psychology of Sport and Exercise, 20,* 40-50.

Cunningham, G.B. (2015). *Diversity and inclusion in sport organizations* (3rd ed.). New York, NY: Routledge.

DiMaggio, P., & Powell, W.W. (1983). The iron cage revisited: Institutional isomorphism and collective rationality in organizational fields. *American Sociological Review, 48,* 147-160.

Dowling, M., & Smith, J. (2016). The institutional work of Own the Podium in developing high-performance sport in Canada. *Journal of Sport Management, 30*(4), 396-410.

Edwards, J., Mason, D.S., & Washington, M. (2009). Institutional mechanisms, government funding, and provincial sport organizations. *International Journal of Sport Management and Marketing, 6*(2), 128-149.

Frontiera, J. (2010). Leadership and organizational culture transformation in professional sport. *Journal of Leadership & Organizational Studies, 17*(1), 71-86.

Gammelsæter, H. (2010). Institutional pluralism and governance in "commercialized" sport clubs. *European Sport Management Quarterly, 10*(5), 569-594.

Greenwood, R., & Hinings, C.R. (1988). Organizational design types, tracks, and the dynamics of strategic change. *Organization studies, 9*(3), 293-316.

Greenwood, R., & Hinings, C.R. (1993). Understanding strategic change: The contribution of archetypes. *Academy of Management Journal, 36*(5), 1052-1081.

Greiner, L.E. (1967). Patterns of organizational change. *Harvard Business Review, 45,* 119-130.

Horch, H.D. (1994). Does government financing have a detrimental effect on the autonomy of voluntary associations? Evidence from German sports clubs. *International Review for the Sociology of Sport, 29*(3), 269-285.

Kikulis, L.M. (2000). Continuity and change in governance and decision making in National Sport Organizations: Institutional explanations. *Journal of Sport Management, 14,* 293-320.

Kikulis, L.M., Slack, T., & Hinings, B. (1995). Does decision making make a difference? Patterns of change within Canadian National Sport Organizations. *Journal of Sport Management, 9,* 273-299.

Lawrence, T.B. (2008). Power, institutions, and organizations. In R. Greenwood, C. Oliver, R. Suddaby, & K. Sahlin (Eds.), *The SAGE handbook of organizational institutionalism* (pp. 170-197). London, UK: SAGE. http://dx.doi.org/10.4135/9781849200387.n7

Lawrence, T.B., & Suddaby, R. (2006). Institutions and institutional work. In S. Clegg, C. Hardy, & T.B. Lawrence (Eds.), *Handbook of organization studies* (2nd ed., pp. 215-254). London, UK: SAGE.

Le Clair, J.M. (2011). Global organizational change in sport and the shifting meaning of disability. *Sport in Society, 14*(9), 1072-1093. doi:10.1080/17430437.2011.614765

Legg, D., Fay, T., Hums, M.A., & Wolff, E. (2009). Examining the inclusion of wheelchair exhibition events within the Olympic Games 1984–2004. *European Sport Management Quarterly, 9*(3), 243-258.

Legg, J., Snelgrove, R., & Wood, L. (2016). Modifying tradition: Examining organizational change in youth sport. *Journal of Sport Management, 30*(4), 369-381.

Lewin, K. (1958). Group decision and social change. In E.E. Macoby, T.M. Newcomb, & E.L. Hatley (Eds.), *Readings in Social Psychology* (pp. 197-211). New York, NY: Holt, Rinehart & Winston.

MacIntosh, E. & Doherty, A. (2005). Leader intentions and employee perceptions of organizational culture in a private fitness corporation.

European Sport Management Quarterly, 5(1), 1-22.

MacIntosh, E., & Doherty, A. (2010). The influence of organizational culture on job satisfaction and intention to leave. *Sport Management Review, 13*, 106-117.

McShane, S.L., & Steen, S. (2012). *Canadian organizational behaviour* (8th ed.). Toronto, Canada: McGraw-Hill Ryerson.

Misener, L., & Darcy, S. (2014). Managing disability sport: From athletes with disabilities to inclusive organisational perspectives. *Sport Management Review, 17*(1), 1-7. http://dx.doi.org/10.1016/j.smr.2013.12.003

O'Brien, D., & Slack, T. (2003). An analysis of change in an organizational field: The professionalization of English rugby union. *Journal of Sport Management, 17*(4), 417-448.

Pettigrew. A.M. (1987). Context and action in the transformation of the firm. *Journal of Management Studies, 24*(6), 649-670.

Scott, W.R. (2001). *Institutions and organizations* (2nd ed.). Thousand Oaks, CA: SAGE.

Skirstad, B., & Chelladurai, P. (2011). For "love" and money: A sports club's innovative response to multiple logics. *Journal of Sport Management, 25*(4), 339-353.

Slack, T., & Hinings, B. (1992). Understanding change in national sport organizations: An integration of theoretical perspectives. *Journal of Sport Management, 6*, 114-132.

Slack, T., & Parent, M. (2006). *Understanding sport organizations: The application of organization theory* (2nd ed.). Champaign, IL: Human Kinetics.

Soebbing, B.P., Wicker, P., & Weimar, D. (2015). The impact of leadership changes on expectations of organizational performance. *Journal of Sport Management, 29*, 485-497.

Theodoraki, E.I., & Henry, I.P. (1994). Organisational structures and contexts in British national governing bodies of sport. *International Review for the Sociology of Sport, 29*(3), 243-265.

Thibault, L., Slack, T., & Hinings, B. (1993). A framework for the analysis of strategy in non-profit sport organizations. *Journal of Sport Management, 7*(1), 25-43.

Wagstaff, C.R., Gilmore, S., & Thelwell, R.C. (2016). When the show must go on: Investigating repeated organizational change in elite sport. *Journal of Change Management, 16*(1), 38-54.

Washington, M., & Patterson, K.D.W. (2011). Hostile takeover or joint venture: Connections between institutional theory and sport management research. *Sport Management Review, 14*, 1-12.

INDEX

perceptual screens 169
performance rewards 76
personal conflict 154-155
personal growth 103
personal integrity 33-34
personality
    assessments of 47-48, 53
    attributed charisma 115
    case study on 57
    cognitive concepts in 52-53
    and emotional intelligence 51-52
    and leadership 114-115
    motivational concepts in 53-54
    successful teams and 53
    understanding 48-51
Philadelphia Eagles 187
Player Assessment Tool 49
players. *See* athletes
Playing With Fire (Fleury) 90
polarization, group 134
political messages 185
Popovich, Gregg 161
posttraumatic stress disorder (PTSD) 89-90
power 160-162
prejudice 24-25
pressure 134
problem-solving teams 141, 145-147. *See also* teams
procedural conflict 155
professional sports teams. *See* enduring sport organizations
programmed decision making 124. *See also* decision making
Project Implicit website 25
PTSD (posttraumatic stress disorder) 89-90
public speaking 177. *See also* oral communication
punishment 62-63

Q

quality of life 5
question asking 170

R

racial diversity 23
random socialization 101. *See also* socialization
rational model of decision making 124-126
RBV (resource-based view) 4
Real Madrid 190
reciprocal exchanges 99. *See also* socialization
recognition of stakeholders 7, 78, 80
Red Sox Foundation 33

Reebok 17
referent power 160
Rehabilitation Act (1973) 23
relatedness 77
relationship goals 158
resistance to change 197-199
resource-based view (RBV) 4
resource management 156-157, 195
reward power 160
rewards for performance 76. *See also* job satisfaction
Ringelmann, Max 148
rituals 185
Robinson, Jackie 203
Rokeach, M. 182
role management 99-100. *See also* socialization
Rookie Transition Program 107
Rosenberg, D. 32-33
routine decision making 124. *See also* decision making

S

sales 67-69
San Antonio Spurs 25, 161
Sandusky, Jerry 31, 133
satisficing 126
scandals 31-32, 133. *See also* ethics
Schein, Edgar 181
Schultz, Gary 133
Seau, Junior 200
Sections 501 and 505 of the Rehabilitation Act (1973) 23
self-awareness 6
self-censorship 134
self-determination theory 77
self-efficacy 64, 94
self-managing teams 141-142. *See also* teams
self-monitoring 53
self-serving bias 55
Selye, H. 93
senior-level teams 142-143. *See also* teams
sequential socialization 101. *See also* socialization
serial socialization 102. *See also* socialization
servant leadership 115
sexual abuse 31, 89-90, 133
sexual harassment 17
silos, functional 141
situational favorableness 114
situational leadership model 114
SMART goals 64, 65
Snapchat 41
Snyderman, B.B. 74
social identity 18

socialization. *See also* job satisfaction
    of athletes 106-108
    case study on 107
    challenges of 102-103
    contexts 103-104
    importance of 100-103
    internationalization and 106-108
    process of 98-102
    in temporary vs. enduring sport organizations 104-106
social learning theory (Bandura) 63-64
social loafing 148
social media. *See also* technology
    ethical challenges of 41
    external communication and 173-174
    responding to 9
social responsibilities 33
social roles in teams 145
Spain, Sarah 41
Spanier, Graham 133
sport events, staging 11
sport management
    ethical challenges in 40-41
    as a field of study 4, 10-11
    knowledge and experience in 10-11
    strategic thinking in 7
sports
    stress and trauma in 89-91
    universal appeal of 16
Sports Business Solutions 67
sports organizations
    internationalization of 106-108
    performance in 64-67
stakeholders. *See also* employees; interns; volunteers
    job satisfaction of 78-81
    organizational change and 198-199
    recognizing 7
    work of 4
statues 184
stereotypes 24, 134
stimulation, intellectual 115
stress
    and burnout 93-95
    case study on 96
    causes of 86-87
    in the competitive sport environment 87-89
    coping with 91-93
    in sports 89-91
    stigmatization of 91-92
    types of 87
Suárez, Luis 190

ABOUT THE AUTHORS

Eric MacIntosh, Ph.D, is an associate professor of sport management at the University of Ottawa in Canada. Dr. MacIntosh researches and teaches on various organizational behavior topics, covering concepts such as culture, leadership, satisfaction, and socialization. His principal research interests delve into the functioning of the organization and how a favorable culture can transmit positively internally and outwardly into the marketplace. Dr. MacIntosh has consulted for and conducted research with many prominent national and international sport organizations (e.g., Commonwealth Games Federation, NHL, Right to Play, U Sports, Youth Olympic Games). He is well published in leading peer-reviewed sport management journals and is a member of several prominent editorial boards. He is also the coeditor of *International Sport Management*.

Photo courtesy of the University of Ottawa.

Laura J. Burton, PhD, is an associate professor of sport management in the department of educational leadership within the Neag School of Education at the University of Connecticut. Her research interests include understanding leadership in organizations (particularly sport organizations) and exploring development, access, and success in leadership. Her work focuses on issues of gender in leadership contexts, specifically how stereotypes and discrimination affect women in sport leadership. She has served as the editor of the *Journal of Intercollegiate Sport* and serves on the editorial board of the *Journal of Sport Management*. She has been published in the *Journal of Sport Management*, *Sport Management Review*, and *Sex Roles*. She is coeditor of *Women in Sport Leadership: Research and Practice for Change*, published in 2017, and the textbook *Sport Leadership in the 21st Century*, published in 2014.

Photo courtesy of the University of Connecticut.